The Golden Thirteen

The
Golden

Naval Institute Press / Annapolis, Maryland

Thirteen

Recollections of the First Black Naval Officers

Edited by Paul Stillwell

With a Foreword by Colin L. Powell

The articles "First Negro Ensigns" and "Negro Rights" are © 1944 by
Life magazine and appear courtesy of *Life* magazine. Reprinted by permission.

Library of Congress Cataloging-in-Publication Data
The Golden Thirteen: recollections of the first Black naval officers
    / edited by Paul Stillwell, with a foreword by Colin L. Powell.
        p.   cm.
    Includes index.
    ISBN 1-55750-779-1
    1. United States. Navy—Afro-Americans. 2. United States. Navy—Officers.
    I. Stillwell, Paul, 1944– .
    VB324.A47G65 1993
    359'.008996073—dc20   92-37273

Printed in the United States of America on acid-free paper ∞

9 8 7 6 5 4 3 2

First printing

Contents

Foreword

In March of 1944 America was in the grip of world war. The U.S. 5th Army was fighting its way up the Italian peninsula. Men and equipment were assembling in England for a massive cross-channel invasion of Normandy. American forces were girding for a major amphibious assault on the Marianas.

Two and a half million men were serving in United States Navy uniforms that month. One hundred thousand sailors and recruits were bursting the seams of the naval training base at Great Lakes, Illinois. Over three thousand brand-new ensigns were commissioned in the first six months of 1944 alone.

The story of one small group of twelve of those new ensigns—plus one Navy warrant officer—might well have been forgotten in the sweep of world events that spring.

After all, none of those thirteen officers ever engaged an enemy in combat. None of them went on to achieve flag rank. They hardly knew one another before they were thrown into an officer-training class at Great Lakes, and they went their separate ways afterward.

Nevertheless, those thirteen men made history. When they posed together for the photograph that appears on the dust jacket of this book, they had just become the first African-Americans ever to be allowed to serve their country as naval officers.

The history they made was more than just an event frozen in time, more than just a curiosity of naval lore. These thirteen men—the Golden Thirteen, they have come to be called—in fact helped to change the very face of America's military. On active duty in the United States Navy today are more than three thousand black officers who walked through the door that the Golden Thirteen opened in 1944.

The Golden Thirteen were not activists. None of them had sought to make history. The Navy's leaders had simply decided that it was past time to bring down the barriers to opportunity in the fleet; and as a consequence, these thirteen sailors were plucked out of their separate lives to learn the ways of officership.

Yet from the very beginning they understood, almost intuitively, that history had dealt them a stern obligation. They realized that in their hands rested the chance to help open the blind moral eye that America had turned on the question of race.

And they recognized that on their shoulders would climb generations of men and women of America's future military, including a skinny seven-year-old kid in the Bronx named Colin Powell.

This is their book, and Paul Stillwell has aptly named it. It is not the *story* of the Golden Thirteen, it is their *recollections*. And it is not just the recollections of their time in the Navy, but rather their sense of what it was to grow up, to make a living, to be American, and to be black in the middle years of this century.

This is a history of our country with the vivid insight of people who have rolled up their sleeves and really lived it, and Paul has done an extraordinary job of making these recollections as vivid in print as they were in spoken words.

You will be touched by this book, as when you read about George Cooper's mother, "Miss Laura," feeding the hungry—white and black—in Washington, North Carolina.

You will laugh, as when Frank Sublett describes learning to sleep in a hammock in boot camp.

You will cheer when the all-black crew of the USS *Mason* "wins" its duel with a U.S. submarine in an exercise off the East Coast.

You will burn with anger when James Hair recounts the lynching of his brother-in-law in 1935.

Most of all, though, you will be reminded that none of our lives is written on a clean slate. The opportunities that come our way, the privileges we enjoy, the very direction that our lives often take are shaped by men and women—like the Golden Thirteen—who came before us and who toiled to make the path a little clearer.

COLIN L. POWELL
Washington, D.C.
September 1992

Acknowledgments

Although he could scarcely know it at the time, my father, Carl Stillwell, put my footsteps on the path toward this oral-history project and book nearly half a century ago. By a coincidence of timing, I was born in Dayton, Ohio, during the same week in April 1944 that *Life* magazine published a one-page feature on the commissioning of the men who would later be named the Golden Thirteen. My father was then the preacher of a church in Dayton and perceived that some of the members of the congregation harbored racial prejudice. Rather than delivering a conventional sermon on the subject, he provided an object lesson. He asked a black minister, Reverend George W. Sherard, from a local church to come baptize me in front of the congregation.

In later years, when my brother and I were growing up in Springfield, Missouri, Dad provided still more object lessons. In particular he focused on the life of George Washington Carver, the great black scientist who worked at Tuskegee Institute in the early years of the century and developed many useful products from such sources as the peanut and sweet potato. Sometimes Dad was missing from the family supper table because he was off delivering an after-dinner talk about Carver to a church group or civic organization. He also took the family to visit Diamond, Missouri, where Carver was born near the end of the Civil War. We listened to the curator of the scientist's birthplace talk about Carver's slave origins and later achievements.

In 1954, when I was ten years old, the Supreme Court directed the integration of the public schools on the reasoning that separate facilities were inherently unequal. That fall the first black students showed up in our classes. Some of them lived only a couple of blocks from us. Now we could go to the same school together; they no longer had to trek to Lincoln, the city's school for blacks. Our parents never suggested that going to school with black children was anything other than a normal experience. Prejudice is not innate; it has to be taught. Our parents taught just the opposite.

And so it was with that background that I moved into the Golden Thirteen oral-history project some years later. I was receptive when Lieutenant Mark Crayton broached the idea of interviewing the first black officers, and I became increasingly enthusiastic as I got to know the members of the group better. They are a great bunch of men, and I am privileged to count them as friends. All have been enormously helpful in sharing their recollections and photos for use in this book. I have enjoyed their hospitality on a number of occasions. It is a measure of these men that they have agreed to donate their share of the royalties from this book to establish a Golden Thirteen Scholarship Fund to perpetuate the memory of the group and allow it to do good works in the future. The other half of the royalties will be plowed back into the Naval Institute's oral-history program as a means of supporting future interview projects.

Other individuals have been helpful as well. One is Bernard Nalty of the Office of Air Force History. He is the author of *Strength for the Fight: A History of Black Americans in the Military.* He has been a source of wise counsel and encouragement throughout the project. He also introduced me to Morris MacGregor, author of a superb book titled *Integration of the Armed Forces: 1940–1965.* Nalty and Mac-Gregor also compiled a multivolume set of documents on blacks in American military service; it is an invaluable source for scholars. Another individual who has provided frequent support and encouragement is Ms. Gina Akers of the Naval Historical Center. She has done important oral-history work with black naval personnel.

Ms. Anne Jones of Twayne Publishers played an instrumental role in the formulation of this book, while Jim Sutton made sure that it eventually wound up being published by the Naval Institute Press. Thanks go also to General Colin Powell for generously agreeing to write the foreword and to Captain Peter Swartz, a special assistant to General Powell, for his role in bringing the subject to the general's attention. Special thanks to Lieutenant Commander Niel Golightly, Swartz's relief as special assistant, for seeing the foreword through to completion. Captain Lee Womack, Jackie Paschal, and the late Ester Boone—all of the Navy Recruiting Command—provided valuable information and photographs. Rear Admiral Norm Johnson provided recollections of his role in helping bring about equal opportunity in the Navy of the late 1960s. William Dermody of the Public Affairs office at the Great Lakes Naval Training Center was particularly helpful. He unearthed and provided photos of the 1987 dedication of the Golden Thirteen recruit in-processing facility.

James Hair, Jr., son of one of the deceased members of the Golden Thirteen, was helpful in providing photos from various periods in his father's life. E. Hall Downes, Jr., supplied pictures of his father. Generous in contributing both recollections and photos have been the three white officers whose memoirs are included in the book: John Dille, Norman Meyer, and Paul Richmond.

Anthony Chiffolo of the Naval Institute Press has done his usual fine job of editing the manuscript for the book, and Karen White produced the attractive design, including the superb front cover of the dust jacket. Several members of the oral-history staff at the Naval Institute were involved in putting together the oral histories of the Golden Thirteen members and also deserve mention: Sue Sweeney, Joanne Patmore, Deborah Reid, and Linda O'Doughda. Sue Sweeney was an enthusiastic supporter from the beginning of the importance of including the memories of the Golden Thirteen in the program. She was deeply touched by their stories. Tears rolled down her cheeks as she listened to the tape recording in which James Hair described the lynching of his sister's husband.

On the home front, my wife, Karen, and sons, Joseph, Robert, and James, have been patient during the long process of assembling the oral histories and book. Joe has already shown that the object lessons have reached another generation. During his senior year in high school, Joe entered a Black History Month essay contest. His essay was about one of the members of the Golden Thirteen.

Black sailors gather on the deck of the USS *Miami* during the Civil War to talk and mend uniforms. Blacks constituted approximately 25 percent of the Navy's enlisted force in the Civil War.

Introduction

The nineteenth century is a good place to start tracing the background of events that led up to the commissioning of the first black officers. Back then the Navy was essentially an integrated service, with black and white sailors living and working together. There were, however, no black officers. Many blacks served as enlisted men because there were no formal quotas or restrictions. During the War of 1812 the Navy's enlisted force was between 6 and 10 percent black. During the Civil War, fought in part to abolish slavery, some 25 percent of Navy enlisted men were black.

The Navy's personnel policies and practices were much less formal in the nineteenth century than they became in the twentieth. For example, mariners often moved back and forth between the Navy and commercial service rather than making a career of the Navy. They usually came from coastal regions and in many cases were foreign born. The Navy was more concerned with manning its ships and shore stations than enforcing rigid segregation. And that is the real explanation behind the enlistment of blacks, not any great policy of enlightenment. The pool of potential recruits was so small that the Navy was willing to take whomever it could get. Even so, those black

These enlisted men were in an integrated mess in the cruiser *Newark* in the latter part of the nineteenth century. The lanyards around their necks suggest they were boatswain's mates.

sailors were almost all in cook- and servant-type roles or in engineering ratings such as machinist's mate or oiler. It was a time when service in engineering was clearly considered less desirable than on deck. There were a few black sailors in the deck specialties—right-arm ratings, as they were known—but those men were exceptions.

In 1899, as the Navy faced the prospect of manning its new steel Navy, including a growing force of battleships, recruiting practices changed. The service inaugurated a category called "landsman for training." In this program the Navy would take civilians without maritime background and train them for naval duty. Now men across the entire country became eligible for naval service. No longer would the Navy have to place as much reliance as before on foreign-born sailors, many of them illiterate in English. And, as Professor Fred Harrod has pointed out in his book *Manning the New Navy,* it was also no longer necessary to enlist black sailors.

As the nation moved into World War I, the war to make the world safe for democracy, the Navy became increasingly restrictive in its use of black sailors. Blacks still worked in food-service jobs and cared for officers, but the engineering-type petty officers were more and more relics of a bygone period because those who retired or otherwise left the service were not replaced. It was essentially a segregated service because black sailors were likely to live and work in restricted enclaves on board ship rather than being spread throughout ships's crews. As time passed the Navy also decided it would prefer to have servants from some other race besides American Negroes, taking in Chinese and Filipinos as cooks and stewards. In August 1919 the Navy completely stopped enlisting blacks. The nadir was reached in 1932 when attrition had reduced the number of blacks in the Navy to 0.55 percent of the enlisted force.

In January 1933 the service again began enlisting blacks as messmen, this time with the rationale that a war in the Pacific might eliminate the opportunity to enlist Oriental servants. The Navy preferred to take in Southern blacks because of the belief that Northern blacks were more likely to be educated and independent. Repeating a phrase that appeared in the official correspondence of the era, an officer indicated that recruiting in the South was likely to bring in the "unspoiled young negro."

The Navy steadfastly held to the position of not allowing black

In this turn-of-the-century shot a steward on board the cruiser *Brooklyn* contemplates a bottle of wine. Doubtless, it was for the officers he served, not for him.

sailors in ratings other than messman, believing that if blacks advanced to petty-officer status they would not be able to exert effective leadership over white sailors under them. Even when blacks reached the level of chief steward, they had no authority over lower-rated enlisted men in the general service. Congressmen appointed two black civilians to the Naval Academy as midshipmen in the 1930s, but white officers at Annapolis soon encouraged them to seek careers in other fields.

As World War II loomed over the United States in the early 1940s, Secretary of the Navy Frank Knox believed in the desirability of continued segregation within the Department of the Navy. President Franklin D. Roosevelt had named Knox to the cabinet for political reasons rather than for any great knowledge of naval affairs.

Knox thus depended for advice on the senior admirals, a group that wanted to uphold the tradition of a segregated service. However, political pressures from outside the government were calling for increased opportunities for blacks in a country that seemed on the verge of war. Roosevelt thus responded to the threat of a planned march on Washington by directing that the defense industry implement equal opportunity. Pressures mounted on the Navy as well, so a committee was established to investigate the opportunities for blacks in the Navy and Marine Corps. The committee reported in December 1941, a few weeks after the beginning of U.S. involvement in World War II, that no changes needed to be instituted with regard to race.

However, organizations outside the government, including the National Association for the Advancement of Colored People (NAACP), continued to exert pressure. President Roosevelt, more attuned to such political forces than Secretary Knox, began in January 1942 to push the Navy toward providing greater opportunities for black sailors. A factor in the process of raising the President's awareness of the need to increase opportunities for black citizens was the influence of Eleanor Roosevelt, his socially conscious wife. On April 7, 1942, the President's prodding finally yielded results when the Navy agreed to begin accepting blacks for general-service ratings on June 1. But that was only half a loaf, for these enlistees could serve only ashore or in small local-defense craft, not in seagoing ships. Black enlisted men in the fleet would continue to be messmen only. Blacks already serving as messmen were precluded from transferring because of a shortage of servants.

In late 1942 mobile construction battalions, the Seabees, began taking black enlistments. In February 1943, because of increasing demands for manpower, the Navy began receiving all its recruits as draftees through the Selective Service System rather than taking volunteers. Whereas the Navy had been able to turn down potential enlistees previously, it now had to take whatever men the system produced. That meant that the number of black sailors would increase until they represented 10 percent of the Navy, roughly proportional with the population as a whole.

To accommodate the influx, the Navy created "base companies" for overseas duty. These were essentially groups of laborers: steve-

Secretary of the Navy Frank Knox looks none too happy on the occasion of giving the oath of enlistment to twenty-nine-year-old William Baldwin of Washington, D.C. On June 2, 1942, Baldwin became the first black to join the Naval Reserve under a new program permitting blacks to enlist for general-service ratings. At right is Rear Admiral Randall Jacobs, Chief of the Bureau of Naval Personnel.

dores, ammunition handlers, construction workers, and maintenance men. In effect, the Navy established a separate branch to absorb black enlisted personnel—to avoid integrating the fleet. Black sailors in these positions resented their status because they were like the messmen, separated from the Navy as a whole and offered neither integration nor equal opportunity. White sailors resented the setup too because they had to face the hazards of combat duty and black sailors did not.

Meanwhile, the Navy was instituting a new program to beef up its training of officers for wartime service. This program, scheduled to begin on July 1, 1943, was known as V-12 and combined college education with officer training. Applicants for the program were due to be tested on April 2. Those pushing for the inclusion of black students in the testing program met resistance from the Bureau of Naval Personnel and Secretary Knox. Knox passed the buck upward to President Roosevelt, who directed in late March that the Navy include blacks in the testing. A number of blacks had excellent scores on the admission tests and were admitted to the V-12 program. Thus it was that the first blacks were on the path to receiving commissions as line officers. It was a change in Navy policy that was kept extremely low key. As James Schneider wrote in his history of V-12, the Navy issued no publicity, with the result that many organizations with an interest in the subject were not made aware that blacks were eligible for V-12. It was tokenism at best. Probably no more than a dozen blacks were involved in the program in 1943.

By the fall of 1943 the number of black enlisted men within the Navy was increasing rapidly, but the V-12 program was not scheduled to commission the first black officers until March 1944. Responding to external pressures, Adlai Stevenson, then serving as an assistant to Secretary of the Navy Knox, and others urged in 1943 that the Navy consider commissioning blacks as officers even more quickly than V-12 could produce them. Stevenson, who later distinguished himself as governor of Illinois, two-time candidate for President, and ambassador to the United Nations during the Cuban Missile Crisis, wrote a memorandum to Knox, suggesting that, as soon as possible, the Navy commission a dozen black men as officers. (The memo is reproduced as appendix A.) In fact, the first black V-12 officers did not come along until later in 1944, a group that included such people as Samuel Gravely, who eventually became the Navy's first black flag officer, and Carl Rowan, now a journalist of national stature.

In response to the urgings of Stevenson and other individuals, Secretary Knox did agree to commission twelve black enlisted men as officers. These were the men who came in time to be known as the Golden Thirteen. On a quiet basis, the hierarchy of the Navy put out the call for qualified candidates. To a man, those who did become the first officers do not know how they happened to be chosen. The best guess is that they were men who had distinguished themselves by their performance and attitude while serving as enlisted men. One of those who was among the first group commissioned, Dennis Nelson, later wrote a master's thesis that was published in 1951 as *The Integration of the Negro into the U.S. Navy*. Nelson wrote that Commander E. Hall Downes, officer in charge of the Naval Training School at Hampton, Virginia, chose eight of the sixteen officer candidates. Commander Daniel Armstrong, officer in charge of black training at the Naval Training Station at Great Lakes, Illinois, selected seven, and the Commandant of the Eighth Naval District selected one. Great Lakes was the site of recruit training for black sailors; Hampton provided advanced training in specific occupational specialties. All of the men considered for the program—certainly more than the final sixteen chosen—were thoroughly screened, and the Federal Bureau of Investigation conducted detailed inquiries into their backgrounds.

Despite repeated requests for information dealing specifically with the selection and training of these first black officers, no documents have emerged from official sources such as the National Archives, Bureau of Naval Personnel, and Naval Historical Center. Perhaps the publication of this book will lead to the unearthing of such records from wherever they have been stored since 1943–44. Lacking such documentation, one can make several observations after reviewing the oral recollections of those who successfully completed the program. One observation is that even though Secretary Frank Knox was obviously reluctant for the service to have blacks in general-service ratings and later as commissioned officers, the Navy did carry out the officer program in good faith once Knox agreed to the proposal put forth by Stevenson and the Bureau of Naval Personnel. Another observation is that all of the candidates had proved their proficiency as enlisted leaders. There were other common denominators, such as the evident willingness to accept discipline and obey orders. The Navy was not looking for militants in these officer candidates. The preponderance of the officer candidates were athletes, perhaps because the Navy believes there is a correlation between athletic achievement and leadership ability. On the other hand, the officer candidates offered a range of educational attainments: some had postgraduate degrees, some bachelor's degrees; some had begun college but not finished, and some did not have a college background. With approximately one hundred thousand black sailors available at the time of the selections, the Navy could have picked, for instance, sixteen men with master's degrees as officer candidates, but that would not have been representative of the overall population nor comparable to the individuals in the white-officer-training programs of the time.

In January 1944 the sixteen black sailors began their training at Great Lakes. The rationale for training sixteen men was that officer-training programs, including the Naval Academy, generally lose a certain percentage of candidates, so some extra men were included to reach the desired total of twelve.

All sixteen men successfully completed their training at Great Lakes in March 1944, but only thirteen of them became officers. In *Strength for the Fight,* an excellent book on the history of American blacks in the military, author Bernard Nalty argues that the choice of thirteen was arbitrary. The Navy had expected that one-fourth of the men would not pass the course, but all did. Rather than making officers of all sixteen men, the Bureau of Personnel gave commissions as ensigns to twelve of the men and made a warrant officer of a thirteenth, a man without a college education. If the records of the Golden Thirteen do eventually emerge, they may well shed some light on Nalty's supposition. His claim of arbitrary treatment makes considerable sense, although it was hardly palatable to the three men who passed the course but didn't get the expected reward. These three remained on active duty as enlisted men and were reassigned to other duties within the Navy.

Finally, 146 years after the establishment of the Navy Department in 1798, the service had its first black line officers. They were also the first active-duty black officers, but not the first overall. On June 18, 1942, the Navy had awarded a reserve commission to a black medical student named Bernard Whitfield Robinson. He was a light-skinned individual, but it's possible that the officer who commissioned him did not actually see him. The Navy was competing with the Army for medical officers and decided to commission a number of students during their final year of medical school so that they would be available to serve on active duty once they became physicians. An internal memo in the Bureau of Naval Personnel explained that Robinson's commissioning was the result of "a slip by the officer who signed up medical students at Harvard." One officer, according to the memo, "says this boy has a year to go in medical school and hopes they can get rid of him some how by then." Robinson did remain a Naval Reserve officer and became a doctor but did not begin his active service until after the commissioning of the group at Great Lakes.

For some thirty-five years after they were commissioned, the thirteen men of Great Lakes were known only as "those Negro naval officers" or later as "those black naval officers." That is, if they were known as anything at all. In keeping with the low-key approach toward the blacks who entered the V-12 program, the Navy greeted the commissioning of the thirteen with little fanfare. It had reluctantly made officers of the men, but it wasn't going to accord them any special treatment. For many years they really had no group identity. They had been together briefly in 1944, then had gone their separate ways.

The first of the original thirteen black officers to die was Charles Lear, probably by suicide, shortly after World War II. Next was Phillip Barnes, who returned to his home of Washington, D.C., following his naval service; he died in March 1955. Reginald Goodwin had a successful career as an attorney in Chicago before he died in 1974. After his retirement from naval service, Dennis Nelson settled in San Diego and was active in the Urban League; he died in 1979. Dalton Baugh got bachelor's and master's degrees after leaving the service, then set up his own engineering firm in the Boston area; he died in 1985.

Lewis Williams, who went through the training but was not commissioned, had a master's degree by 1944 and had worked before World War II as a union organizer for railroad redcaps. These baggage handlers were not employed by the railroads and thus depended entirely on tips for their income. They had no salary, no medical coverage, and no pension benefits. Thus they had to work as long as they could to provide income for themselves and their families. Following his wartime naval service, Williams returned to civilian life in his hometown of Chicago and pursued a career in social work. I have no information on the men named J. B. Pinkney and A. Alves who also were trained with the Golden Thirteen but did not become officers.

In the mid-1970s Dennis Nelson brought about a reunion of the group of men who had trained together and been commissioned together in 1944. He tracked down all but one of the surviving members of the group and arranged for them to get together in 1977 at Monterey, California. Captain Edward Sechrest, who was assigned to the Navy Recruiting Command at the time, was involved in that first reunion. Vice Admiral Sam Gravely, one of the early V-12 graduates, recalls that it was Sechrest who coined the term "Golden Thirteen" for the first black officers. It was a master stroke because that label gave the group an identity. By the late 1970s the Navy was far more racially aware than it had been in 1944. Now it was desirable to play up the service's equal-opportunity success stories.

As a result of Nelson's efforts in bringing the group back together, the service retroactively made heroes of the Golden Thirteen. It publicized their achievements and began sponsoring reunions on an annual basis. They were called to meet the Secretary of the Navy, called upon to aid Navy recruiting, and in 1982 sent aboard the modern guided-missile destroyer *Kidd* in a highly publicized visit. Interestingly, the members of the group are now much closer than they were in 1944. Back then they were so focused on passing the officer training that there was little time for socializing. In recent years they have gotten to know one another as friends rather than as members of the same brief training course.

In 1986 Lieutenant Mark Crayton of the recruiting office at the Great Lakes Naval Training Center visited the Naval Institute. His immediate interest was to promote coverage of black naval veterans of World War II, who were due to have a reunion at Great Lakes, the site of their training more than forty years earlier. Lieutenant Crayton really set in motion much more than that. He inspired a series of interviews with the still-living members of the Golden Thirteen. In effect, this book is "the story of the Golden Thirteen, told by the Golden Eight," because by 1986 only eight of the men were still alive. All eight were interviewed as part of the Naval Institute's ongoing oral-history program. In addition, the program has come to embrace three white officers who were connected with the group in various capacities.

As valuable as oral history is for preserving recollections of events not included in history books and official documents, it is certainly not infallible. We all know that memory can play tricks on us and that it grows increasingly hazy with the passing of years. Moreover, memories are reflections of the perceptions of a given time. Thus if individuals perceived an event differently, they will remember it differently. A good example from these stories is that some of the Golden Thirteen recall their Great Lakes instructors as condescending, while others do not. The documentary records of the group's training, if they could be located, would be a valuable adjunct to the memories of the men who went through that training. Another pitfall of oral history is that the interviewer may not ask all the right questions. Fortunately, the men of the Golden Thirteen have been cooperative on this score. All agreed to a second round of interviews, at which time I was able to ask more knowledgeable questions than the first time. In addition, since they knew me better the second time around, they were more forthcoming in their answers.

Altogether, the memoirs of the eight black officers and the three white officers in this project constitute more than two thousand pages of transcript taken from the oral interviews. In condensing that much material to fit the confines of a book, an editor must choose what to include. In general, the format emphasizes their entire lives rather than focusing only on their experiences together at Great Lakes in 1944 or even on their total Navy service. I have chosen to carve out excerpts that way for two main reasons. The first is to demonstrate the backgrounds that these men brought to their naval service—the experiences that had formed them and shaped their attitudes, the sort of guidance they had gotten from their parents, teachers, and associates. The second is to describe what sort of lives they led after leaving the Navy. As a by-product, we learn much about society's treatment of its black citizens over the years.

Since none of the interviewees made a career of the Navy, we must view them mostly in terms of their achievements in civilian life. By that standard, the Golden Thirteen are an outstanding group of men. And I think that a description of those civilian achievements helps demonstrate the caliber of men that the Navy chose for this program. They had a combination of native ability and motivation that made them successful. In other words, giving each man the opportunity to tell his story in broad, overall terms lets us put his Navy service in the appropriate context. Still another facet of the editing is the desire to avoid duplication. Concentrating only on the events of 1944 would result in telling the same story over and over.

Television producers have expressed an interest in dramatizing the story of these first black officers. Because of the nature of the medium, a TV drama will have to deal largely with the events of early 1944. It will depict the conditions under which the men were trained, the ways they confronted the challenges of an unfamiliar environment, and their interactions with one another. These were men of varying personalities, as will be apparent when actors portray them. That sort of dramatic focus will draw on other facets of the two thousand pages of material than this collection does. Both approaches can complement each other. In a way, we might compare this editing process to cutting a diamond. The way in which the jeweler carves the rough stone determines the facets that sparkle in a given setting. Here, then, are the carved-out stories of the Golden Thirteen.

The Golden Thirteen

Chapter One

The Importance of Inspiration

Graham E. Martin

For many years Graham Martin and his wife, Alma, have lived quietly in a white frame house five miles north of the Indiana state capitol and the Hoosier Dome, home of football's Indianapolis Colts. Greeting a visitor in the mid-eighties, Martin pointed out that one of his legs was bowed and the other straight. Both knees had been damaged during the course of playing football; only one had been repaired surgically. By the late eighties Martin had been largely confined to a wheelchair and required regular visits from a physical therapist in an attempt to restore some movement to the damaged joints.

In a room nearby, Mrs. Martin was as friendly as her husband but unable to get out of bed because her long-time experience with multiple sclerosis left her immobile. Mr. Martin's physical problems have worsened because his unstinting devotion to his wife has frequently included lifting and carrying her. But as a proud and loving husband, he wasn't one to push off that chore on others. In recent years relatives and friends have, of necessity, provided a good deal of care for the Martins. Also, the Martins have chosen to remain in their long-time home rather than availing themselves of the treatment they might find in an institution. Caring for the house is a difficult chore.

Sadly, Martin is no longer able to attend the annual reunions of the Golden Thirteen. Even in his absence, though, the other members of the group think of him often, for he has earned their high respect.

Seeing Graham Martin in a wheelchair is a saddening experience, particularly when one thinks back on his earlier life as a football star and as the sort of man who would run through an obstacle course several times a day for recreation. During World War II he was skilled enough to play semipro football for the San Francisco Clippers. He held his own with linemen who had played in the National Football League before World War II. He competed under the name Jim Patterson, taking his wife's maiden name as a pseudonym because he preferred not to call attention to himself. In a way, that epitomizes Graham Martin, who is a person of quiet dignity and pride. Throughout his life he has looked for the opportunity to excel, but on his own terms—not in a flashy manner.

That same quality explains why he spent the bulk of his adult life as a high school teacher and coach, even though he had earlier had aspirations of being a college teacher and even a college president. For Graham Martin, the most important goal has been to make a contribution rather than to seek glory or recognition. Certainly his educational attainments qualified him to pursue a career as a college professor. In part he was denied that goal by circumstance. At a time in his life when he might have sought a doctorate, World War II sent him to a much different existence. After the war, a job at his high school alma mater in Indianapolis looked promising after a short stint as a college coach in West Virginia. He and his wife experienced racial discrimination in West Virginia and so decided to return home. Achievement was more important than status, and so it was that he remained in Indianapolis to serve as the best sort of influence for two generations of students.

Some members of the Golden Thirteen participated in the oral-history interviews with torrents of words. Graham Martin was much more reserved because he is not the sort to boast. Indeed, he needed to be drawn out because he prefers to let his actions speak for him. Those actions speak eloquently on his behalf.

I was born in Tennessee, January 18, 1917, in a small town called Tobacco Port, which was near Hopkinsville, Kentucky, on the Cumberland River. My mom was named Carrie Martin, and my dad was Charlie Martin. I had two sisters and one brother— four of us. We lived on a tobacco farm, and I recall as a very young child, four or five years old, helping my dad by pulling the worms off of tobacco. I was trying to get a can full of them so he could pay me a penny for it. I remember walking behind him in the field, following the plow and seeing the things that he'd turn up sometimes: a nest of little rabbits or a nest of snakes.

When I was a little boy, I would catch catfish in the Cumberland and go hunting with my collie dog. One fall day my father and I were walking back from work about dusk, and he noticed a couple of squirrels in a tree. He sent me home to get his shotgun. By the time I returned, it was almost completely dark. He shot up into the tree, and two squirrels came down. That sticks very vividly in my mind because I thought he was a superman. He didn't kill indiscriminately; it was always something we could use.

I think I was about seven or eight when my father died. I saw him open his mouth and gasp for breath, not seeming to get any. The older people took me out of the room, and that was the last I saw of him. I presume it was a heart attack or stroke. His loss weighed heavily on me and posed a real problem for my mother. She didn't think she could keep the farm up, so she decided to come to Indianapolis and get a job. We knew some other people who had come here previous to that time, and we just followed them.

The rest of the family stayed in Tennessee because they were older, so it was just my mother and I living together in Indianapolis. She got work as a seamstress and a maid—a domestic servant. While I was living on the farm, I had gotten a little education in a one-room country school. When I came here, I went to Public School 64 on the south side, and then I went to various schools throughout Indianapolis over the years. They were all 100 percent segregated. I wasn't a very good student initially because I was always playing hooky and doing other things.

I didn't have many outside interests, except maybe skipping school and going to cowboy movies for ten cents—if I paid at all. There was definitely a Jim Crow setup in Indianapolis during the 1920s and 1930s. For instance, when we went to a show downtown, we had to sit in the balcony. In order to prevent somebody from being burned up in a fire, they had those outside ladders that had weights on them and would swing down when people got on them. We would get a whip from an ice man, whip it up there, and pull the end of the fire escape down. Then we could go up and slip in the show.

During those early years, I belonged to a gang. We would get together and do little mischievous things. We didn't do anything that was really bad at first. It started out as something to do for fun, but, really, it got beyond that. From the time I was in the fourth or fifth grade, I began getting into more serious things, including stealing and breaking windows. My mother was definitely concerned about my being in the gang, but it was kind of hard to do anything because she had to work. Then I started to get in trouble with the courts.

I guess the worst thing I did was walk in a store and take some money. I went behind the counter and grabbed it and then ran down an alley. But what do you know? That alley had to have a dead end. I was busy trying to climb the wall, and a policeman was standing down there with his gun. He said, "Come down here, boy. How old are you?"

I said, "Twelve."

He said, "I wouldn't shoot you, but maybe somebody would, because you're big for your age. You're going to get killed."

I think that was the final straw. That was about my third time before the judge. He decided that since my mother had to work to make a living, he'd better put me in an orphans' home. That turned out to be my salvation, although I did take a while to adjust. I ran away a couple of times before I realized that this was really the best place for me.

Up to that point I didn't particularly like school, and when I got to the orphanage, I was back in the fourth grade. My fourth-grade teacher was excellent, a real inspiration to me. She took a lot of interest in me and suggested that I try to get good grades and behave myself and see how I liked that. So I tried it for six weeks, and I got all As and A+s. It felt wonderful to have teachers praise me, so I said, "I'm going to do this all the time."

From then on I started reading a lot of books. At the orphans' home you had to make up your bed, clean the floors, wash the windows, work in the kitchen, and clean the pots and pans, things like that. But after that, you were on your own. So I'd get a stack of books and just sit down and read them because I decided I wanted to be a teacher. So I'd read the books until everybody else admired what I read. I also acquired something else that I had lacked up to then, a sense of discipline. We had to do certain things at certain times, and if we didn't do those things, we were disciplined physically. So it was a real learning process in a number of ways.

The orphanage was on a big plot of land, and right next to it was school number 37; I went there until the eighth grade. At the end of each reporting period, the superintendent would always get the best report cards and have those kids come up front and stand, and she would say nice words about us. I liked that, so I just kept on trying to get the best grades I could. The principal there was a very positive influence also. She was really giving. She developed a jug band, and I played with it. A jug band involves, as the name would indicate, several jugs, a washboard, thimbles, some wooden sticks, drums, a piano, and a Jew's harp. The jugs had different amounts of water in them and thus different pitches; I played a jug. We performed for clubs all around town. We even went out of town to perform in clubs. We did very well, mostly playing for whites even though all the band members were black. As with the reading, I was getting more and more involved in positive things.

Up to the mid-1920s the schools in Indianapolis were integrated, but in 1926 they started building a new high school for Negro students; it was named for Crispus Attucks. I didn't know much about him at that time, but I learned later that he was one of the heroes of the Revolutionary War, the first man to fall in the Boston Massacre. In fact, I later spent a good deal of my life teaching in that school.

When I was in grade school, I really followed what the people

Martin as a young man.

were doing in Crispus Attucks High School. I would hear about the scholars and the great football players and what they did. So I aspired to do the same thing. I think I had been in that orphans' home about four years when I graduated from the grade school and went into high school. Naturally, we had a black staff, black principal, black everything. The principal was a great, great inspiration. He stressed the importance of education, saying, "That's the way you get out of your cycle of poverty."

The teachers were all that way too. They would spend extra time with us. They didn't give us anything at all; we had to earn it. But they would give you that extra effort to help you, particularly the math teachers, the history teachers, the science teachers, those basic subjects. Their theme was that we had to work harder than white people to succeed. There were two strikes against us to start with, so we had to use that last strike. Go in there and don't ask for anything, just do the job.

As for the segregation, I would describe my attitude then as one of disappointment. I didn't have time for resentment because that wouldn't have served any purpose, but neither did I really accept the situation. For instance, I would have liked to have played the other local high schools in sports to see if we could have beaten them. I think so, but we never got a chance to prove it. We had some terrific teams. That adversity did have an advantage because it got me to St. Louis; to Tulsa, Oklahoma; to Owensboro, Kentucky; to Lexington, Kentucky, so we could play against quality black teams.

Even so, the trips still reminded us of our status. We would take along sandwiches, and, of course, they would give out on a long trip. On one long trip we stopped in a restaurant in Terre Haute, Indiana. Some of the guys on the team were feeling a little mischievous, so they put salt in the mustard and played around a little bit. The proprietor called the police, and they got hold of one of our coaches. He had been a great football player up East. He was a Phi Beta Kappa, and he was really a fine role model. He was trying to explain to the police that we were just boys and that we were just messing around, but they hauled him out of the restaurant and took him somewhere. I guess he was able to explain it to them because eventually he came back and we left. But it was very disturbing to see him dragged out of the restaurant and humiliated.

I must have been in the orphanage for close to eight years. I was about ready to graduate from high school before I got out. I believe I got out in 1936 and moved back with my mother. She had been able to make it during the Depression because when President Franklin D. Roosevelt came in, his administration established some new programs. One of them was called the Works Progress Administration. People worked hard to do whatever they were skilled in, so she was hired away from working in a restaurant to do sewing, which she was very good at. She helped make blankets and things for the Army as well as products like bed linens to be used in hospitals. She got a big check of $38.75 a month.

It was much more money than she could make anywhere else, and that was the thing that enabled me to go back and live with her. She was able to take care of me better then. Of course, by then I didn't need much taking care of because I was older and established in my mind what I was going to do. Besides, I was always trying to find some kind of job myself. While I was in school, for instance, I got involved in the Youth Progress Administration. It was designed for promising youngsters who were having trouble financially. So they would let us work around the school—doing such things as helping in the cafeteria, washing windows, or otherwise making the building look pretty.

By the time I was in high school, I wasn't in any trouble at all because I had completely changed around from my early youth. Since you ask, it might be worth mentioning that I served in several leadership roles because that has some bearing on my later experience in the Navy. I was superintendent of my Sunday school for a while, and in high school I was president of the boxing club, president of the student council, president of the French club—four or five clubs—and president of the graduation class. If I didn't run for a position, somebody nominated me. I learned parliamentary procedure pretty well and acquired some organizational skills, and those qualities stood me in good stead.

During those years I had a vision: I wanted to go to college. I wanted to get a scholarship. I had a particular scholarship in mind; it was called the Foundation. The Foundation is an organization that still exists; it grants scholarships to poor but promising youngsters, regardless of race. I had a chance to go to Fisk University in Nashville, Tennessee, but I heard a lot about the rich boys, the doctors' and lawyers' sons, all the money and clothes they had, so I decided I'd better go somewhere close around. Instead, I went to Indiana University, which is in Bloomington. I think the tuition there was about $50.00 a year. I could handle it, though even that was hard to get. I could have gotten a full football scholarship to Fisk, but it was so far away. At Indiana I got only the academic scholarship from the Foundation. It was worth $1,000, payable over four years, and $250 was enough to see me through almost the whole year. With the work I could do during the summer, I was able to do pretty well.

I guess my best summer was working as a redcap at the Greyhound bus station. I was carrying bags for passengers. I was able to memorize most of the schedules, and when somebody would come and ask when a certain bus left, I could tell them. I got some good tips that way. That summer I was able to buy a footlocker and an extra pair of pants, maybe a suit. I went back to school pretty sharp, pretty clean.

Studying at the university gave me my first chance to prove myself in an integrated situation. I was able to lead or be near the top of most of my classes. Academically, my strengths were in the social sciences, physical sciences, and math. What I learned in high school was the real foundation because I could just build on that.

After I got straightened out from my early troubles, education became my primary thrust. I knew it wasn't going to get me in the front door of a movie theater, but I decided, "There are more important things. What difference does it make where I sit, one place or another?" At Indiana I had a roommate who was a white student, and we'd go to the movie. They'd give me my ticket for upstairs and then ask him where he wanted to sit. He was very angry and said, "Oh, hell, I'm a Negro too." So they'd hand him a ticket for upstairs. But I didn't let all that affect me negatively because I had something else to think about. I was thinking about getting to work and trying to be at the top of the class.

During those same years, Joe Louis was becoming famous in the country as a heavyweight boxer. I'd stand on the street sometimes, and whites would pull by in automobiles and shout racial slurs, especially when Louis was beaten by the German fighter Max Schmeling in 1936. Two years later he beat Schmeling. I felt a great glow of pride in Joe Louis's accomplishments and also those of Jesse Owens, the sprinter who did so well in the 1936 Olympics. Colored people had been told over and over that we were inferior, and that didn't make sense when these men proved that they could beat everybody. I just couldn't equate their talent with being inferior. I began having a better feeling about myself.

A sociology teacher asked me in class one day if I was a Communist. That's back during the time when the Communists were trying to infiltrate Negro organizations and getting Negroes to become Communists. I said, "If you mean by Communist that I think I'm as good as anybody, and I think I ought to have the same rights as you in this country—because my roots here are probably deeper than yours—if that makes me a Communist, then I'm a Communist." He never asked me that question again.

I'll say one thing about the teachers at Indiana. Every one of them, except one or two, was extremely fair; they gave me what I earned. I had As and Bs in almost everything I did, but one instructor gave me a C. I went back to ask him about it, and he came up with a whole lot of reasons. I said, "Those are not valid. You know they're not valid. You only did that because I'm a Negro."

"No, no, no."

I said, "I could beat you up." I was solidly built, small waist, big chest, standing straight. I said, "I could beat you up, but I know what the headlines would say. They'd say, `Big Black Athlete Assaults Little Professor.'" I said, "I'm not going to give you that satisfaction. I'm not even going to go to the dean, because I believe I could get it changed if I went to the dean. But then if I do, some other teacher who probably was going to give me a break along the way would think I was a troublemaker and make it harder on me. So I'm going to accept this C that you gave me." But he definitely had no reason to give me a C because every paper I had was a B or above, and all my tests were a B or above. So it had to be a B, at least.

I never did have him anymore, and I wouldn't have liked him anyway because he was just prejudiced. It was something that he grew up with, and he didn't know anything else. On the other hand, some of my people told me about another man they thought was prejudiced. They said he was always saying "nigger." I had to have his class because it was part of my major. I listened to him closely when I got in class, and when he finally came to that word, I kind of smiled to myself. These other people didn't know what he was saying.

I had read about the pronunciation of some of the Southerners. He was saying "Nigra." Now, the man had a Ph.D. and couldn't pronounce N-E-G-R-O as Negro; he had to pronounce it as "Nigra." He wasn't saying "nigger." So I went to him, and we talked about it. I was doing well in class, so we had a pretty good relationship. I told him what the people were saying about him, and he said, "That's my pronunciation. Nobody ever told me that I should stress Negro." He changed his pronunciation right then.

While I was at Indiana, I played football. Back in high school I had made all-state, but you've got to restrict that. I thought it was great at the time, but—looking back—we only had three schools to choose from—Roosevelt in Gary, Crispus Attucks in Indianapolis, and Lincoln in Evansville. So I was able to make all-state from that group. I went to Indiana University, and I thought I was good enough to play, but I didn't get to play a lot. I would go in to talk to the head coach, Bo McMillin, who later coached in the National Football League. He'd give me an explanation, and I'd go away satisfied, get about a block down the street, and say, "Why, son of a gun, he didn't tell me anything." He was a real smooth talker.

Eventually, I lettered in my senior year. I played tackle at 193 pounds. I was one of the small ones, of course. It was frustrating not being able to play more than I did, but being on the team had some benefits, I guess, because McMillin let me work at his house. I could tell what he was teaching his children because I was out raking the yard one day, and his little five-year-old son came out, looked up at me, looked at my hair, and said, "Are you white?"

I said, "No, I'm not a white."

He said, "You're colored, aren't you?"

I said, "Yeah."

He said, "You can't help it, can you?"

I said, "No. That's the way I was born."

He said, "But you can't help it. You're all right, aren't you?"

I said, "Yeah, I'm all right."

That told me he was trying to do the best he could, even in his family, on the matter of race. So I didn't feel too bad about it. In retrospect, I think that even if I had been white I would have had a difficult time playing more than I did because I was a walk-on rather than on a football scholarship. And McMillin probably had pressures on him from the administration and the alumni that I didn't fully realize at the time. The best tip-off is that I played more time in road games than when we were in home games at Bloomington.

I never actually thought that McMillin was deep in his heart really prejudiced, but he did talk about the color of a person in a superior kind of a way. I heard from some of the white boys that he was making a speech down in one of the small Southern towns, and somebody asked him how his colored boys were doing. He had two of us on the team, and he said, "They're getting whiter all the time." So you could equate that with his thinking about blacks, that black was just normally and naturally inferior, and white was superior. He was saying that we were beginning to act more like them, that we were better accepted.

Academically, I did very well at Indiana. I was hoping to get Phi Beta Kappa, but I guess I played a little bit too much football. I got written up several times as being a leader among the athletes and that my status was comparable to the top 8 percent or 10 percent of the school itself, so I did very well. I got better than a B average. My career objective was to be a history teacher.

I graduated with a bachelor's degree in June of 1941 and sent applications to all the black colleges that I knew about in the South—Virginia, the Carolinas, Georgia, Florida, Alabama, Mississippi, Louisiana, Texas—to every one. I thought maybe I was going to get a chance to go to one of them, but I didn't. In the meanwhile, I was so sure I was going to get a job, I got married in July of that year to a young woman named Alma Patterson. We eloped to Ohio to avoid the three-day waiting period here in Indiana.

Since I still didn't have a job but did get a scholarship offer we decided to keep our marriage a secret. Alma would live at home in Indianapolis while I went to Howard University in Washington, D.C., to work on my master's degree. I've always regretted not finding out how I happened to get that scholarship. The university wrote to me and offered me a fellowship to proceed with my master's degree for instructing one class in freshman history. So that's what I did.

The overt segregation in Washington was much worse than anything I'd experienced back home. Indiana didn't have any signs, but it was sort of tacitly understood that blacks had a certain place. In Washington it was spelled out specifically. For instance, they'd have drinking fountains and restrooms with signs on them for "colored," the term that was used then. I guess they figured not all blacks could read, so the one for us would have a black hand pointing, and the hand over there on the other side would be white.

While I was getting my degree, I had some great professors. One was named E. Franklin Frazier, who was an eminent sociologist, studying the family, the migrations from the South, what they did when they got into the metropolitan areas. A couple of others were Dr. Rayford Logan, Latin American historian largely, and Dr. Charles

Wesley, who was an eminent historian and writer. All these persons were good writers, and they had books that were selling very well at the time.

It was at Howard that I started to learn about black history, which we hadn't covered at all at Indiana University. These new courses opened my eyes and gave me an interest in black history, so I started looking for the books that would tell me a lot about it. I had another interesting discovery at the time. Back then it was just the general opinion that the white schools were much better than the black. And I'm human, so I guess I thought that too. I thought I was going to breeze through Howard because I had gone to big Indiana. But I found out that I did more studying to get the same grades than I had done at Indiana.

For the master's degree I wrote a thesis on the underground railroad in Indiana, tracing the path of slaves as they escaped to the North in the nineteenth century. Indiana was sort of a passageway because it adjoins Kentucky. Quite a few of them came through Indiana, but they were going on to Ohio. Richmond, Indiana, became a real headquarters for them. That's near the Ohio line, so if they could get that far, they were almost home free. I came back here to Indiana a couple of times for research, but I did most of it in the Library of Congress. I was able to dig out records right there, and I became a fixture. Everybody knew me at the Library of Congress because I was there just about every day.

At that time my ambitions went beyond just teaching; I wanted to be a college president. Naturally, it would be as president of a black college; that was in the back of my mind. I had had so much success in organizing everything I had gone in, I thought maybe I could organize a college and could help somebody really do something.

While I was studying at Howard, December 7 erupted. I thought that I was going to be drafted, but they didn't send me my greetings until April of the next semester. I wish I had kept a copy of my reply to the draft board in Indianapolis because I must have been very persuasive. I told them I was as patriotic as anybody, and I didn't in any way shun the armed forces. But since what little money I had was involved in the school, I wished they would let me finish my course. They wrote me back in a very short time and said, "You stay there, and we'll contact you again."

In the spring of 1942 my wife came to Washington to see me graduate from Howard, and then she remained there while I was waiting for my draft call. I decided that I really didn't want to go into the Army because I considered the Army too dirty for me—crawling in all that mud and stuff. Another factor was that the Navy general-service ratings were available so that blacks weren't limited to being cooks. I was supposed to report to the Army on August 1. I joined the Navy July 31 in Washington.

They put me in charge of a group of about ten or twelve young men to go to Great Lakes, Illinois, for recruit training. We got to Great Lakes on a Friday night and missed our evening meal. Saturday morning the Navy served us beans and cornbread. I'd been used to eating eggs and bacon or cereal or stuff like that, but never, never beans. That was always a night meal or a noon meal. I disdained that, of course; I pushed it aside. For breakfast the next Saturday we had beans and cornbread; this time I asked for seconds. I discovered that was a Navy tradition for the Saturday morning meal.

I didn't want to go to the Army because of all the marching, but when I got to Navy boot training, I found that we started marching at eight o'clock and did an awful lot of it each day before quitting time. So I didn't get away from that at all. But I took to it pretty well, and it didn't hurt me. I was made the exercise leader for our company because of my athletic experience. That was basically calisthenics and going through obstacle courses.

We had a white chief petty officer in charge of the company. He was very sympathetic and helpful. The race thing never came up, but I don't think he was in any way prejudiced. He didn't show it, at least. Along with our marching we had a lot of classroom training. Included were remedial classes for those who hadn't done very well. A lot of them came up from the South. They couldn't read too well, and I was among those who tried to teach them how to read.

After I finished boot camp myself, I remained there to help train other men coming through. I was made a company subcommander, working for a white chief petty officer. I served in that role from late 1942 until the end of 1943, a little more than a year. My job was to take care of the drilling and providing for the recruits' academic instruction, which was Navy regs and seamanship. I was just doing the same thing that the commander did from a substitute role.

I did have some trouble while I was in that job. When I was a company subcommander, we were having inspection one day. This chief discovered that one of the black recruits had a cigarette in his jumper pocket, which was against regulations. The chief told me to make the recruit eat it, and I refused to do it. I thought it was a very dubious order, but it wasn't up to me to make that decision. I based my refusal on my experience as a health minor in college. I didn't think it was good for the guy's health to make him eat a cigarette. The chief put me on report, and I had to go before the captain. The captain wanted to know why I would deliberately disobey an order. I told him my reasoning. He shook his head, but he sustained me. That was a very ticklish situation, and I was later scared when they said only thirteen of sixteen were going to make it in officer training. I was very, very much disturbed about that, as to whether they would hold it against me.

While I was in that job, I used to go through the obstacle course three or four times a day for fun, showed the recruits how to do it. I just loved it. So I was in shape when an opportunity came along to play football again. It was also a chance to prove to myself that I was a better football player than the amount of time Coach McMillin played me at Indiana. I tried to play on the Great Lakes team in 1942, but they wouldn't have any blacks. When I was still there the next football season, I tried to play again, starting in about August. They still said, "No, no, no." The team played one game and barely won. Then they played Purdue. I was sitting up in the stands watching the sloppy tackle play. Purdue beat Great Lakes that Saturday. Two days later the head coach came to the black camp.

That was Tony Hinkle, who was a great football star at the University of Chicago and a great coach at Butler in Indianapolis. He came to the black camp and asked if any of us "boys" wanted to play football. We said, "Sure, we'd like to play. We've been trying to get on the team for some time." He had us put on tennis shoes and took us out there on an asphalt drill field. He stood behind us, and he had us get down and demonstrate pulling out, blocking, left and right, and pass blocking. The guys told me later that he was pointing to my feet as I was doing my maneuvers. He let me and three others come out for the Great Lakes team. I met a white player who came out the same day. He was Steve Lach, an all-American running back from

In 1943 Martin was a tackle on the Great Lakes Naval Training Station squad, which was as good as the finest college football teams in the nation.

Duke. He and I met in the backfield because I tackled him for a loss. The coach later told me I made the team that first day. By Saturday I was first string, so that made me feel pretty good.

One time Hinkle called me in and gave me a lecture on race relations. I had a master's degree, and I was pretty well versed in that.

But, of course, I had to sit and listen, and said, "Yes, sir." He was a full lieutenant then, and I was just a petty officer. He told me how to get along without having any trouble with the players. I didn't have any trouble. I didn't have a bit of trouble.

When we were playing Ohio State, they had a two-hundred-pound black tackle named Bill Willis, who was truly an all-American. He is now in the pro football hall of fame. At the end of that game, we were in the locker room, which had some lockers down the middle. The guys on the other side couldn't see me, and I overheard one of them talking about Willis. He said, "John, I couldn't block that nigger any time at all."

I started to become angry. Then I said, "Hey, John, I couldn't block him either." Now, I could have got angry about that and gone over there and wanted to fight. What good was that going to do? I think the humor made everybody laugh, and everybody had a good time. That's the first time I had ever heard that word with that group, and I didn't hear it anymore.

We played Notre Dame the last game of the season, and we were nine and two overall—eight and one in the games I played. Notre Dame had won nine in a row, and they were favored over us by forty points, but we didn't give that any consideration at all. We beat them 19 to 14. The commandant of the base was so pleased that he said, "You boys can go home." He gave us a three-day pass. So we got home the rest of Saturday, Sunday, and didn't have to come back till Monday afternoon.

After the football season, the commander of the base called me in and congratulated me on my trouble-free stay with the team. He said something good was going to happen, but he wouldn't tell me what it was. That was the selection for me to go through officer training, beginning in January of 1944. I had made third-class boatswain's mate by then and was getting frustrated about not advancing any faster. All of a sudden, I jumped to first-class petty officer as soon as the officer class started.

The officer in charge of Camp Robert Smalls during this training was Commander Daniel Armstrong, whose father had founded the Hampton Institute for the education of blacks. I never had much dealing with him, but I think he was fair. I'm pretty sure that he thought he was the great white father, so he knew the significance of what he was doing, and he relished it. Reginald Goodwin from our group was close to him. Goodwin probably was his clerk. So he knew more about him than anybody else. We didn't have many specific dealings with Commander Armstrong, but we had enough to consider him condescending. We didn't say it that way; we just said he thought he was better than we were. I will say that he didn't do anything to harm us.

At times I thought the attitude of the instructors was similar to Commander Armstrong's—condescending. I think they were trying to do a good job because they were concerned about their own advancement. If your pupils do well, that means you've done well as a teacher. But they manifested their attitude toward us in small ways, such as in their mannerisms. I felt that sometimes they envisioned themselves as being sort of like God, trying to pass on this information to people who probably couldn't absorb all of it anyway. Now, I don't know whether that would be a true statement or not, but that was just the way I felt.

These instructors were people who had been in the Navy for some time. We had a chief boatswain's mate, a machinist's mate, and several others for the various courses. They'd teach the courses and test on the courses, and we would try to get as near a 4.0 as we could. We came pretty close because we had a pretty good group of guys. We wanted everybody to succeed. We weren't trying to be at the pinnacle ourselves and everybody else under us. We were trying to go up together. I don't think there was any special joy that I felt when the course was over. Maybe I had too much faith in myself, but I just thought if anybody else was going to make it, I was going to be one of them. That isn't to say that I ever took it for granted; I worked as hard as I could to make sure I would be among those who made it. I did have a couple of advantages. One was that I was among the best educated in the group with my master's degree, and I also had the advantage of being fresh from my time at Howard when I went into the Navy.

I will say that we were under a strain, but I think most of us were too resilient to feel anything but good about what we were doing. Nobody was selfish. I don't remember a one of them who was selfish. We did have one who was cocky and brash. That was Dennis Denmark Nelson II. Dennis was the most outspoken of us, and he would

Martin as a newly commissioned ensign.

push himself into situations where I might have held back and waited to be invited. He felt that he was equal to anybody—more than anybody else in the group felt that way. And he carried himself in that peacock fashion. But make no mistake about it, he was a brilliant man, even though he had those showoff characteristics. I think he was the one that should have stayed in the Navy, and he did.

When we got our commissions as officers in March of 1944, I felt that I had probably had more satisfying moments than that previously. Even so, I felt good about it, and I just wondered what the next step was going to be and how they were going to use us. I know I wasn't thinking about this as being any kind of history-making event at the time. I was just thinking about getting what I was due. I had a master's degree, and I ought to be able to at least get further than a third-class petty officer in seventeen months. After all, I'd known some whites that had become officers right out of high school.

I was retained at Great Lakes as a battalion commander, which was an early tip-off to me that the Navy didn't know what to do with us. Because I didn't need to be a battalion commander, really. Some of the battalion commanders before that time had been chief petty officers, so they didn't need to waste an ensign. I really don't know, but they probably feared incidents, and they didn't want anything to happen. They thought they'd keep us there, sort of protected. I brought my wife up to Great Lakes, and we lived out in town. We stayed until around D-Day, June 6, 1944.

We left shortly after that, but I do remember something from that brief period. I've got to tell this. On a day off once, my wife and I went to Chicago. I was wearing my blue uniform when we went into a restaurant, and the people there looked at us funny. I'd seen that look before. They served us, and no sooner had we gotten out than we had to go to the bathroom. And we had to go to the bathroom for the next twelve hours, both of us, one after another. I think they put croton oil, which is a laxative, into the food. That's the way they treated a commissioned officer in the Navy.

From Great Lakes I went to San Francisco and served with Frank Sublett in *YP-131,* a yard-patrol craft. This was another made-up job because they didn't need two officers. But I said to myself, "Even though I resent it, I'd better go ahead and do a good job because if I

Graham E. Martin   23

Graham and Alma Martin in downtown Chicago, a city where unfriendly restaurant operators put laxative in their food.

don't, that will give them something to talk about." Among our duties—we took nurses out sight-seeing around Alcatraz. Another factor in that duty was that the crew of the patrol craft was white when we reported. As we learned how to handle the patrol craft, they were allowed to go on to other duty. And then we finally got a totally black crew. Maybe the Navy didn't want white enlisted men to have to work for black officers.

After that I was the skipper of a yard oiler, which was a tougher job. There also they went through the process of taking the whites off. Fortunately, I had good people working for me, including one white man who didn't want to leave. One time, however, I did have a problem. I had a warrant officer under me, and I went ashore one time and left him in charge. I told him that if he got a fueling order at night, to give me a call. He wasn't supposed to do it himself. But he tried to make that trip, and he ran against the dock. So I got a bad letter for that because I was responsible, according to the Navy regulations. That was one of the factors that led me to get out of the Navy later, even though my wife wanted me to stay in. With that in my service jacket, I knew I wouldn't be able to live it down.

Most of the encounters that I had with white officers or white enlisted men were very good, but I do remember an incident when I was walking on the base at Treasure Island. A sailor went by who didn't salute, and I was in a particularly devilish mood that day, so I decided, "I'm going to see about this." I said, "Hey, sailor. Would you come back here, please?" He came back and looked at me square in the eye. I said, "Are you supposed to salute officers?"

"Yes, sir."

"Well, you didn't salute me."

"No, sir."

"What's the matter? Why didn't you?" He gave no answer, so I said, "Oh, I see what it is." So I took my hat off, stuck my hat out in front of him, and I said, "Now salute the insignia of the United States Navy."

He saluted smartly and said, "But you understand that I'm not saluting you."

I said, "I understand, but you understand that you're supposed to salute this insignia." That's the only real incident that I ever had because I tried to avoid them, and I imagine most other people did too. A few sailors would cross the street to avoid saluting, but that was all right. I wasn't bothered much about that. That was their problem, not mine.

After San Francisco I was assigned for a while to Hawaii and to Eniwetok in the Marshall Islands. My duties at Eniwetok included being a straw boss for a stevedore gang unloading ships. I was also involved with recreation and physical fitness for the men stationed there. Naturally, I was well qualified for that kind of duty, but it still didn't seem like a real assignment. Again, I felt that the Navy didn't know what to do with us, and they were just trying to make sure that we weren't pushed into any situations where we couldn't extricate ourselves. I don't know whether they were trying to protect us or hold us back. I'd rather be positive and think that they were trying to protect us.

When the war came to an end, I felt a real sense of exhilaration that I had survived, and so had Alma's five brothers. They were all in the war zone too. I got shipped from there back to Great Lakes to write speeches for an admiral and then to Washington, D.C., to work in the Navy's public-information office. But there really wasn't anything to do, so I was eager to get out and get into the career in education that I had prepared for before the war. I had a physical exam at Great Lakes before I got out, and the doctors discovered that my knees were gimpy. That wasn't too surprising after all the football I had played. But there wasn't anything really service-connected, and soon I was on my way back to civilian life.

In 1946 I sent my applications to schools again. I got a favorable response from Bluefield, West Virginia, and from Southern in Louisiana. I chose Bluefield as the lesser of evils because one is near South, and one is deep South. I stayed there only one year. I kept asking the boss about a raise, and he was putting me off. Then I got a letter from my high school principal in Indianapolis, telling me that I could come back and get a job on the coaching staff at Crispus Attucks. I coached from the season of 1947 through 1971.

Initially, the school was all black. Then the public schools were integrated in 1954, and the immediate impact was to lessen our acquisition of good football players. The football team started to suffer, although the basketball team at that time became better. It was not really because of integration because we didn't have any white

Martin takes a hand at steering the destroyer *Kidd* during the Golden Thirteen's reunion on board the ship in 1982.

boys on the basketball team for a long time. Eventually, the school wound up about 60 percent black and about 40 percent white. At the time people were afraid integration wouldn't work. They thought people would stone the school bus and tear up the school, but all that sort of thing didn't happen.

We never did have any powerhouse teams. In fact, my best team was the one in 1965 that finished with a five-and-five record. But they had gotten off to a terrible start, losing their first four games, so it was a real achievement to finish that well. After I stopped coaching, I stayed on as a teacher and counselor for another eleven years until I retired in 1982.

In all of my teaching and coaching, I tried always to stimulate positively. On one of the buildings down at Indiana University there is a saying something like this: "A teacher is supposed to inspire, as well as instruct." That just struck me, and it stuck with me. The way the kids have come back over the years and told me of their accomplishments in life, I know I succeeded.

Chapter Two

Training the Golden Thirteen

Paul D. Richmond

The years have been kind to Paul Richmond. As a result of his success of many years as a stockbroker, he and his wife, Virginia, live in a sumptuous home on the outskirts of Detroit. They are both friendly, gracious people. Fate played a large part in the fact that Richmond spent most of his adult life in the civilian world. Because of vision problems, he served in the Navy only during the war years, rather than making a career of the service. Even so, his graduation from the Naval Academy remains a source of great satisfaction, and he continues to visit Annapolis often.

Unlike two other white officers whose memoirs appear in this volume, Richmond did not volunteer for service in connection with black sailors and officers. Indeed, except for his eyesight problem he might have spent most or all of the war in fighting ships at sea. Circumstance sent him ashore when the war began, and circumstance assigned him to duty training black sailors for service at sea. So deeply ingrained was the Naval Academy ethic that an officer energetically carried out the duty ordered, even if it was not something he asked for.

A central figure throughout the training of the Golden Thirteen was Commander Daniel W. Armstrong, who ran the camp where the black sailors were converted into officers. He was the son of Brigadier General Samuel Chapman Armstrong, a Civil War veteran who in 1867 established the Hampton Institute in Hampton, Virginia, as a college and trade school for blacks. Daniel Armstrong was born in 1893, the same year his father died. He graduated from the Naval Academy in 1915, then transferred to the reserve in 1919. He was recalled to active duty for World War II and reported to Great Lakes in 1942 to supervise the training of black sailors when the general-service ratings opened up in June of that year.

It is interesting to see Armstrong through different sets of eyes and to contemplate the varying perceptions of him. To the white officers working for him, he was a superb officer. To the black officer candidates, he was a self-important, condescending Southerner. With both groups he was the same person, but he came across differently on the basis of the experiences, attitudes, and expectations of those who served under him.

Perceptions are also a key factor in assessing the training provided to the officer candidates. Several of the Golden Thirteen expressed in their interviews the idea that the course of instruction was deliberately made difficult so that they would fail. Paul Richmond's testimony is especially valuable on that point because he was the man who set up that curriculum, and as he explains, the training in 1944 was not a test. He was ordered to make officers of these black enlisted men. In the Naval Academy tradition, he said, "Aye, aye, sir," and set out to make of them the best-trained officers he could. It was not a grudging project on his part. He developed a genuine admiration for these men who came to be called the Golden Thirteen. He continues to take pride in his association with them nearly fifty years ago.

*f*or the most part, I grew up in Highland Park, Michigan, a section of Detroit that was famous as the site of the factory in which the Model T Ford was built. When I graduated from high school in 1938, I had a principal appointment to the Naval Academy. It had been a long wish of mine to go to the academy, so I was just delighted. I passed the entrance exam, the physical exam, and entered the academy in the summer of '38 as part of the class of 1942.

Because the war was developing during my time as a midshipman, the academy programs were accelerated so that our class was scheduled to graduate on December 19, 1941—almost six months early. We did graduate and get our commissions on that date, but in the meantime the Japanese attacked Pearl Harbor on December 7. Along with all the other damage, they knocked out the ship I was slated for, the battleship *Nevada*. In addition, my eyesight had deteriorated while I was at Annapolis, so I was given a Naval Reserve commission. Because I wasn't considered eligible for sea duty at that early stage of the war, I was reassigned to the Great Lakes training station.

I reported in on January 2 and got involved right away in the training of recruits that were coming in. Even though my commission as an officer was brand-new, I still had the advantage that few Naval Reserve officers did at that point—nearly four years of Naval Academy training. The station itself was still quite small, but it soon began expanding at just an unbelievable rate. I would say there were probably just two recruit-training regiments at the beginning of 1942. When I left the station in '44, there were close to forty regiments.

It was in the summer of '42 that the Negro was accepted for general ratings in the Navy, and a special regiment was developed to take care of them at a new camp built to the west of the regular sta-

Richmond as an ensign, newly graduated from the Naval Academy. He was a member of the class of 1942, which left Annapolis in December 1941 because of the onset of World War II.

tion. It was part of the station, but the facilities where we went in at Camp Robert Smalls—barracks, recreation hall, drill hall, and so forth—didn't even exist when I went there six months earlier. The camp was named for a former slave who had been a hero for the Navy during the Civil War.

I don't know how I happened to be chosen when the training program was set up for black recruits. It wasn't something I sought,

Commander Daniel W. Armstrong, officer in charge of Camp Robert Smalls, where black sailors were trained at Great Lakes.

nor did I have any desire to avoid it. It was the duty assigned, and I really thought it would be quite a challenge and very interesting. I never regretted it.

There was a special officer assigned to take care of the Negro regiment, Lieutenant Commander Daniel Armstrong, a Naval Academy man. Just four other officers were assigned to help Armstrong develop Camp Robert Smalls: Donald Van Ness, Vance Kauffold, John Dille, and myself. Van Ness was a lieutenant (j.g.); the rest of us were ensigns. With the five of us we had a regimental commander and four battalion commanders—and empty barracks to go along with them. To a great extent, we followed the training routine that had been established for the white recruits over on the main side—as it was called—of the Great Lakes station. But Commander Armstrong was a very innovative officer. His father had started the Hampton Institute for Negroes, so Dan Armstrong himself had a great sympathy for their cause.

I can remember writing home to my mother that he was certainly the best officer that I had ever run into up until that time. And I guess that takes in all the ones that were at the Naval Academy when I was going through the training. So he was a very outstanding man, very imaginative, and an inspirational leader. He was working there all the time. I don't know whether he was divorced or a widower, but he was not married. So he had the time to be there at the regiment, and he was.

He participated in the program in every way possible. He attended the ceremonial reviews weekly. When the men graduated, he was there to pass out a diploma and honor certificate to the outstanding recruit in each company. When we had happy-hour entertainment programs, he always attended and generally had a few remarks for the men. Commander Armstrong brought in black entertainers and other celebrities for the benefit of the recruits. He set up musical programs that were the envy of white sailors on the main side. He installed an E (for excellence) award at Camp Robert Smalls before any of the white regiments had such an award. He was a "can-do" officer who was sincere in his work with the black sailors; I'd say he gave about 102 percent on their behalf. Under his leadership we just developed any number of interesting programs.

For example, we tried to outfit our camp with as many practical

A military policeman checks in the first recruit to enter Camp Robert Smalls for training in the spring of 1942.

training devices as we could think of. I remember we had a 5-inch gun moved into the drill hall for the recruits. We had classrooms set up to teach the signal flags. We had gunnery drills with a gun-loader machine that they could practice on. We built an obstacle course that really was the pride of the Great Lakes station. We had a wooden model of a ship so recruits could go aboard and visualize what a real one would be like. When President Roosevelt came to visit in September of '42, he really spent most of his time while he was at Great Lakes visiting our camp and observing the innovations that we had there. In my opinion, the training facilities at Camp Robert Smalls were comparable to those on the main side and perhaps even better.

Training was only part of our job. From the middle of '42 and into '43, our primary concern was getting the recruits through their basic requirements and out to the fleet. And so there were many things that had to be done, like getting them vaccinated, dental examinations, uniforms, service numbers, dog tags, service records, and so forth. The original recruit-training program, I think, at one time had been three months. Then it was cut down to two months or eight weeks. Still later, I remember putting many companies through in three weeks so we could get them out to the fleet. You don't do a lot of curriculum training when the need for manpower is so urgent.

It was a hectic setup and undoubtedly far different from what many of the men had experienced as civilians shortly before. We call it culture shock now, but as far as the Navy was concerned, the blacks had no different problems than the whites had. The whites were just as upset and felt just as strange about coming into the training program as the blacks. The blacks just didn't know that the whites were experiencing exactly the same things that they were. Of course, in the case of the whites there could be no charge of racial discrimination. But fundamentally the problems were the same. We treated the blacks just like we treated the whites.

For running the individual companies in the recruit battalions we had a group of young men who had been successful athletes in college but not graduates. They had been recruited by Gene Tunney, the former heavyweight boxing champion, and given direct appointments as chief petty officers. There is actually a tunny fish, so the old-line Navy chiefs labeled these new young fellows the "Tunney fish."

They had been promised that they would get commissions directly after coming in as chiefs. It didn't work out that way. I can remember that they still hadn't received their commissions two years later. It was a little bit of a problem when the candidates for the black officers were announced, and some of the white chiefs realized that these brand-new black people were going to be commissioned ahead of them. They developed some resentment of the blacks as a result.

Naturally, these new chief petty officers didn't have any Navy experience when they arrived. So it took some training at the beginning to prepare them. We had a system that was called "shadowing." The new man shadowed the man with more experience by following him around and watching what he did. After six months or a year, as we got into the program, the new men were shadowing somebody who had been shadowing somebody else just three to six months previously. Also, of course, we had a standardized curriculum and training routine, and those were helpful.

I did not have a hand in picking the white chief petty officers who worked with these companies. With few exceptions, they were capable and willing. If we did run into somebody that was antagonistic or didn't measure up to our standards, he was relieved of his duty and sent elsewhere. We didn't try to force this duty on them, although we did have any number of white chiefs there who were very amenable to the program. I remember an occasion when Dorothy Donegan, a black singer and pianist, came to put on a concert. I said to this one chief who was from down in Louisiana someplace, "Come on, let's have dinner with Dorothy Donegan."

He said, "Not on your life. If a picture was ever taken of me having dinner with her, my name would be mud. I couldn't go home."

And I said, "Well, come on. There'll be no pictures." He did come, and there weren't. I think that a great many racial barriers were broken down that way. And when the whole thing was over, we had a better country for it.

Along with my other duties, I was from time to time a shore-patrol officer as well. I had taken white shore patrols to Waukegan and Milwaukee and occasionally to Chicago. We did this even though Chicago had its own white shore patrol down there, so it wasn't part of our responsibility. Our new black regiment necessitated another requirement. When we did finally give liberty to the recruits who had finished their training, we ran a train down to the south side of Chicago for them. I was the only white person on the train when I went on the first black shore patrol the weekend of that liberty.

I had a regular black chief from the old Navy who went along with me. On the train ride down, he said, "When we get there, I'm going to introduce you to'The Man.' 'The Man' will take care of you." And that's all he told me. So when we arrived in the south side of Chicago, we turned the sailors loose and established our patrol. The men were patrolling around the streets and going in and looking at the bars and so forth.

After a while, this chief said, "Come on. We'll meet 'The Man.'" So we went over to a nightclub, where we were ushered right in because this chief seemed to know the people there very well. The next thing I knew, we walked into the back office, and there was "The Man." It was Joe Louis, the famous Negro boxer. I was introduced to him, and the chief said, "The lieutenant here is in charge of the shore patrol, and he wants to have things run properly."

Joe Louis said, "I'll tell you what, Lieutenant. If you have any trouble, you just come to me. But there ain't going to be any trouble." And there wasn't.

In early 1943, after I had been working with the black recruits for more than six months, I decided to write an article about our program and submit it to the Naval Institute *Proceedings* magazine. When I wrote the article, I was actually looking for recognition of the job we had done. I thought it might alert the fleet that these fellows were being trained for regular assignments, that they were no longer just mess attendants and steward's mates. They were sailors. As an example of what black Navy men could do, I wrote about Doris Miller, a mess attendant who operated a machine gun so successfully on board the battleship *West Virginia* at Pearl Harbor that he was afterward awarded the Navy Cross for heroism.

I submitted my article through channels in my effort to get it published. Then the recruit-training officer called me in and wanted to know why I was writing such an article and what was so special about the blacks. He made several comments that he didn't think we needed this extra publicity. I think there was a little jealousy on the part of the whites, an attitude of, "Why make such a thing out of it?" I was told, "You can send it in to the Institute if you want to, but we advise against it." I wrote home to my mother that I lost the argument, but I thought it was more prudent to go along with their thinking than raise a ruckus when it wasn't absolutely necessary.

After a while we began to develop a cadre of men who had been through the program at Camp Robert Smalls and were held over to help administer and train those who came along later. And there were a good many other colored ratings that came along. Eventually, we organized our own service school, right there at Camp Robert Smalls. I would say it was probably towards the end of 1943 that we opened up two more regiments. And so, having started out with one, we now had two recruit regiments, and the 18th regiment housed the service school.

It wasn't until after I left Great Lakes in mid-1944 that the segregated camps were abolished. Up until that time, it was the Navy policy. I would say that maintaining the segregated setup was the wish of Commander Armstrong. He certainly wanted it that way, and it was his baby. He was happy the way it was running.

At one point, I recall, a number of Negro personalities came to visit the camp. They seemed to think that the Navy should do something about breaking the color barrier in sports—for baseball, as an example. They would have liked for just one of our people to play on the white team, as opposed to having an all-black team. Their objective was to be able to use this as a lever after the war to integrate professional baseball, reasoning that if black and white men had played together in the Navy, they should be able to play together afterward. In football, Graham Martin played for the Great Lakes team. Shortly after the war ended, professional baseball and football began integrating.

In late 1943 Commander Armstrong told me that we would soon have the first black officer candidates coming to Camp Robert Smalls for training. By that time, I had been made the commanding officer of the regiment. So really the training of the black candidates fell kind of naturally to me. By that time I was the only one who had been to Annapolis that was there for it. So I got a new challenge. I had probably no more than a month to get ready for yet another training program.

I had nothing to do with the selection of the candidates, and I don't to this day know the particulars of how they were chosen. To

Richmond, shown here after promotion to lieutenant (junior grade), had to put up with the cold Great Lakes winters while serving as a battalion officer at Camp Robert Smalls.

my recollection, nearly all of them had gone through Camp Robert Smalls for basic training. What we tried to do was to set up a program that would parallel the program for the so-called "ninety-day wonder" reserve officers that were trained at Columbia and other universities.

In putting together the curriculum for the course, I made it up by thinking back to my own training. I was only two years out of the Naval Academy, and what I tried to do was to give the officer candidates an abbreviated course in the professional naval subjects that we had studied at Annapolis. Nearly all of these men were college graduates to start out with. In effect, I gave them U.S. Navy 101. I selected subjects like seamanship, navigation, gunnery, naval regulations, and naval law. They spent a little time with the recruit companies to practice their leadership skills.

In my classroom experiences with the black officer candidates, I recall that they were very serious. We'd have question-and-answer sessions. At Annapolis we got a quiz and a grade every day, and essentially the same thing applied in my classes for the black officer candidates. Now, maybe in the classes that some of the other teachers had, they didn't do it that way because they had gone to civilian colleges and whatnot. But I think I gave the candidates a quiz at the end of every program and gave them a grade. And I know that they were all graded on their class performance. Those grades were sent to Washington, and I've heard that they were pretty much in keeping—and maybe a little bit better—than the average white grades.

I had to gear the training to the time available. In the navigation course, for example, I used a textbook that had been published to help yachtsmen and whatnot. I thought it would be easier for the group to tackle this than Benjamin Dutton's well-known text that we had used at the Naval Academy. We taught them basic navigating and things like the points of the compass and dead reckoning. I can remember we had sextants in the room that I was able to get from the main side to show them how star sights were taken and gave them a description. But I don't think that we really ever taught them to work out a star-sight program. In our few weeks together, I gave them an overview of what the problem was. By contrast, I had taken navigation for a whole year, trying to learn what it was all about; it's not an easy subject to grasp for the uninitiated.

In picking instructors, we took the men that were best qualified for it. We had lawyers there who were in the legal department, and they taught the subjects in naval regulations and law. I taught the classes in navigation and gunnery because I figured I was the most qualified. We didn't give the instructors any specific coaching on what sort of attitude to adopt in dealing with the black officer candidates. I suppose in our school at Great Lakes we had some that were excellent, and there may have been some that weren't too good. We didn't assign them a bum instructor on purpose—I'll tell you that. We were trying to assign the best that we had.

Lieutenant John Dille, as he has pointed out in his own interview, was sort of a morale officer and a counselor for the group, and he really spent more time individually with the men than I did. That was his job, and he was excellent at it. It wasn't my job to do that, I didn't feel, and I never did socialize or fraternize with the black officer candidates. I didn't think it was proper for a schoolteacher to be in that capacity.

I didn't think of this program as an experiment. It was a fact. We were making them officers. The assignment was, "Train them, and they're going to be commissioned." I personally tried to make it as difficult for them as I possibly could so that they would get the best training. If I might have scared them a little bit by letting them think that they weren't going to make it, it was on purpose—a way of motivating them. I had no intention of purposely flunking anybody. It was my hope that they all pass.

There was a great divergence of ability and previous training so that some of them learned some things faster than others. I had no objection to their working together in the barracks. I just wanted them to learn the material. I think it was great that they were helping each other. I wasn't aware of the extent that they may have stayed up late at night, but we did that at the Naval Academy too. They were bright, serious men, and I was impressed by their degree of motivation. I recall that Dennis Nelson was a little bit more of a cutup and more gregarious than some of the others, and some were more reserved.

We shied away from trying to foster the sort of competition that is so important at the Naval Academy. At Annapolis the midshipmen are reminded frequently that their class standing can have an effect on their entire careers. With the black students, we made it a group effort. I wasn't trying to have one fellow be ahead of the others. No way.

I've heard that they felt that they were confined in a small area. They were, I guess, but it wasn't to put a hardship on them. That was all the space we had. All the rest of the training was going on. This was in addition. We had the full service school there. They weren't supposed to mingle with the service-school people. We had the recruits there, and they weren't supposed to mingle with the recruits. That sort of necessitated them being confined to their barracks and schoolroom. And they were. They were supposed to be there studying. My God, they were supposed to learn all this technical detail in a very short time. And it probably was tough on them because they were older. Every single one of these men I was teaching was older than I was.

One area that was sensitive was the matter of how these black officers would be treated once they got their commissions. The white officers on the station certainly didn't want the blacks in the officers' club. So I tried to say, "For Pete's sake, you want to be successful. Now, don't be bringing up a lot of things that would quash the program." I don't think I ever told them they couldn't go there. I think I probably told them that it wouldn't be wise for them, and it would be foolish actually, because they would be jeopardizing the program by antagonizing the white officers.

I had a feeling that they wouldn't push things. I still have a copy of a letter I wrote to a friend in April 1944. Among other things, I said of these first black officers, "They are all good leaders and they are not radical in any sense of the word. They were picked because we knew that we could count on them to benefit the Navy and they will not raise racial issues, I am sure, such as coming to the Officers Club or anything of that nature. They are loyal to the Navy."

The member of the group whom I particularly recall is Graham Martin. One incident stands out the most in my mind, and it was really a very serious incident, where he was shadowing a white company commander in order to learn from him. During a Saturday inspection, a white chief petty officer discovered one of the recruits that had a package of cigarettes in his jumper pocket, which was wrong, of course. The chief pulled the package out of his pocket and gave it to Martin and said, "Make him eat these." It was a ridiculous disciplinary tactic that he apparently thought might impress somebody. I don't know how.

In any case, Graham Martin was a fine athlete and an intelligent man that had been trained in physical education, and he knew what the damage would be, so he refused. And the chief said, "You either do it, or you're on report." Martin was put on report for failing to carry out an order. This was reported to me as the regimental commander, so I called Graham in. I said, "From what I have heard, you did the right thing. I don't blame you, and I wouldn't have made the man eat them either. I think it's ridiculous. Let's forget the whole thing." And I didn't discipline the chief either. I took the attitude of, "Instead of looking for problems, let's ignore it."

But the chief didn't ignore it. He told some people on the main side of the camp. The next thing I knew, Commander Armstrong had been called over to explain what kind of an outfit he was running where the Negro candidates weren't obeying orders. Well, I think he changed his mind when he heard the circumstances of the orders, but in any case, Commander Armstrong called me in and said that he had to discipline me in some way for not being more positive. He asked me to write an essay on what I had learned at the Naval Academy about following orders.

In my essay I gave an illustration about the manner in which Lord Nelson, the famous British admiral, carried out some less-than-desirable orders. In the Battle of Copenhagen in 1801, he was ordered by flag signal to withdraw. Nelson, who was aggressive, wanted to keep fighting, so he put a telescope to his blind eye when looking toward the flagship's signal. Commander Armstrong accepted that as my explanation, and the whole matter was dropped.

It's unfortunate that the chief picked on Graham Martin because he picked a pretty great guy. He was tampering with something over his head, and he got defeated. Martin was an Indiana University graduate, and he had a master's degree as well. Then for him to be able to play on the Great Lakes varsity football team was, in my opinion, remarkable. I really felt that Martin was a better man than I was, and I told a lot of people that too. I said, "You wouldn't have this racial prejudice if you really thought this fellow was superior to yourself."

They'd say, "You don't really believe that, do you, Paul?"

I'd say, "My God, the record looks that way. He's done a hell of a lot more than I have."

When the training ended, I wasn't at Great Lakes, so I don't know what factors were used in deciding which men would make it and which wouldn't make it. I wasn't consulted in that. I taught the class, gave them the grades, turned in the grades, and that was the extent of my responsibility. At the time the men were commissioned in March of 1944, I was on leave. I hadn't had any leave in about two years, and so I went to Florida. I was really quite tired out, to tell you the truth, after this intensive program of training the officers and writing a lot of the program. I was just very happy to go down to Florida and lie on the beach for a while. The candidates were commissioned during that time, and I never saw them again, though I was always curious about what became of them. Years later, I contacted them when I learned they were having a reunion on board the destroyer *Kidd*.

Some months after their training ended, I arrived in Hawaii, where Jack Dille was stationed at an ammunition camp. Dan Armstrong was out there. He'd been promoted to captain by that time and was still coordinating the Negro-in-the-fleet program. And he was helpful. The Navy personnel office was considering whether I'd be assigned to something still in the Negro program. I expressed a desire to see some fighting, and the Negroes weren't where the fighting was going on.

I think Captain Armstrong appreciated my request and probably pulled some strings which got me onto Rear Admiral John L. Hall's staff that went in on the Okinawa invasion in April 1945 on the USS *Teton*. After the war was over, I left active duty. Since I didn't have the experiences of my classmates who had spent the entire war in combat or combat-related duty, I would have started out behind in the postwar Navy and stayed behind. That's why I chose to pursue a career in civilian life, and it has been a very satisfying one.

In looking back at Camp Robert Smalls and my role in training the officer candidates, I remember it as a very gratifying experience; I thoroughly enjoyed it. I didn't want to have that as my only experience in the Navy—to become an expert on race relations—but it was a pleasant experience for me.

Chapter Three

Living a Respectable Life

Samuel E. Barnes

Dr. Samuel Barnes lives only a few blocks from the Army's chief medical facility, Walter Reed Hospital, though he is neither a physician nor an Army man. The tree-lined street in northwest Washington, D.C., is in a comfortable old neighborhood. The welcome mat on the doorstep of the brick-and-stucco home suggests the hospitality of those who live there. Upon entering the house, one feels the sense of going into a Golden Thirteen museum. The foyer just inside the front door is lined with pictures, plaques, and other indications of Barnes's role as one of the Navy's first black officers.

Just off the foyer is a living room that serves a similar function for the Barnes clan, displaying dozens and dozens of family photos. This is no accident, for family is important to Sam Barnes and his wife, Olga. They were married just before he entered officer training, and Mrs. Barnes is quick to point out that theirs is the only one of the Golden Thirteen families with a second-generation member of the Navy, son Michael. Artwork done by architect Alexa Donaphin, one of their daughters, also adorns the room. Their other daughter, Michele Barnes Welch, is a professor at the University of Tennessee.

Like most of the members of the Golden Thirteen, Sam Barnes was an athlete. Unlike the rest of them, he spent virtually his entire professional life involved in some sort of sports. Even today he has the slim build of the sprinter he was sixty years ago. He majored in academics as well as athletics; he was the only member of the Golden Thirteen to earn a doctorate. As a result of the combination, he distinguished himself in the field of sports administration, serving as both coach and athletic director. A measure of his achievement in the field was his selection as the first black member of the governing council of the National Collegiate Athletic Association.

The professional manner that enabled Dr. Barnes to achieve success in his chosen field is apparent in his approach to oral-history interviews. At times he seems to be giving a speech, for he has doubtless given many of them over the years. Rather than simply relating anecdotal information, he puts the actions of the Golden Thirteen into the perspective of overall race relations. He doesn't just talk about the collegiate sports of his era but compares them with the current sports environment, in which athletics seem to have become an all-too-powerful end in themselves, rather than avenues to fitness, character-building, and school spirit. Of all the oral histories comprising this collection, Dr. Barnes's is the most thorough. That is partly a result of his geographical proximity to the Naval Institute and partly his willingness to make the record as complete as possible. He has a genuine desire to see history recorded while it is available. He spent more time than any other member of the Golden Thirteen in editing his transcript—perhaps a reflection of his academic habits. He also spent more time than anyone else in discussing the details of the group's time together at Great Lakes in 1944. Scholars researching that period would do well to examine his entire transcript.

In recent years, as part of the legacy of the Golden Thirteen, Barnes has been active in fostering minority recruiting programs to get more blacks into naval service. One occasion symbolized more than almost anything else the interests he still holds. At a Washington Redskins' game in Robert F. Kennedy Stadium he helped swear in a Redskin company of Navy recruits. That moment captured two major themes of his life, sports and the Navy.

*M*y brother and sisters and I were born in Oberlin, Ohio. My father was from North Carolina, and my mother was from Kentucky; however, they decided to raise and educate their family in Oberlin because it was one of the most liberal communities in the United States. It was a halfway station for escaping slaves who were traveling to northern cities in the nineteenth century as part of the underground railroad.

Oberlin was a town of about forty-five hundred people when I was growing up, and we enjoyed many rich experiences there. My father was a chef at the Oberlin College dormitories. My mother, who was a college graduate, owned and operated our family laundry. She was active in women's programs and in church activities. She was also active in politics. For instance, she was an alternate delegate in 1936 to the Republican Party national convention, at which Alf Landon was nominated as the presidential candidate to run against Franklin D. Roosevelt.

I had one brother and three sisters. All of us finished college, which was one of the ambitions of our parents. Therefore, they provided a great deal of the financial support for our education. I always admired my older brother, James, who was named after our father. He was an outstanding athlete, both in high school and college. James died in 1935 while he was the director of athletics and head basketball coach at Virginia State College in Petersburg. He impressed on me the importance of conditioning. That has followed me throughout my life; my weight has not varied five pounds since 1932. I am still 5 feet, 10 inches and weigh 175 pounds.

Our parents emphasized cooperation in all family chores: helping with the garden, canning fruit, and so forth. Mom taught my brother and me how to sew and iron our clothes. From the time we were nine years old, she never did any of those things for us. Dad taught us to cook, so I've been pretty self-sufficient around the house ever since. Mom always said, "You'd better learn all you can, because you don't know who you may marry." On the question of race, she taught us other lessons. For instance, she pointed out that Oberlin was more liberal than a lot of places we might grow up. However, she often said, "What exists here, you will not find everywhere, so you must learn to adjust to wherever you may be. But never lose your dignity." She and Dad constantly preached this idea to all their children.

I don't want to imply that we were always angels as children. We often joked that the only reason we weren't juvenile delinquents was that we didn't get caught doing wrong. We did "borrow" apples, grapes, and other fruits from time to time. And we did engage in the mischievous things that some kids do as they grow up. Sometimes we would get into fights, especially when we were called "nigger." Now you hear people speak of "blacks." I don't know how many fights I had early in my life because I was called "black," especially when I was competing on sports teams. Our mother talked to us about this issue of race: "You're not better than others, but you're as good as others. You must live the kind of life that will make people respect you, regardless of your color. You don't have to be liked, but be sure you are respected."

As a family we spent a lot of time in church while we were growing up. We'd go to Sunday school in the morning, and then we would attend the church services. In the evening we would return to church for a meeting of the BYPU, the Baptist Young People's Union. So we were in church all day on Sundays; we were involved in clubs, we were involved in church activities, and we sang in the choir. While Dad would be working on Sundays, the rest of us went to church and sat in the same pew. Next to Mother was my eldest sister, then my brother, then my other sister, then my twin sister, and I was on the end. I believe my mother had the longest arm in our church because if she saw me doing something, she could reach across those four other children and strike me, never taking her eyes off the minister while she was doing it. We never dared to question the authority of our parents.

Our values were established early at home and were reinforced both in the church and in the community. If we ever failed to live up to those values, our parents gave the adults in the town the option of correcting us on the spot. Then we could expect another lecture when we got home. We learned early what discipline was. I never forgot, for years later, when I became an ensign in the Navy, the officer who gave me the oath of commissioning said, "Now you are an officer and a gentleman."

I replied, "Sir, I wish to say one thing. I was a gentleman before I entered the Navy. You can make me an officer, but my parents made me a gentleman."

In 1932 I was elected to our high school honor society. That fall I enrolled in Oberlin College, which was, and still is, a very selective institution. It enrolled only those high school graduates who were at the top of their classes. I still believe that one of the reasons I was admitted to the institution was the fact that my family lived in Oberlin, and we were known. I graduated in 1936.

While I was growing up, I was very much involved in sports. I was selected to all-conference teams in football, track, and basketball in both high school and college. In track I established a broad jump record at Oberlin College that may still stand: 23 feet, 6 inches. My brother held the record previously. James was a better athlete than I ever was. Whatever I may have achieved was because I tried to emulate him in everything I did. I played the same positions he did in team sports. I was a guard in basketball and an end in football. In track and field I was a sprinter and broad jumper because he had participated in both. As a sprinter I ran the 100-yard dash, the 220-yard dash, the 440-yard dash, and one leg on the mile-relay team. I was a busy man during track meets.

While in high school I once ran in a state meet against Jesse Owens, the sprinter who later won gold medals in the 1936 Olympics. I don't need to tell you what the result was; he ran away from me. Even so, it was great to be in the same race with him. His style was just picturesque, he ran so effortlessly. Jesse, in my judgment, was one of the cleanest-cut persons I have ever known. He was neither boisterous, nor was he a showoff or a braggart. As he did in the Olympics, he let his actions speak for him. I regret now that so many of our current youngsters have not emulated more of his style. Many of our present athletes and coaches are too concerned with winning. Seemingly, they don't realize the value of having athletes do the best they can, regardless of the outcome. Also, individuals too often put their own achievements ahead of those of the team. During the period of time when I was competing, the coaches seemed to be more concerned with developing their players than gaining accolades for themselves.

When I graduated from college I decided I wanted to be a teacher. Nothing else interested me as much. So I accepted a position at Livingstone, a small college in Salisbury, North Carolina. It had perhaps 200 to 250 students enrolled. My starting salary was $75.00 a month. My college classmates were amazed that I was able to find a job in 1936 because the Depression was still with us. While at Livingstone I coached football during the fall and both men's and women's basketball during the winter months. I taught all the physical-education classes, both theoretical and practical; directed the intramural programs; and served as an assistant to the dean of the college. I also taught courses in biology and mathematics when there was a need for assistance in those departments.

I recall that when I started out with my first football team, only twelve players appeared for practice. I had to go around to the dorms and elsewhere on campus to find students who were both available and interested. We finally had about thirty players on the team. I accepted the efforts they made and the fact that each man played as well as he could. We played a number of the well-known black colleges in the South, although we weren't able to travel far enough to play a power such as Florida A & M. When we had to travel to an away game, we had to go around town and find people with cars who would help transport the team. We carried the football uniforms in the car trunks. If we had to stay overnight somewhere, we were housed in a college dorm.

Segregation existed in North Carolina, to be sure, but I avoided situations that could have caused problems. I was sensitive to the situation and didn't get involved in anything other than teaching, coaching, and helping our students. I avoided contacts with white people unless absolutely necessary. I used my initials at that time, "S. E.," because in that area people were on a first-name basis. If white people had known my name was Sam, that's exactly what I would have been called. So when they asked me what my name was, I replied, "S. E. Barnes."

"What does the S. stand for?" they'd ask.

I said, "It doesn't stand for anything."

"What does the E. stand for?"

"It's just E. My parents named me S. E. Barnes, so that's my name." So I was never called Sam, but they did call me "Professor." White people would rather call a black man by a title such as "Doctor" or "Reverend" or something like that rather than say, "Mister." I accepted being called "Professor," for it was a lot better than some of the things they might have said. I'd meet with some white people and chat with them, but there was never any real socialization. That suited me as well as it probably suited them. I deliberately avoided situations that might have led to unpleasantness.

I remained at Livingstone from 1936 to 1941, after which I accepted a job as the boys' work secretary at the Ninth Street YMCA in Cincinnati, Ohio. There, among other duties, I helped youngsters earn and save money so they could afford to go to summer camp. I had to resign that position because of the beginning of World War II. My twin sister, Becky, had a friend at the local draft board, and she warned me that my name was due to come up in the next call. The day before I would have been drafted, I enlisted in the Navy. My principal reason was that the Navy's training bases were mostly in the North. If I had been drafted into the Army, I didn't have any idea where I might be sent, probably in the South. Getting away from that kind of environment was the reason my parents had moved to Oberlin years earlier.

My recruit training was in Camp Robert Smalls at Great Lakes, Illinois. I recall quite vividly the first night I spent in boot camp. We slept in hammocks that we slung between posts in a large open bay. All night long, people were falling out of their hammocks. We were all new recruits and didn't know how to get into the hammocks or how to stay in them. Gradually, we got the hang of it and adjusted to this new way of life.

One thing I found appealing about boot camp was that—as I expected—the Navy was such a clean service. We washed our uniforms daily and hung them up to dry. There was never anything dirty because we washed so often. During our inspections, which were held daily, the inspecting officer wore white gloves. He'd run his hands under the tables and other out-of-the-way places. If he ever got his gloves dirty, the company got a bad mark. During personnel inspections, he checked our uniforms, haircuts, and shaves. We had to be ready for inspection at any time, which developed good discipline.

While in training, I was selected the company clerk and later was chosen as honor man of my company. During recruit training I'm sure that I benefited from being a college graduate and having had several years of work experience. As honor man I was given the choice between going to a service school as an aviation machinist's mate or staying on the base as part of the ship's company—as it was called—at Great Lakes. I chose the latter because it gave me an opportunity to stay in recreation and athletics, both of which I was familiar with. Later I was transferred to the service-school-selection office, where I was involved in interviewing recruits. The purpose was to determine what fields in the Navy best matched up with their backgrounds and capabilities.

The head of Camp Robert Smalls was Commander Daniel Armstrong. My only contact with him was in a recreational situation, which wasn't surprising because of my background in sports. I was on duty in the drill hall one day when Commander Armstrong came in and asked me, "What's your name, sailor?" I told him, and he asked, "Do you play badminton?"

I answered, "Yes, sir," although I had never played badminton in my life.

He said, "Well, I want you to have the nets up tomorrow. I'll be here at twelve o'clock, because I want to play badminton."

I said, "Yes, sir," and immediately went to the library and found a book on badminton. Then I spent some time practicing what I had read. I had enough athletic ability that I picked the game up pretty quickly. After that first day, Commander Armstrong began coming every day at noon to play badminton. I'd have the net up, the rackets and birds out, and we would play for about an hour. He was a good player and enjoyed winning; he was very competitive and really battled over every point. I tried to make the games interesting, but as I got better at it, I had to be careful that I didn't win more than he did. For instance, if we played four games, he'd win three and I'd win one. If we played six, I would win two, and he would win four. He always came out on top. He had more knowledge and experience with the game. I knew just the bare fundamentals, but I did have the advantages of youth, speed, and coordination. He had the advantage of being the boss. I tried to make each game competitive without embarrassing him. I don't think he ever knew that I was deliberately missing points to let him win.

During the time we were at Great Lakes, I viewed Commander Armstrong as someone who was straitlaced. He was the kind of a person whom you couldn't joke with, for he wouldn't ever stoop to frivolity. Commander Armstrong always walked straight and carried himself in a dignified manner; his uniform was always immaculate. He gave the impression of being a rooster presiding over a bunch of hens. He was pompous, although not to the point of strutting. He was proud of his position and rigid in his interpretation of the rules, but I respected him because he was fair and he was consistent.

Back while I was teaching at Livingstone College, I had met and dated a lady named Olga Lash. At some point we decided to get married. She had a teaching job in New Jersey, and we really had to do some figuring to determine how we would make it financially because I wasn't getting paid a lot as a third-class petty officer in the Navy. I was able to do some moonlighting to supplement my Navy pay. The Johns-Manville Company had an asbestos plant near the base at Great Lakes, and they hired people on a part-time basis. I went to their office and was hired. After dinner in the evening, when I was not on duty, I'd go to the plant in Waukegan and work until midnight, five nights a week. The asbestos plant didn't operate on weekends, so on Saturdays and Sundays I worked in the Campbell Soup factory in Chicago. I'd catch a few hours of sleep at the USO shelter on Saturday nights. I followed this routine for three months to save enough money for the wedding and a honeymoon.

Olga and I were married in North Carolina on December 19, 1943. After we enjoyed a reception in Oberlin, I returned to Great Lakes. One day soon after returning to naval duty, I was sitting in the interviewing office when Commander Armstrong came in and said, "Barnes, you are relieved. You must report immediately to the main side." Naturally, I was concerned because the only time black seamen were summoned to the main side was for something unusual. The main side was a part of the base strictly for whites only. I reported along with two other men from the interviewing office, Reginald Goodwin and Lewis Williams.

The wedding of Olga Lash and Samuel Barnes in December 1943.

When we reported to the commanding officer's office, we saw several other blacks waiting, none of whom we knew. Finally, we were asked if we knew why we were there, and we said we didn't. Then we were told, "The Navy has decided to commission Negroes as officers in the United States Navy, and you have been selected to attend an officers' indoctrination school." We were told that in order to be considered, we had to be at least first-class petty officers. I had been a third-class petty officer for almost a year, and in less than a minute I was promoted to first class. That was a nice boost.

Many, many times since that day I have been asked, "Why were you selected?" The simple, truthful answer is that I don't know why or by whom. I'm sure there were many qualified Negro sailors who could have been selected.

After we changed our rates, we returned to Camp Smalls, where we were housed in a barracks separate from the rest of the black sailors being trained there. We attended classes in our barracks from eight in the morning until noon, when we had chow, then returned to our barracks to go to class from one to five. At first we were concerned about being completely isolated from the other sailors on the base. But we were told, "You are here for a specific purpose. We want to see what the situation is, and we don't want any distractions."

Soon after we began this routine, we gathered as a group in our barracks and held a meeting. We came to the conclusion that we were involved in an experiment, and we determined that we were not going to fail. It was then that we vowed to follow the motto of the Three Musketeers: "All for one and one for all." When we first got there, George Cooper was a chief petty officer, and the rest of us were first-class petty officers. Since he outranked us, he suggested that the rest of us march behind him on the way to the chow hall and back. That's when Jesse Arbor piped up and said, "Hell, don't let them stripes go to your head. I ain't walking behind you. Don't forget that you're one of us." Cooper agreed, and nobody was ever designated as the leader for the group.

At an early meeting, while discussing our studies, we decided that whatever knowledge any one of us had on a given topic would be shared with everyone else. We decided not to compete with other members of the group, so we had many study sessions together. We were determined to succeed in spite of the burdens that would be placed on us. We knew that we were the foot in the door for many other black sailors, and we were determined not to be the ones who were responsible for having the foot removed.

In the evenings, after lights were supposed to be out in the barracks, we went into the head and grilled each other. What we had in class that day, we would go back over. That reinforced the things we had learned that day and prepared us mentally for the next day. The subjects we studied dealt with professional Navy topics such as navigation, gunnery, aircraft recognition, naval history, Navy regulations, signaling by flags and Morse code, seamanship, and survival techniques. We learned all of these subjects from classroom lectures. We rarely left the barracks and never went aboard ship. We did receive rifle-range practice and leadership duties with assigned recruit companies. For the most part, though, we had to learn vicariously rather than through actual experience.

We worked constantly at a fast pace because we were given an intensive course. We didn't have much of a personal relationship with the instructors during the entire program; it was all business. They never made us feel inferior, but they let us know they were there for a purpose. They wanted us to realize at all times that they were in command, but they didn't have to force that upon us. We respected their positions of authority. When the program was over, one instructor, Lieutenant Richmond, admitted to us that he had not asked to work with us but had been assigned to do so. He said, "I deliberately made the course work difficult for you. When you finished the courses, you actually had completed the equivalent of a semester at the Naval Academy. I want to congratulate you for the way you have handled the pressure and did so well under the circumstances." His statements helped us realize that what we had done went beyond the expectations of many people.

The most talkative member of our group was Jesse Arbor. He was entertaining, but once in a while he talked too much, so we'd tell him, "If you don't shut up, we're going to put you in the head and lock the door." Another one who talked a lot was Dennis Nelson, who was also the most flamboyant and the most pompous. Nelson was a very precise person and had several idiosyncrasies. One of the things that I recall about him is that he never carried anything but new money. When he was paid, he would take his money to the bank and exchange all of it for brand-new bills. He washed his car every day. He was always very neat, almost to the point of being obnoxious. Once he became an officer, his uniforms were always cleaned and pressed. He was the only member in the group who had every conceivable type of uniform, formal and informal.

After we took our oaths as officers, we were told to go to the base store and buy our new uniforms because we had been given an allowance to cover the cost. Instead, we went to Chicago and had our uniforms individually tailored in a store downtown. Of course, that cost a little more, but when we came out our uniforms were really spick-and-span, which reflected our pride in being officers.

At the time we were commissioned, each of us received a letter from the Secretary of the Navy, Frank Knox, on our new status as ensigns. That was ironic, since Knox had been dragging his feet on getting Negroes commissioned. About a month after we became offi-

Newly commissioned Samuel Barnes poses with his father, James, who worked for many years as a chef at Oberlin College. Margaret S. Barnes, mother of the naval officer, was active in church work and Republican Party politics.

cers, Knox died. We had a little laughter about that. We weren't laughing about the fact that he had passed away, but the little joke among us was that once the Navy commissioned Negroes, it was just too much for him to accept. It was an unkind thought, but we were not serious. At the time it happened, someone said, "Do you think our being commissioned had anything to do with his death?"

And somebody else said, "Well, maybe it sort of expedited it."

A few of us were assigned duty at Great Lakes after we received our commissions. One of these was Reginald Goodwin, who was quite a mature person. Those of us who went through the training together really looked up to him, not because he was older but because he was one of the first Negroes to receive a petty-officer rating at Great Lakes. He was an astute man and someone who didn't involve himself in any kind of frivolity. As officers, he and I lived in a house in the town of Lake Forest with a man and his wife. We were roommates and went to the base together every morning as officers.

Under the watchful eye of Ensign Barnes, lower left corner, hundreds of recruits go through calisthenics at Camp Robert Smalls in 1944.

So I got to know him better than I knew the other fellows. I had a great deal of respect for him because he was very businesslike and very impressive. When he walked into a room, he made an instant impression because he was a nice-looking guy and carried himself at all times with a great deal of pride.

As an officer I was placed in charge of both the recreational and athletic programs for the Negro sailors at Great Lakes. For instance, the renowned singer Lena Horne once came out to Robert Smalls to entertain the sailors and officers. I was responsible for setting up her visit and for acting as her escort. I arranged all of the sports activities, such as individual and company competitions. I set up all of the schedules for games and arranged for the use of the large drill halls. I enjoyed that duty because we had plenty of equipment, and it fit right in with my previous experience in recreation and coaching. I have a photograph from those days that I value very much; it shows me and a whole drill field full of cadets going through exercises.

There was another aspect of the job that wasn't so pleasant. After we had settled into a routine as ensigns, the honest-to-goodness reality set in. In a number of instances we were embarrassed and made to feel that we weren't really bona fide naval officers. For instance, we were denied the privilege of going to the officers' club on the main side at Great Lakes. We were also denied the opportunity to become officers of the day. In our initial assignments, we acted as junior officers of the day; the officers of the day were white. We would wear a web belt while a white officer would have a web belt, a gun, and the complete authority. We junior officers just trailed around behind the white officer while on duty; it was a demeaning position to accept. We also learned that the Negro sailors were unhappy to see Negro officers not being treated with the same respect shown white officers. We felt that we were certainly capable of handling more responsibility, so we pressed for recognition. Finally, the naval authorities decided to advance us to full-fledged officers of the day with complete authority while on duty. But we never were permitted to visit the officers' club.

I remained on duty at Great Lakes until I received orders that I was to report to Williamsburg, Virginia, for training and further reassignment. While there I received training as a logistic-support commander, including the administrative duties involved when working with a group of men. During the indoctrination, we went to a firing range for rifle and pistol practice, received additional equipment, and were assigned a company of men.

At that time a logistic-support company was an all-black stevedore gang, intended to unload cargo from the ships that transported supplies and equipment to distant bases. After several months at Williamsburg, I was transferred to San Francisco. It was there that my company and I boarded a troop transport bound for overseas duty. While the ship was being readied to depart, I happened to look across the deck and saw that an oil tanker had come up alongside. I looked down, and there, to my surprise, were Frank Sublett as the commanding officer and Graham Martin as the executive officer. I hadn't seen them since we were all together back at Great Lakes. We had a joyous reunion just before my company set out for new duty overseas.

The transport took us to Eniwetok in the Marshall Islands. After three weeks there we proceeded to the island of Okinawa, which had been captured from the Japanese. I became personnel officer of our battalion. I was the only Negro naval officer on Okinawa from the time I arrived until I left. One of the white officers in our battalion was Lieutenant Steve Belichick. After the war he worked for many years as an assistant football coach at the Naval Academy. His son Bill is now the head coach of the Cleveland Browns in the National Football League. Steve was from Youngstown, Ohio, and I had known him because he played football in Cleveland at Western Reserve University. The first time I walked into the officers' club in Okinawa, all the officers but one walked out. The only ones left were Steve and I, so I said, "Well, Steve."

He said, "Hell, Sam, don't even worry about it. Let's enjoy having the club to ourselves." He was one of the most unprejudiced persons I'd ever met. After several similar incidents, I guess the white officers got tired of leaving when I came in. Finally, they would remain when I appeared, and nothing unpleasant ever happened. The way they walked out hadn't really bothered me because I wasn't any more anxious to meet them than they were to meet me.

In situations like that, I wasn't eager to push myself forward. I tried not to be conspicuous. I didn't seek out people as if I needed their companionship. I had been taught that people couldn't be

Lieutenant (junior grade) Barnes gives instructions to one of his chief machinist's mates in a machine shop on Okinawa in 1945. Barnes was a division officer of a logistics-support company attached to the 3rd Special Construction Battalion.

forced to accept someone, so I didn't try to cultivate them. On the other hand, I wasn't about to stop going to the club. I suppose the white officers finally realized that I didn't have a tail and wasn't going to bite them. I wasn't going to disappear either, so they decided to stay around even when I did show up. Eventually, I think they came to the conclusion about me that "he isn't as bad as we thought he might be."

In addition to Steve Belichick, the commanding officer of our unit was also a nice person. He was Lieutenant L. W. Musick, and he came from Arlington, Texas, where he had been a civilian lawyer. He and the other white officers in our specific unit were congenial and supportive. We ate together and slept together, and there was never any feeling of uneasiness. Perhaps the fact that they were willing to serve with a unit made up of black enlisted men made them more willing to accept me than the men in the officers' club had been.

At that point, late in the war, Okinawa was being set up as a supply base for the planned invasion of Japan. My company of 120 men was assigned to unload ships. We would leave the base at ten o'clock at night and work until seven o'clock the next morning, when we were relieved by another shift. Each night I would assemble my men and assign them to duties such as driving trucks and unloading cargo. I assigned others to go into the ships and bring the materials out of the holds. Some would load supplies into landing craft, and others would bring them ashore, and still others would transport them once they were on land. I didn't need to go out to the ships because the ships' officers handled that area, but on shore we were responsible for getting the supplies to the proper bases. When my unit was relieved each morning, we would return to the base and have breakfast; then we would try to sleep. As hot as it was out there, that was not the most pleasant kind of experience.

The war ended, of course, without any invasion of Japan. I felt a sense of relief, the same as everybody else. It was unfortunate that the war ended the way it did with the atomic bombs, but it would have been a very, very bloody and extended war if we had tried to invade Japan. On Okinawa we did still have a problem because the island was hit by two typhoons that fall. The velocity of the wind was at least 150 miles an hour. That's where the needle dropped off. The wind shuffled the tin off the Quonset huts in which some persons lived. It was dangerous to venture out during the storms. We couldn't walk around because two-by-fours and other objects were flying through the air like toothpicks.

Once the war was over, the cargo didn't stop coming, but it did slow down. Then I found out that I had accumulated enough points through my service that I was eligible for an honorable discharge. I decided to get out, even though a Navy directive came out that promised a promotion to the next rank for anyone who was willing to reenlist for a minimum of six months. That would have meant the lieutenant rank for me, but I'd had enough of Okinawa by that time.

After my discharge at Great Lakes in early 1946, I went back to

THE SECRETARY OF THE NAVY
WASHINGTON

January 23, 1946

My dear Mr. Barnes:

I have addressed this letter to reach you after all the formalities of your separation from active service are completed. I have done so because, without formality but as clearly as I know how to say it, I want the Navy's pride in you, which it is my privilege to express, to reach into your civil life and to remain with you always.

You have served in the greatest Navy in the world.

It crushed two enemy fleets at once, receiving their surrenders only four months apart.

It brought our land-based airpower within bombing range of the enemy, and set our ground armies on the beachheads of final victory.

It performed the multitude of tasks necessary to support these military operations.

No other Navy at any time has done so much. For your part in these achievements you deserve to be proud as long as you live. The Nation which you served at a time of crisis will remember you with gratitude.

The best wishes of the Navy go with you into civilian life. Good luck!

Sincerely yours,

James Forrestal

James Forrestal

Mr. Samuel E. Barnes
221 N. Main St.
Oberlin, Ohio

Like hundreds of thousands of other Navy men, Barnes received a letter of appreciation for his wartime service from Secretary of the Navy James Forrestal. Secretary Forrestal did much for black naval personnel after taking office in April 1944.

Oberlin, Ohio, to help my parents because my mother wasn't well. While I was there, I decided I might as well get my master's degree. I could have relied solely on the GI Bill for financial support, but I decided to work anyway. So I was the athletic trainer and the supply manager in the athletic department at Oberlin College during the year that I was getting my master's in physical education and administration. After that, a friend of mine from Howard University in Washington, D.C., recruited me to go there as a coach and a physical-education instructor.

I was an assistant coach for the football team and worked with the ends, which was a natural because I had been an end myself. Then they also said I would be the boxing coach, wrestling coach, and the assistant track coach. I did all these things, and I'm very happy because my boxing team was quite successful. In fact, I had an Olympic champion. In 1952 Norvel Lee won the light-heavyweight championship over in Helsinki, Finland. I was never a boxer myself, so I learned it the same way I had picked up badminton back at Great Lakes. I read a book and then stood in front of a mirror and worked on the moves in the book. I also went up to the training camp of Jersey Joe Walcott, a black professional boxer, and also attended other local matches and clinics. So I learned things and passed them on to the members of my team.

Washington was not a hospitable city for blacks in that era. There was no place you could go. You couldn't go into any of the hotels or movie theaters downtown. You couldn't eat in most of the places downtown. I understand from some of the women that they would go into Garfinkel's department store, and they would have to put a shield over their heads in order to try a hat on. You had to ride in the back of the buses and all that sort of thing. It was even worse when you traveled. I can remember driving from Washington to New York and not being able to stop anywhere on the way to go to a restroom. It was very embarrassing, and it was difficult.

After seven years at Howard, I was eligible to apply for a sabbatical leave. That meant I could get a full year off at half pay, so I decided to get my doctorate. Even before then, I was taking extension courses from New York University and Columbia University, in addition to some doctoral courses at Howard. I went to New York City to visit the schools from which I'd been taking extension

A number of black naval pioneers gather in this photo taken at Howard University in the late 1980s: a master chief petty officer, at the top of the enlisted rate structure; Samuel Gravely, first black flag officer; one of the first black women naval aviators; Samuel Barnes of the Golden Thirteen; Wesley Brown, first black Naval Academy graduate; and Captain Eugene Bailey, among the relatively few black four-stripers.

courses. I found out that the person in charge of the physical-education program at Columbia had made a declaration to the effect that no black would get a doctorate in that department while he was there. NYU wasn't much more receptive, so I decided to go to Ohio State University, which was in my home state.

I put in a year on the campus at Columbus, and then the following summers I did additional work toward the degree. I spent some of the time at home in Oberlin, writing the dissertation, and my twin sister typed it for me so that my committee could review it and make corrections. Finally, my degree in administration was awarded. My mother had died by that time, but fortunately, my father was still living, and he and my wife were present when I got my doctorate in 1956. The title of the dissertation was "Criteria for Evaluating the Administration of Intercollegiate Athletics." It had to do with setting standards whereby an individual school could evaluate its program in terms of the level of competition that it could maintain with some integrity. That education and practical training proved valuable for me, since athletic administration was the field in which I spent the rest of my career.

The objective that I tried to follow was one put forth by the president of Oberlin: "Winning is not something you should be ashamed of, but winning in the context of the philosophy of the institution is important." If you ask me, "What was the score of the Oberlin-Wooster game in 1936?" I don't remember. But I remember something that I learned from that game that helped me later in life. When you look at collegiate sports today, we've lost a lot of that ideal. As we go back through the history of athletics, you'll find that the rationale was to be a recreational outlet for the students. Those who had the skills were to participate at the level of others who had the same skills. But it shouldn't be to the extent that sports overshadow the purpose of being in school in the first place. You come to college to get an education, ostensibly, but it often doesn't seem to be that way anymore.

As the years passed, I did the best I could in trying to follow what I thought was the proper approach to college sports. After I'd been there a while, I was selected to be Howard's athletic director and the chairman of the physical-education department. Being the director is much more difficult than being coach because you're responsible for the whole operation, including hiring personnel, arranging schedules, handling the budget, maintaining the physical facilities, and making sure the players meet the academic requirements. Whether things are right or wrong, you are the one responsible.

You have to deal with a lot of personalities, including athletic directors from other schools and the coaches of the various sports in your own school. The coaches are competitive people, or they wouldn't be in those jobs. Just like every crow thinks his child is the blackest, every coach thinks his sport is the most important. The football coach wants a whole lot, the basketball coach, the track coach, the golf coach, the wrestling coach—all of them are looking for more and more. There are only so many pieces you can get out of the pie. In coaching the satisfactions are on a more personal level as you watch individuals grow and develop in their sports. As athletic director you are looking for institutional growth. For that reason, I would say that I got more satisfaction from coaching than I ever got from administration.

One big change during my time at Howard University was the gradual process of desegregation in collegiate sports. We did have a few white players while I was there, but more important was the fact that we scheduled and played white schools. The situation was a good deal different from what it was at Livingstone College when I started out. At Livingstone you didn't even consider playing against a white team. At Howard University, because of its name and recognition, it was not difficult to schedule other schools. I left it to the coaches to determine at what level we would play. For instance, we weren't going to schedule Notre Dame or Ohio State. We looked for games that would be equitable for both teams. I made enough good contacts with other athletic directors that we were able to maintain the kinds of schedules we wanted.

I had a break in this routine in 1957–58 when I took a one-year sabbatical to go to Iraq. It was part of a people-to-people program sponsored by the State Department. The purpose was to pass on American coaching techniques and physical education programs to Iraqi students. I was based at Baghdad and traveled to schools throughout the country. About a month after I left, the government was overthrown by a military coup. I was sorry to learn that many of my new friends were killed.

In 1971 I became the first black to be an officer of the National Collegiate Athletic Association. I was on the council for ten years in the NCAA. Subsequently, I was elected to the Athletic Directors' Hall of Fame and the Oberlin College Hall of Fame. I stayed at Howard for twenty-four years until leaving in 1971 to go to the District of Columbia Teachers' College, where I was also athletic director and physical-education chairman. Then the Federal City College was just forming, and I was interim athletic director there for a while.

My goal throughout my work in the universities has been to use my own experiences to help others who were coming along. What really counts is the ability to affect the lives of young men in a positive way as they mature. When honors have come my way, I feel perhaps that I have made a contribution somewhere to somebody. That, to me, is very important. So I accept these things with both pride and humility, grateful for the opportunities that I've had. It hasn't always been easy, and that makes it even more satisfying.

I think a lot of it has to do with relationships between people of different races and how they conduct themselves. I don't like the idea that someone will say to me, "You know, you're different." I'm not different because I don't think there's any color on sincerity, honesty, dedication, and commitment. No one race has a monopoly on class and dignity. It's amazing to me that people make so much fuss over skin color, which to me is insignificant because you had nothing to do with the color you are. But what you do, you have a great deal of control over. It goes back to what my mother told me: "People will respect you if you're respectable."

Chapter Four

Producing Something the World Wants to Buy

George C. Cooper

The Navy picked well by including George Cooper in the first group of black officer candidates because he is exceptionally able as a leader. He is not the sort of individual who talks loudly and demands attention. Rather, he is someone who quietly looks at problems and finds creative, pragmatic solutions. He has the ability to achieve results when most of the rest of us see only challenges.

Cooper's own description of his naval service underscores his creative approach. As he explains, his method of dealing with racial injustice was to confront prejudice in constructive ways and thus try to turn negatives into positives, while others of the Golden Thirteen members generally sought to avoid unpleasant situations. He is a serious man, which is not to say that he is dour. He is as willing to laugh and smile as anyone else, but there is no frivolity about him.

At the time of the oral-history interviews, George Cooper and his wife, Margarett, lived in a spacious ranch house in Dayton, Ohio. In 1992 Cooper underwent surgery to replace a painful hip joint that inhibited his mobility. The couple then moved to a more compact home in nearby Centerville because it requires less maintenance than the ranch house in Dayton. In the winter they become snowbirds and fly off to a condominium in Tampa, Florida. By any standard, they have achieved success in American society. Unlike the home of Sam Barnes, the Coopers' house in Ohio is not filled with family mementos and photos. Instead, the decorations and art collection are an appreciation of the family's African-American heritage. Such things are important to the Coopers, but so also is family. They are proud of their daughter, Peggy Davis, who is a law professor at New York University and is married to a fellow attorney.

George Cooper is forward-looking and energetic at a stage of life when most people are willing to settle back for a relaxing retirement. Thus it is that he continues to coordinate all sorts of things, whether it be a civic project in Dayton or a program of the Golden Thirteen. He maneuvers people into doing the right thing with his oft-repeated statement, "Here, I'll get him on the phone for you. Let's see what you can work out." It's a quality of diplomacy that brings people together to achieve something toward a common purpose. At other times he makes his point in public forums, for he is an articulate speaker. Particularly important is his attitude. Where some individuals might be inclined to say, "I've got mine; it's up to you to get yours," Cooper does not. His approach is to find ways of helping others help themselves.

Underneath Cooper's urbane exterior is an individual in his mid-seventies who still seethes when he sees a nation in which the color of one citizen's skin makes a difference in the way he or she is treated by fellow citizens. For that reason, George Cooper's work is not finished.

*I*n September 1916 I was born in the little town of Washington, North Carolina. I was a member of a family of eleven children, one of whom died shortly after birth. My father was a sheet-metal worker by trade and, in the early part of my life, worked for a white shop. As I understand it, he went in one day and said to his boss that he had this big family, he had to make more money, and he'd like a raise. The man told him he could not afford to give him a raise, so my father said, "Well, in that case, I've enjoyed working here. Thank you for the opportunity you have given me, but I think I'll start my own shop."

According to the story, the man said to him, "There's no way a black man could run a business like this. But if you think you can do it, I will even help you. Go back in the shop, and if you find some pieces that in your judgment are obsolete or stuff that we no longer use, if you think that you can use it, you can have it." It was this kind of a relationship between employer and employee. He did, in fact, start his own business.

That sort of relationship was unusual in little Washington sixty-plus years ago. Jim Crow was the name of the game. Everything was separate; nothing was equal. Segregation was in full swing. There were white and black drinking fountains, white and black sections in the railroad station, the bus station, everything. And there was no choice but to accept it. The only "choice" that you had was to try to make the best of it or get in trouble. Prejudice was something we lived with every day of our lives.

I remember, for instance, an experience when I was very young, probably eight or nine. My dad, in addition to running his sheet-metal shop, cultivated every vacant lot in a five-block radius of our house. We had a cow. I had to milk the cow twice a day. I had to deliver this milk in the morning, and in season I had to deliver the

Cooper when he was about five years old.

excess produce from our various gardens downtown to sell to the merchants.

On one of these trips, taking some produce downtown, I had a conflict with a little white boy on Market Street. It was the wrong day for him to call me a "nigger," and we had it out. Even though I won the fight, nothing resulted from it then. His father got in touch with my dad, but nothing really ever came of it—just a fight among kids. It's interesting, though. Some twenty years later that was thrown back at me during officer training in the Navy.

In terms of formal education, my father stopped school in the third grade, but he was truly a self-educated man. He always stressed to each of us, his children, that the only thing that anybody would pay for in this world was production. If you were not in a position to produce, don't expect too much in return.

Our parents were determined to instill the work ethic in us, so we children used to go out and work. I can remember, for instance, working in tobacco fields as a youngster, handing tobacco. (When you hand it, you pick up three leaves and hand them to the person who ties them.) And these would be adults. They would frequently bring their kids to work with them because there weren't any day-care centers back then. They'd bring the kids to the farm, and they'd sit on the ground until Mama got through working. You'd see these black kids playing with the farmers' kids, and there was pleasant interaction. That kind of thing went on until the children got up to a certain age, and then there would be a separation, and it would be very clear. After a certain period we couldn't have anything more to do with the white children.

Whereas Pop taught us about earning our way in the world, Mama taught us humanity and compassion. She was a housewife who worked her fingers to the bone, not only trying to keep the family together and keep us together as a unit, but helping everybody in the neighborhood. We had a garden in every vacant spot in a five-block area, and she just fed the neighborhood, basically. If somebody came by and told Miss Laura that he or she was hungry, Mama fed them—white or black. There was no such thing as a welfare system as we know it today, so people just helped each other. And she was one of the forerunners in providing that kind of help. Fortunately, Pop made a decent living in his sheet-metal shop. And with the gardens and a cow, we were never hungry.

One of the things I did at the time I started high school was work as a bellhop in a hotel to make some extra money. The people who were traveling and staying in hotels in "Little" Washington, North Carolina, were, for the most part, salespeople—drummers, we called them. And the hostility that you would encounter there would just

Cooper as a high school student in 1934.

make your hair stand on edge. Hostility not because you did anything to anybody, but hostility simply because of prejudice and because of the fact that you were black.

I remember one situation, for instance, where I was helping a man register and showing him to his room. I had put his bags in the elevator, and he tried to get on the elevator. This guy inadvertently got caught in the door the wrong way. I thought the man was going to hit me, really. He called me everything derogatory that came to his mind. From my perspective it was obviously an accident. But if anything went wrong in the lobby, it was considered your fault as the bellhop. It was never the manager's fault, who was behind the desk. That kind of thing was just a part of living as a black person.

George Cooper's parents, Edward and Laura Cooper, at home in North Carolina in 1940. Cooper learned the work ethic and values for life from his parents. George Cooper followed his father's trade as a sheet-metal worker.

I had to learn how to accommodate that kind of situation. Pride is certainly something that every person should have, but I think that in any person's lifetime, there are innumerable occasions when one has to swallow that pride to do what one thinks he needs to do and has to do if he's going to really accomplish anything in life. I sincerely believe that.

My dad was hell-bent on education, saying, "You've got to have an education because without it you're simply not going to make it." There was never any question in any of our minds that we were not going to finish high school and go to college. This was just a fore-gone conclusion.

After I had graduated from the segregated high school in Wash-ington, then I went to Hampton Institute in Tidewater, Virginia. When I was there, the faculty was predominantly white. Because of that, the quality of Hampton's faculty was probably a little bit better than an all-black faculty in a black institution such as Howard Uni-versity, because the exposure of the Hampton faculty had been broader. I don't think that says anything against the black faculty because they were exposed to what they were exposed to. The white faculty had been exposed to so much broader an educational process. Many of our teachers were really dedicated people.

During my time, Hampton had a program where you would come in and during the first year take a very light load, maybe six semester hours a semester, because you worked full-time in an effort to pay your way that year and hopefully have some money to start the fol-lowing year. Some of my brothers and sisters were already out of col-lege, and they helped to the extent that they could. My dad helped to the extent that he could.

Fortunately, I had a fairly decent singing voice and got to be a member of the Hampton Choir, the Trade School Singers, and the Hampton Student Quartet. This gave me an opportunity to make some money and do a fair amount of travel because the quartet trav-eled rather extensively, singing a repertoire made up primarily of gospel songs and spirituals.

For instance, we would go on one singing trip as a sort of fund-raising effort, and that would obviously attract a certain kind of per-son to the performance. We'd go to the Chamberlin Hotel, right on the point at Fort Monroe, and we'd sing just for the hotel crowd, which would attract a different kind of clientele and, incidentally, help raise a little extra money for our school expenses. From each different kind of exposure, you learned something else.

For instance, from one of the things where we would go sing as a fund-raising effort, we came to recognize that there were people in the world who were interested in perpetuating education and, partic-ularly in this case, education for blacks, and were, therefore, willing to put some money behind that. On occasions of that nature, it was possible to have social interaction with them. So in spite of preju-

Cooper as a student at Hampton Institute in 1937.

dice, in spite of discrimination, we saw people really concerned and willing to back up that concern with their checkbooks.

I can remember writing home and saying to Papa I needed some money to buy a pair of shoes. And you could get a pair of Thom McAn shoes then for $3.15. He'd send $3.00 and say, "You ought to be able to get the fifteen cents yourself," and he was serious. So the $10.00 that I made singing at the Chamberlin Hotel meant a lot.

Hampton, of course, was noted for its trade school. So I went in and took the trade, and then I went on and got a degree in what at that point was called vocational education, because I didn't know whether I'd want to teach it or work at it or what. After I got my degree, I went back to North Carolina to go in business with my dad. Of course, having taken sheet-metal work in the trade school at Hampton, I took drafting and was able to draft whatever I needed. Dad, on the other hand, had a pattern for everything that he made. If he needed to make an elbow and he didn't have a pattern, he'd just take an old elbow and tear it apart and make a pattern from that, and then go ahead and do it. Because I wanted to draft everything and lay it out my way, and he wanted to do it his way, there was something of a conflict. We stayed together for about six months.

At this time, which was in 1939, I knew about a black insurance company, North Carolina Mutual Life Insurance Company. They had an appreciable amount of property in Wilson, North Carolina, a little town which was about fifty miles from my hometown in Washington, and they needed somebody to come in and do some sheet-metal work for them. I talked it over with my dad, and he gave me the same kind of start his previous employer gave him, letting me take a lot of stuff out of his shop to start my little business.

I had by this time married Margarett Gillespie, a librarian whom I had met while at Hampton. I was able to get enough work to keep the shop open, and between the two of us we were making enough to live on, but by this time it was beginning to get hard to get metal to do the kind of work I was doing. You could get metal if you were doing defense work, but for maintenance and upkeep of houses, I found it difficult to get the materials that I needed.

In the early forties, the National Youth Administration was coming into focus. It was a federal program for training young people, ostensibly for defense work. Somewhere I saw an ad in the paper that the NYA facility at Wilberforce University in Ohio needed a sheet-metal instructor. My wife had gone to college there, so I wrote and got some information and applications. I sent the application in and was invited for an interview to teach aircraft sheet-metal work.

When I walked into the supervisor's office at Wilberforce, he said, "Mr. Cooper, somebody made a mistake."

I said, "What do you mean, 'Somebody made a mistake'?"

He said, "I'm going to be perfectly honest with you. We thought you were white."

I said, "I thought you were looking for a sheet-metal instructor."

He said, "We are. I'm going to be honest with you again. I've never seen a colored sheet-metal worker. I just don't believe you can do the job."

I said, "Well, you have my credentials in front of you. Obviously, I didn't fabricate these things. And I've come a long way." Because from Wilson, North Carolina, to Dayton, Ohio, at that point in time was a pretty good trip, which I had made at my expense.

So he said, "You have, in fact, come a long way. I'll tell you what I'll do. I don't really believe you can do this job, but we have a fully equipped shop here. I will give you a set of blueprints for a simple thing like a metal locker, and if you can make one in a week, I'll give you the job."

I said, "I don't really think it's fair, but if that's what it takes to find out whether or not I'm qualified for it, I'll go for it."

Two days later I asked him to come look at this locker, which I had built with the help of three students who were there with the previous instructor. He said, "I thought you were going to take a week to do it."

I said, "No, that was your suggestion. I didn't say how long it was going to take me to do it." To make a long story short, I got the job.

Then World War II broke out and started breathing down our necks. In the fall of 1942 I got an opportunity to apply for a job teaching metalsmiths at the naval training school at Hampton Institute. That particularly appealed to me because it offered an opportunity to return to the college where I had done my undergraduate work. I also reasoned that it would keep me out of the military service. To the extent possible, I like to be my own boss, so I had no desire to submit to the regimentation of the service, particularly when blacks were permitted only menial roles in that era.

The skipper at the naval training school was Commander E. Hall Downes. He had graduated from the Naval Academy but resigned his commission shortly after World War I to pursue a civilian career in education. When World War II came along, he was recalled to active service in the Navy as a reserve officer. When I met him for an interview, Commander Downes said, "Mr. Cooper, we would like to have you take this job because we need you, and there aren't many of you around, white or Negro. If you take the job, I'll see what I can do to keep you from being drafted. I can't promise you anything, obviously, but I do know we need you here. And what you can do here may have a little bit more weight than what you're doing at Wilberforce in terms of keeping you in your civilian capacity."

So I went there and started training metalsmiths for the Navy in this Class A training school which had been set up; it was an all-black school. At that point in time the Navy staff of the school was 80 to 85 percent white. About half the civilian instructors were black, the other half white. So we went to work there.

One day Commander Downes came in, and he said, "I want you to go to Great Lakes. I can't keep you out of the service any longer. But if you'll agree to go into the Navy, I think I can guarantee you chief petty officer right off the bat. And I think I can bring you back here to do the same job you're doing now." He did indeed have enough clout to get me a chief petty officer's appointment right away, so that's how I got into the Navy in June 1943. I went to Great Lakes, Illinois, signed some papers, and came back to my job at Hampton.

Then, late in the year, he called me in again and said, "You've got orders to go to Great Lakes, and I think you will not be sorry." He couldn't tell me any more than that, but I had the feeling that it must be fairly important for him to agree to let me go because he and I had by then developed a very fine working relationship. Once I got to Great Lakes, I met fifteen other men who were there under the same set of circumstances, not knowing what to expect. We had been chosen as the first black Navy men to undergo officer-candidate training.

Commander E. Hall Downes, who had graduated from the Naval Academy and then earned a master's degree in education, was well qualified to run the naval training school at Hampton, Virginia, in World War II.

Fortunately, at least one member of our group was already familiar with almost every subject we were exposed to during the course of training. We decided early in the game that we were going to either sink or swim together—even to the point of studying together after we were supposed to be in bed. I can remember being in those barracks and sitting in the head after lights out, just drilling each other back and forth until it hurt because we were convinced that if one of us made it, we were all going to make it.

Here I am reminded of one of my favorite quotations: "All that is needed for evil to flourish is that good men do nothing." While we didn't think of ourselves as "good" men, we knew to the man that if we failed in this endeavor, the evil of segregation in the Navy, as related to black officers, would be set back for only God knows how long. We had to do *something,* and that something was to make it work!

I think that the Navy as an institution was making a good-faith effort in our training because it had been ordered to do so by the commander in chief. Unfortunately, the institution was made up of people with their personal likes and dislikes. I don't believe that the brass in Washington said, "Make these men fail." I think the way our instructors—who were predominantly white—dealt with us was the result of what I would call institutional racism and how those individuals felt in their hearts. I don't think that the Bureau of Naval Personnel said, "Send them through the mill. Give 'em hell and flunk 'em." I think it was more the institutionalized racism, which, incidentally, in my judgment, is still alive and well in this country.

We experienced a million little things that are hard to describe but which you could see and feel almost immediately if you were in that situation. I am sincere when I say that a person has to be black himself to really appreciate what we went through. Prejudice is exerted in so many subtle and unobvious ways that a black person senses it and smells it and feels it. It's in a glance, it's in a tone of voice, it's in an attitude. We had learned instinctively, after years of living in a segregated society, to have our antennas out. You just sense what's going on.

A request can be made of you to do this, that, or the other. And the mere tone of voice and the approach that the person uses in making that request is demeaning, suggests a sense of relative superiority and inferiority. And it's so frequently done by people who, if you're on the bitter end of it, are so much your inferior in so many ways that it takes a hell of a lot to stomach it. What we experienced there at Great Lakes often took me back to what Mama used to say: "Son, it ain't no sin being colored, but it's darned inconvenient."

The entire training period was an ordeal because of that attitude of the men who were teaching us. We did have two or three good instructors, but the shining exception to the norm of those working with us was Lieutenant (junior grade) John Dille, a Naval Reserve officer who came from a newspaper family in Chicago. He went over and above the call of his duty as a battalion officer to be an inspiration to us. John was perceptive enough to recognize what was going on, and he went to bat for us time and again, probably sometimes at risk to his own prospects. John knew and understood what we were up against and gave us a hell of a lot of support when we really needed it. He was understanding and helped us think through situations that arose in the course of that training.

After we had gone through our indoctrination class, I was called to main side one day, to Commander Armstrong's office. In the course of the conversation, he said, "I don't know what kind of an officer you'd make for the Navy. In the first place, you're what we call a hell-raiser."

I said, "Sir, I don't recall having raised any hell since I've been here, and certainly not at Hampton when I was down there as a chief petty officer."

He said, "This goes back to when you were eight years old and the fight you had with a white boy in Washington, North Carolina."

So I said, "Well, there's nothing I can say about that, sir. If you're aware of it, you must know the circumstances, and that's all I can say." What I didn't know was that he had my commission on his desk at that time.

So then in the course of twenty-four hours, as I remember, thirteen of us had our interviews and got our commissions. Three of the original sixteen didn't make it, and I don't know why not. I was the only one of the thirteen who could go into the Navy store and put on a uniform and walk out with it. Everybody else had to have it altered. I was the first black man to wear a naval officer's uniform because my size was just right.

Fortunately, over that weekend we had liberty, so I was going to see my wife, who was in Hamilton, Ohio, getting ready to have our baby. I walked into the railroad station in Chicago, and that whole station stood still—literally. As I would walk through, everywhere I'd go, everything would stop. The same thing happened on the train.

Cooper in March 1944, at the time he was commissioned.

That was the beginning of a real experience.

Commander Downes had made arrangements for me to go back to Hampton, to the naval training school, and made me his personnel officer. All of the trainees were black, and the preponderance of base personnel, known as ship's company, was white. Again, I ran into racism. Many members of ship's company just simply refused to salute. If they'd see me coming, they would cross the street and get on the other side.

My wife and I were walking down the street with our daughter one day in Newport News. A sailor got a foot away from my face, and he said, "You black son of a bitch, I read about you guys, but I never thought I'd meet one."

That's the one and only time I ever lost my cool. I really started after him. My wife grabbed my arm and said, "George, it's not worth it." But if she hadn't been there, I'd have been in trouble.

I very quickly thought and said, "Peg, you're right. Thank you."

How do you deal with situations like this? You can't go in to the skipper and say, "I want to resign." There's no such thing as resigning. So I developed a technique that if I ran into difficulty with someone, I had the opportunity, as personnel officer, to develop something that would require us to be together. I did that time and time and time again, in the hope that as we sat down man-to-man to solve a problem, that the other fellow would recognize me as a human being.

For instance, if a guy needed to go on emergency leave, he didn't have to come through the personnel office. It was normally just a routine thing. If his mother was dying, he had to go home, but I made it so that he had to come through me to get that leave to go home. When I would start empathizing with this guy, he began to see me as a human being and not as a black son of a bitch wearing officer shoulder boards. It would work almost invariably. In a situation like that, particularly in a training school, you could think up a thousand reasons to see different people, and I did. And after I had some of these positive experiences, the men that I talked to would go out and spread the word that I wasn't a bad guy after all. There was a positive ripple effect.

Commander Downes was an enlightened leader and was extremely supportive. The Navy chose well in sending him to that command, both in terms of his educational abilities and his qualities as a human being. Let me tell you a story which would document where he came from. I was officer of the day. I went in to pick up a Navy captain who was coming in on temporary assignment. (White officers were frequently sent to Hampton to get some indoctrination in dealing with black naval personnel prior to going to another assignment.) I went to the airport and picked up this officer. He looked at me and said, "You obviously are assigned to the school."

I said, "Yes, sir."

He said, "Well, where am I going to stay tonight?"

I said, "You're going to stay in the BOQ."

He said, "Where do you stay?"

I said, "I live in an apartment, sir."

He said, "Good. But before I go to bed, I want to see the skipper."

I said, "Sir, you can't see the skipper tonight. You can see the skipper at quarters tomorrow because I'm not going to call him tonight."

He said, "Well, I've got a problem."

I said, "Can I help you with the problem?"

He said, "You are the problem."

I said, "There's nothing I can do about it then. I'm sure that I'm not going to call the skipper tonight, and you'll have to, sir, see him at quarters the next morning." I took him to the BOQ and put him up for the night.

Commander Downes was the kind of guy who always got to work forty-five minutes to an hour before time. He was always in his office. When we officers got to quarters that morning, Commander Downes said, "We had a new officer come in last night. George met him, and he came in this morning early to see me. He told me that if he had known there was a Negro officer on this base, he would have asked not to be sent here because he never wanted to see another nigger as long as he lived." Downes said, "I've been in touch with BuPers, and he won't stay here. He's going to Alaska."

I felt confident in talking with the captain as I did because I'd have bet my bottom dollar that he would support me, and, of course, he did. By this time, I'd worked with Commander Downes for better than two years, and we'd really gotten to be good friends.

One of the things that the skipper used to win friends and influence people was the metal shop. We had a Class A training school, and in the metalsmith shop we had a black man named Joe Gilliard. He was in the art department at Hampton Institute and was a whiz at metal spinning. We set up a lathe so he could spin. Commander

Downes would have him make items such as candlesticks and minia-ture coal scuttles out of copper and brass. Whenever Downes went to Washington, he would drop one of these items on an officer's desk, and whatever he wanted, he walked out with it.

Commander Downes knew how to win friends and influence peo-ple, and he knew how to play whatever game needed to be played to get what he wanted done accomplished. I'm sure it was through him that I got to be in the first group of officer candidates.

After I had been in the job as personnel officer about a year, I received orders to go overseas because the war was still in progress in the Pacific. I never made it because of an injury I suffered back when we were in training at Great Lakes. A contraption had been built up over the swimming pool to teach men how to abandon ship. Well, some joker had left a bar of soap up there, and I stepped on this bar of soap and fell in the pool and hurt my back. I was in and out of hospitals for outpatient treatment. They wanted to operate, but I wouldn't consent to it. I'd fake it and say, "I'm all right," and go back to duty.

But finally, I was ordered to the Pacific and went to Norfolk, where I got the first real examination I'd had since I'd joined the Navy. The doctors discovered this back injury and said, "We can't send you out. You've got to go." So I got a medical discharge, and that's how I got out of the Navy.

I sort of looked forward to going overseas because I felt that I wanted that experience, that exposure. So that when I found out that I did have this physical problem, it was something of a disap-pointment. I must be honest enough to say it didn't last too long because after the initial disappointment I was able to stay with my wife and baby daughter, and that was a real pleasure for me.

In the years after that I was in a variety of jobs, trying to support my family, serve the community, and overcome the effects of racism, which unfortunately continue to this day. After leaving active service with the Navy, I stayed at Hampton Institute. My first job was as counselor for returning veterans, helping them readjust to civilian life and to learn what educational benefits were available to them under the GI Bill. I had that job for a year and a half. Then they asked me if I would take over as director of the department of trade training at Hampton, which was the old trade school. So I went into that and took that over and worked at that for about four years.

In the early 1950s I took a leave of absence and went to Dayton, Ohio, not far from my wife's home in Hamilton, Ohio. In the course of visiting her family I had become very friendly with a family in Dayton, Cal and Evelyn Crawford. My wife and they had been in school together at Wilberforce. Crawford was in the house-cleaning business, and it looked as if I could help him make a real go of it. I took a half-year sabbatical to help him get set up. We developed it into a really professional operation and were just getting started on the idea of franchising it through the state of Ohio, and our business started jumping.

Then I got sick. I came down with spinal meningitis. The doctor said, "I don't know what you're doing for a living, but whatever you're doing, you ought to get out of it. Do something with a little less stress."

Shortly after that I saw an ad for a housing inspector for the city of Dayton. By that time I had decided to stay there. I was just going to quit Hampton despite the tenure. I was tired of the academic world, and I needed something a little different. I went downtown and took an examination. A couple of weeks later I discovered that I had come out on top, and they offered me this job as a housing inspector. It was a natural for me because of my background at Hampton, where I had at least a speaking knowledge of all the building trades.

One of the men I worked with in that job was a fellow named Ken. He came on the job after I got there, and he knew that he was better than anybody else. I decided to see if I could find a way to turn Ken around. So I began arranging, deviously if necessary, for us to go on inspections together. While we were out on an inspection, I might say, "Let's stop by the house and have a hot dog, Ken." And Ken learned to recognize that I lived pretty much like he did. He came to realize that he could appreciate me as a human being and not as a black man, and we developed a real kinship. It was like that old song we sang in church when I was a child, "You bring the one next to you, and I'll bring the one next to me. And in no time at all, we'll win them all. We'll win them one by one."

That inspecting job lasted a year, until I was offered a job in city planning. I was riding on the elevator one day with the director of

Cooper works with a young assistant during his time as a city planner in Dayton, Ohio, during the 1960s.

planning for the city. He said, "George, how would you like to work for me? We need the kind of expertise that I've seen come from you as you work with community groups. We need that input into the planning process."

I worked there for about six or seven years. Then in the early 1960s I moved over to Antioch College in Yellow Springs, Ohio, not far from Dayton, and became director of the international work-study program. We would bring people in—businessmen, teachers, and engineers—from various parts of the world, keep them on campus for ninety days of indoctrination, and then put them out somewhere in the country to work from eighteen to twenty-four months at their profession or business. It was a challenging and enjoyable job, and I worked at that for about seven years.

Then I got a call from Jim Kunde, the city manager at Dayton. I had known him when I was with the city as a planner. He said, "It's time for me to appoint some black department directors. I'd like for you to be the first one." So we talked about it, and I decided that I would accept his offer to become his director of the Department of Human Resources, which took in corrections, housing, health, consumer protection, parks, recreation—about nine hundred people in seven divisions. I worked at that job until my retirement in the early 1980s.

After I retired, I decided that I wanted to do something about getting blacks into the mainstream of American business and industry. I believe the only way you're going to do that is to produce something, to make something, to provide opportunity for employment. I thought about it a good deal. Twenty years ago, if you needed an energy engineer, you'd have difficulty finding one because there weren't that many around. Today I know six good black energy engineers. As I got thinking about that, it occurred to me that in almost any skill that you needed now, you could find it in the minority community pretty well developed, having developed over the past quarter of a century.

To help further this trend, I joined with a number of other individuals to set up an organization called Community Industries, Inc. We have obtained a rent-free lease on an empty school building and have already started using it as a combination factory, day-care center, and training facility.

In this instance we are not only doing day care, but we're training paraprofessionals for the day-care industry. There is a very severe shortage of people in that line of work now, which simply leads me to say that everything that we do in this school building is going to have a training component connected with it. We're going to use that not only to produce some things and to develop some minority businesses, but to train in-school youth working with the Dayton Board of Education and out-of-school youth working with the Dayton Urban League and the Community Action Agency. Each of these three entities has indicated a very sincere interest in this approach and in cooperating to make this thing possible.

I don't believe that one is capable of pulling oneself up by his own bootstraps. If I've had any success in my own life, it's been because somebody helped me along the way. I therefore have a responsibility to do whatever I can to help somebody else. We can't live in this world alone.

Since the Golden Thirteen began holding annual reunions in the late 1970s, we have often met with the National Naval Officers Association. It is a group of black officers serving in today's Navy. When I go into one of those meetings and see four or five hundred good-looking, obviously bright, up-and-coming naval officers, I like to remember that I played at least a little part in making this possible by being one of the first black officers and going through some of the things that we went through to make it work. Seeing all these bright people gathered together makes the buttons just pop off my shirt because I'm so proud of them.

There is a lot of compensation from the fact that we as a group played a part in making this become a reality. In addition to that, we recognize that while—in my judgment, at least—institutional racism is still alive and well in America, the Navy and the other services have come a long way in trying to address that. The door is open now, and probably a little bit more in the service than out. Anybody now can go in and do pretty much what he's capable of doing, and become pretty much what he's capable of becoming. That was not the case when the Golden Thirteen went to Great Lakes.

I'm egotistical enough to believe that we had something to do with that by virtue of the way we responded to the challenge in 1944, because if we had screwed that thing up, it would have been screwed up for a long, long time after that. We determined that we would not, in fact, screw it up, but we would make the best of it, and to the extent possible, make it work. So that I perceive of the short period of time that I spent in the Navy as having made a contribution to something worthwhile.

Chapter Five

The Golden Thirteen
Plus One

John F. Dille, Jr.

Through some combination of heredity and environment, John F. Dille, Jr., wound up in the newspaper business just as his father had. John F. Dille, Sr., may not have been a household name, but one of his creations most assuredly was. In the late 1920s he created a comic strip called "Buck Rogers in the 25th Century." It featured interplanetary warfare and communications and employed futuristic weapons such as death rays and rocket pistols. Dille developed the concept for the adventure strip and supplied story ideas that were executed by the writer and artist. More than sixty years later a "Buck Rogers idea" still connotes something futuristic, and the Dille family is still in the newspaper business.

Despite his positions in what have now come to be called the media, John Dille, Jr., carries with him neither arrogance nor pretentiousness. In Elkhart, Indiana, there is no splashy new corporate headquarters complex for Federated Media, only the sturdy, five-story brick building that has been the home for many years of the *Elkhart Truth*. That suits Dille's style. The walls of his office attest to the honors that have been accorded him over the years; photos depict the great and famous he has known. But he is not inclined to dwell on such things, for he is eager to talk about his association with the Golden Thirteen, both in 1944 and all these years later. The members of the group remember him warmly from their days together at Great Lakes because he was able to give them a great deal of moral support at a time when they were concerned that they had been set up to fail. They were able to look to someone outside themselves as a source of strength, and one of those who supplied it was John Dille. He treated them then as he does now—with respect—and the feeling is reciprocated.

Dille is a tall, friendly man, now showing signs of the passing of years. He will soon be eighty, as his knees tell him frequently. His recollections of being with the black officer candidates nearly fifty years ago are not so precise and detailed as theirs are. In a lifetime of achievement, their two-month period together at Great Lakes in 1944 probably does not loom as large for him as it does for the men of the Golden Thirteen themselves. And while he saw them frequently, often daily, he did not experience the twenty-four-hour-a-day togetherness that they did. Though Dille was not one of the Golden Thirteen, his attitude, his approach, and his sense of humanity helped shape them, helped them believe they could succeed when they might otherwise have had doubts.

*B*ack in 1913 I was born in Chicago. During my primary grades in school we moved to the suburb of Evanston, and I really grew up there. I went to Evanston High School, and from there to the University of Chicago. While I was in college, I met the girl who became my wife; she is also a graduate of the University of Chicago.

For many years I was in the newspaper feature-syndication business—from the time I finished school until I had an opportunity to buy an interest in the daily newspaper in Elkhart, Indiana. In 1952 I moved to Elkhart and took over the responsibility for the operation of the daily newspaper, and it had an AM radio station at that time. As the years have gone by, we built the organization considerably. My son, John III, is actually the head of it now. We're operating two daily newspapers, the other one being in Greencastle, Indiana. He has also added two radio stations, AM and FM in Tulsa, Oklahoma, to increase our group to a total of ten; that is, AM-FM combinations in five markets, Southbend-Elkhart being the original home market, and subsequently Fort Wayne, Grand Rapids, Cincinnati, and now Tulsa.

My son was born in August of 1941, which was four months before the United States went to war against Japan. At the time I was working for the National Newspaper Service. It was not affiliated with any of the newspaper chains, as a number of the syndicates were. It was an independent my father had started, and it handled some very well-known newspaper features at that time, including columns, comic strips, panels, cartoons, and articles.

Because of my father's role in the organization, I started as a trainee, with the goal of working into a job in administration. I did a lot of editing of newspaper columns for accuracy, policy, and tastefulness. And I developed an amusing feature of my own, which I syndicated. I put together puzzles that were called Brain Twizzlers; they were credited to one Professor J. D. Flint, Flint being my middle name. The feature proved to be quite successful, amusing, and entertaining and ran in a substantial number of outstanding American newspapers.

In the process of working with the features syndicate, I traveled the country a great deal—calling on managing editors and publishers to try to persuade them to buy more of National Newspaper Service's features. Then the Japanese bombed Pearl Harbor in December 1941, and I had a decision to make in terms of my own position. I was free of any obligation in terms of the draft law because I was married and had a child. My official classification meant there was little likelihood of being called to active duty. But it's been traditional in our family to serve if needed. We've had a number of military men in past generations. I knew that I would feel better in my own sense of obligation by volunteering for service.

I had had years of military training in high school and university through ROTC programs. So in 1942 I applied for a direct commission in the Navy. One of the reasons for my choice of service is that I'm something of a germophobe, and I'm very, very high on hygiene and cleanliness. To me, the Army meant visions of crawling through the mud on my stomach while cradling a bayoneted rifle in my elbows. That vision did not appeal to me at all. Nor did flying. Being by that time in my late twenties, I thought it was a little late to start to learn to become an aviator. Also, since I was over 6 feet, 3 inches tall and wearing size-thirteen shoes, the typical airplane cockpit and I would not be a very comfortable match. On the basis of my previous training and a letter of recommendation from the president of the University of Chicago, the Navy granted me an ensign's commission.

During my physical examination, I passed all of the tests required, but the Navy determined that I was at least partially defective in color perception. (That came to be an interesting joke later on when I got involved with the training of black sailors.) Curiously, even in the wake of the bombing of Pearl Harbor, the Navy was using a test for color vision invented by a Japanese scientist named Ishihara. Because the Navy wasn't sure that I would read signal flags correctly, it did not intend to give me any sea assignments, and that was per-

Dille as a lieutenant during World War II.

A chief petty officer marches at the head of a company of black recruits at Camp Robert Smalls during training in World War II.

fectly all right with me. Actually, I can tell any shade of color, but the Navy wasn't taking any chances.

After being commissioned, I was ordered to the Great Lakes Naval Training Station, which was conveniently close to home. As a matter of fact, I think the commuting from my home, then in Highland Park, to Great Lakes took less time than it had commuting to my newspaper office in downtown Chicago. When I first reported for duty, I was ordered to the recruit-training command. After a short period of indoctrination, I was put in command of a battalion of approximately five or six hundred recruits, that is, new men in the Navy, for their initial boot-camp training. To a limited extent, I was learning along with the enlisted men, becoming familiar with those terms and activities that are peculiar to the Navy. However, basic military procedure is pretty standard, and I'd had a lot of that, so it was a quite easy adaptation for me. And boot training is largely a matter of teaching some elementary subjects and marching the men around. At that point, because of the massive number of enlistments following Pearl Harbor, the Navy was inundated with recruits, so my background and ability to train them meshed with the Navy's needs.

As I think back, the strengths I brought to the job were knowledge of military protocol; military courtesy; fundamental military maneuvers; and the structural organization of battalions, companies, platoons, and squads; and the ability to command. The job required some administration in the sense of evaluating disciplinary problems and decisions on how to mete out punishment because in any group of hundreds of men, you're going to have some recalcitrants who will go over the edge and break the rules.

The marching and inspections and other activities of boot camp were a means of inculcating a sense of discipline and order-taking. That was the first step in bringing a man into the Navy; later he would be taught the specific skills that would be needed on board ship. Perhaps most importantly, recruit training instills a feeling of group oneness. The man marching beside me and in front of me and behind me is my brother, so to speak. We are no longer individuals but part of a unit.

I was still involved in recruit training when the Navy announced in 1942 that, for the first time in its history, it would accept general enlistments from Negroes. Up until that time almost all blacks were limited to being steward's mates or food-preparation personnel. There were a few black petty officers in specialties—machinist's mate, for example—but not in purely naval ratings such as gunner's mate, quartermaster, and boatswain's mate. With the integration of the general-service ratings, the Great Lakes Naval Training Station was suddenly to be inundated with large numbers of black recruits. This obviously brought up a great many elements of a new situation for the Navy administration because it came as something of a surprise to the command of the Navy.

I'm sure that this development was influenced strongly by President Franklin D. Roosevelt and his wife, Eleanor, who were very sympathetic to and worked a good deal with the NAACP and the Urban League and those organizations that were pushing for greater and greater equality for the black person. So suddenly new barracks were being erected at Great Lakes. A whole new territory was established and named Camp Robert Smalls, and the blacks were all assigned to this new camp.

While the barracks buildings were going up, I went to the recruit-training commanding officer, Commander William Turek, and said that I would like to be assigned to Camp Robert Smalls. I suppose I was motivated to volunteer by a combination of things, some selfish, some of a more generous feeling. If it was selfish motivation, it would be that perhaps it was an opportunity to distinguish myself in a new climate, a new territory where other officers might not do as well as I was sure I could. I hoped I could bring positive attention to myself and therefore, perhaps, bring promotion. I thought I might do better than some others because I would start with a friendly, sympathetic, and understanding attitude toward the black recruits as a result of my past friendships with minority individuals. I also genuinely felt that these men would need all of the help and understanding that could be mustered by the officers in charge of training them because of it being a whole new environment. I perceived that it would be an opportunity for them, if they would work at it.

The Navy was obviously moving cautiously. Even though it was accepting blacks in the general-service ratings, the training and housing of recruits were still segregated. The Navy felt that putting blacks and whites together in the same barracks would breed a whole lot of problems, so the hierarchy didn't feel that was the way to approach it. Incidentally, it was my observation, during my nearly four years in the Navy, that a surprising number of high-ranking naval officers—meaning, for the most part, Naval Academy graduates—were from the South. They had to take their orders to accept these new general enlistments of blacks, but I'm sure that many, many of them did not want any part of it and, therefore, did not have a friendly, receptive attitude in trying to set up the necessary training to absorb them.

The basic structure of Camp Robert Smalls included four battalions of black recruits. Each battalion was commanded by an officer with the rank of lieutenant (junior grade) or ensign. When I applied for the assignment, I was told that it was for Naval Academy graduates only. A number were available who had some sort of physical problem, perhaps transitory, that prevented them from being ordered to sea. So they were used in that capacity. Commander Turek told me he was sorry he could not put me over there, but he'd keep me in mind. Then one of the four men who had been assigned originally to a black battalion managed to overcome the problem on his physical exam and was ordered to sea. Commander Turek called me and ordered me to the duty I had requested.

Once I got to Camp Robert Smalls, I was reporting to the officer in charge, Lieutenant Commander Daniel W. Armstrong. He was a Naval Reserve officer, a Naval Academy graduate who had not stayed in the Navy. He came from a distinguished family, basically a Southern family, although I think he had a minimum of prejudice resulting from his geographical background. Because of his father's role in founding Hampton Institute to provide college-level training for blacks, Dan Armstrong was a natural choice for the Navy. There couldn't have been half a dozen like him in the entire country to call back to active duty and put in charge of this program. I always considered him a fair man, one with a genuine interest in the concerns of the black sailors.

I think the choice of Commander Armstrong to run Camp Robert Smalls was a particularly good one because he was a kind of a man of all seasons. He was a handsome man, and he fitted into the Lake Forest high-society framework very readily. That was a plus because the Navy was frequently in the position of cultivating that society,

Lake Forest being the most conspicuously fashionable community of those on the North Shore. The admiral and captain running Great Lakes would at times include Dan Armstrong when they mixed with local civilians, and I think it gave him good exposure, kind of an inside track. Whether the admiral liked it or not, I think he had to recognize that this man Armstrong was different, unusual, capable, an academy man, Southern aristocracy, and should be listened to before spoken to. Having that kind of entrée probably helped him achieve things for Camp Robert Smalls that other officers wouldn't have been able to.

When I joined the organization in the spring of 1943, I was still an ensign. There was one lieutenant named Donald O. Van Ness, who was a Naval Academy graduate. He had been out of the Navy but came back to active duty when the war was approaching. He was essentially the executive officer to Commander Armstrong, and then there were four of us in command of battalions. Because the command hierarchy in Camp Robert Smalls was limited to a few officers, we were a close-knit group. Commander Armstrong held meetings at least weekly to compare notes on problems, how they'd arisen, how they were best handled, and ideas for improving the training.

Each battalion broke down to companies, and, in my case, for example, I had a chief petty officer assigned to each company and several regular Navy petty officers, first class, second class, third class, and the requisite number of yeomen. I think we had three yeomen in the battalion office. Most of these enlisted administrative and training personnel were white simply because there weren't yet very many blacks who had made petty officer.

In terms of selection of white chiefs and petty officers to perform with the black units, there was a very definite attempt to be sure that none of them expressed overt antipathy toward the men being trained. The personnel office of the Great Lakes Naval Training Station made those selections. They might seek recommendations, if any were available, from Commander Armstrong or from any of us. Otherwise, they would just be by interviewing individuals and discussing with each man what the assignment was and determining whether or not he had an antipathetic reaction. There were a few cases where such chiefs or petty officers had to be told that a certain attitude could not be displayed—that they must treat the black recruits in the same fashion they would the whites, or else they would not be assigned to Camp Robert Smalls. That approach solved the problem.

Having just come from training the white recruits on the main side, I was in a position to make comparisons and observed that the new black sailors were getting the same sort of course the whites were. Now, bear in mind, this recruit training was conducted under the pressures of war and the need for men. It was about an eight-week period of training, which was shorter than the standard course before the war. During the course of training, the men were given aptitude tests and then sent on to appropriate schools for further training in the field in which they had aptitude. I think that the quality of blacks who came into the Navy at that time was at least equal to the whites because they'd been barred from it for so long. It looked like a new opportunity, something previously unavailable. As a result of both the opportunity and their sense of patriotism, these black recruits had a great deal of enthusiasm for the program.

As for recreation for the sailors, I'm taxing my memory a little bit, but it seems to me that the provisions made for liberty involved sending the men into Chicago rather than flooding the local community. There was just a string of suburbs, starting at Great Lakes, being very small and getting progressively larger down toward Chicago. As I remember, it seemed best for everyone's sake to provide transportation for the sailors. I believe that not only was there bus transportation, but trains as well. The Chicago and North Western Railway ran immediately adjacent to Great Lakes, and it pulled into a station on the west side of downtown Chicago. In the case of the black recruits, they could get home to see family if they came from that area. If not, they often found their liberty recreation in Chicago's black community.

I hesitate to make comparisons with white sailors in terms of behavior, but I'm inclined to say that perhaps we had more disciplinary problems with the blacks. But that was only because they had been uprooted, so to speak, and cast into a totally new, strange, and, in many respects, not particularly friendly environment. And among men who have quality of character or strength at all, this is apt to produce some rebellious activities, and you'll get individuals who will be rebellious and, therefore, require discipline. You're bound to have some who are simply against the system, who felt that the Navy wasn't really friendly to blacks now any more than it had been for its whole history up until then, so I think some of those things were inevitable. But I would not attribute them to a basic racial distinction.

As we looked for leaders among the recruit companies, I suppose, in a sense, you could say they selected themselves. By that I mean that a limited number of individuals would distinguish themselves in terms of their bearing and the way they looked, the way they acted, the way they respected military courtesy, the way they performed whatever duties they had, and, to the extent that they took tests, the way they performed on the tests. One young man who pops into my mind was a squad leader named Duncan. He was a very good look-ing man and had the bearing of a military man. His bearing, in terms of his ordering the squad to do this, that, or the other, was outstand-ing. He did not turn out to be one of the first officers; I don't know whether he ever became an officer, but he certainly went on to petty-officer rank in a hurry and, I'm sure, performed very well to his own satisfaction and the Navy's.

The next major step, as far as my activities as a naval officer were concerned, came when the Navy announced, to the great surprise of a great many people, that it was going to commission a dozen black officers. My understanding is that the Navy was thoroughly screened in picking the men who would undergo this training. There were many capable men to choose from because the entire United States Navy was screened for potential candidates. For several reasons, this was very important to the Navy. The Navy recognized that the White House had a substantial interest in this kind of project. The Navy realized that it would look better if it did a good job of selecting the men so that the men themselves could perform well and make the Navy look good. The result was that there were sixteen men ordered to Great Lakes for training as officers.

Here again, I quickly identified myself to the command at Great Lakes as someone interested in working with these men, in the belief that I could serve primarily to indoctrinate these men in protocol, military courtesy, the new kind of relationship in which they would find themselves as commissioned officers. Because of the combina-tion of my sympathetic attitude with my experience in recruit train-ing, I felt I could be helpful.

The officer candidates I encountered in January 1944 were extraordinary men. Several held degrees from highly accredited universities; they were not primarily, as some officers of the Navy might have feared or claimed, from small Negro colleges in the South. Graham Martin, for example, had a master's degree from Howard University, an outstanding black school in Washington, D.C. Syl White and Lewis Williams had degrees from the University of Chicago, my alma mater.

Many officer-training situations are competitive, but I didn't find that to be the case with the Golden Thirteen. I think I would call them much more supportive of one another than competitive. They had many things in common, including their leadership capacity, but also whatever problems or handicaps go with being born to a minority group. Now, cast in roles where they might be striving for, say, the same command or the same position, it might be a different story. But they'd approach it differently, quite differently, because their personalities are quite different. There would be the few who would exhibit the tiger approach to being competitive, and others who would use the approach of study, study, research, come to a conclusion, then push it.

Many of these men were athletes. A number of them would be perfectly at home on a platform, as master of ceremonies or speaker. They simply were superb. But they were going to face problems, and they knew it and I knew it. To the extent that I could be helpful, I tried to articulate these circumstances and set up warning signals. I was not involved in the training of the officer candidates in professional subjects because I didn't really have the background that the Naval Academy graduates did. The part that I felt most involved in and interested in was indoctrination of conduct as a naval officer, anticipating the eligibility, all of a sudden, for officers' clubs and the reaction of the current membership of officers' clubs to suddenly having black members. I talked about Navy regulations, in terms of how they applied to being an officer, how to conduct oneself toward both officers and enlisted personnel. And I suppose I made some general observations on when to speak and when to wait to be spoken to, and yet to accept gladly and proudly the full rank, as a commission indicates, and enjoy it.

Formally, I never had anything written down to be sure to talk about this potential situation or that because it would inevitably come up in discussion. More often than not, being the intelligent, educated, and, for the most part, sensitive men that they had to be to be qualified, they would anticipate various situations and bring things up themselves. Sometimes it was with me, sometimes among themselves and then asking for a reaction from me or from someone else involved in that training. These were just things we talked about man-to-man, not part of any structured curriculum. In giving such advice I got virtually no policy guidance from superiors other than Commander Armstrong. I may be thoroughly unjust, but I concluded that from the beginning of their commissioned days, most higher-ranking naval officers really felt that the less contact they could have with the whole subject, the better off they would be.

Three men of the original sixteen were not commissioned, including Lewis Williams, or "Mummy," as he was known. I regret to say that while I remember Mummy Williams, and if I passed him on the street, I'd know him today, I do not remember the story on him. Before these thirteen men finished their training, I was transferred to other duty. I was disappointed that I didn't have the pleasure of being around for their commissioning. I was also not involved in the process whereby thirteen of the sixteen were selected to become officers, and I am not in position to explain how the choices were made. That would have to be done by whatever individuals formed the group that selected them. I don't know what criteria they used. I do know the results that the thirteen produced and that the quality of the men who were commissioned was extraordinary.

It wasn't long after I became well acquainted with these men that I was ordered from Great Lakes to the Hawaiian Islands in command of an ordnance battalion that was largely black. We were at a naval ammunition depot in the mountains north of Honolulu—really up above a little town called Waipahu. The Navy had blasted tunnels into the sides of the mountains in the valley going up, and in those tunnels were stored torpedoes. I think I am correct in saying—it certainly was true up until I left—that we handled all the torpedoes for the Pacific Fleet.

After that I was switched into the Navy's public-information organization. The Navy wanted more recognition of what the blacks were doing for the war effort, and that meant public relations. I guess this

After leaving Great Lakes, Dille was involved in publicizing the activities of black Navy men in the Pacific. Here, members of a labor gang perform stevedore duties under the watchful eye of Dennis Nelson, a member of the Golden Thirteen.

is where my newspaper background and experience at Camp Robert Smalls came together. I was ordered to the staff of Commander Service Force Pacific Fleet, where the senior public-information officer said, in effect, to me, "You can have just about anything you want, but get some pictures and stories back to the American press that show and say that these sailors are doing well in the Navy and are performing worthwhile missions."

The Navy, at my request, searched for some men who were experienced as black journalists, whether for black newspapers or white. By the latter part of 1944 I had put together several such men and a couple of photographers. Then I had the cooperation of the Commander Service Force and was able to locate where blacks were performing in different kinds of Navy activities, where we could get a story and/or pictures on them. We began by publicizing activities in Hawaii and then moved farther and farther west, covering a lot of territory in the process. Commander in Chief Pacific was at Guam, and so I moved on out to Guam, and we covered activities in Guam, Tinian, Saipan—the Marianas group—and then we went to the Philippines and covered the activities of black Navy men there. By the time we were finished, we had produced many pictures and stories about black naval personnel and what they were doing.

I was also a press-liaison officer and had to deal with a number of problems in that regard. One involved some black newspapermen who were covering events on Guam when I was there. I knew Enoch Waters, who was a very fine newspaperman, because he was with the *Chicago Defender.* With him was Charlie Loeb, a war correspondent for a group of black newspapers. They came to Guam to perform their chores for their own newspapers, and they were housed in barracks with some black personnel. When I talked to them, they said, "Well, we can't work normally, Jack. Normally, we would be in the BOQ, where the other correspondents are, and that's where we all get together and compare notes and get ideas and give ideas and so on. But here we're stuck off to the side."

I said, "Let me see if I can do anything about that." So I went to my superior in this capacity regarding the press and explained the problem. He sent a memorandum at my request to Vice Admiral Charles McMorris, who was the chief of staff to Fleet Admiral Chester Nimitz, the commander in chief of the Pacific Ocean Areas. McMorris, who was from Alabama, sent back the memorandum regarding Enoch Waters and Charlie Loeb and said, "This is addressed to the admiral," meaning Nimitz, and he said, "I will not bother the admiral with such trivia." So that came back to me.

So I instigated another memorandum and got it back up to Admiral McMorris. It said, "With great respect, the admiral views this as trivia, but I can assure you from knowledge that you would have no reason to possess that this would not be considered trivia in the

White House with *the* commander in chief." That made an impression, and so Charlie and Enoch wound up in the BOQ. That was one of those side issues, but it's an example of the kinds of problems that minority individuals must overcome in order to get things accomplished. In many ways, I would say they have to be superior to their white counterparts to achieve any reasonable parity.

After the war ended with VJ Day in 1945, I was able to make contact with the Washington headquarters and request assignment to return to assemble some of the journalism work that had been done, and I got it. So I was fortunate to get orders back to the United States quite soon after the war itself had ended. I got back to my family in much shorter time than most men were able to and was really able to put the finishing touches on the work we had been doing.

Our brief time together in 1944 was the beginning of my relationship with the men of the Golden Thirteen. They have been holding reunions in recent years and have been gracious enough to include me in their reunions. As we visited in later years, I got to know them much better than I had during World War II. For instance, I was reminded that Dennis Nelson was a very proud man. Of course, I liked every one of them, but Dennis Nelson would be one of the ones I would find most easy to get into an argument with. And that's to his credit because he was always a positive person. He knew what he felt, and he articulated it, and he did it very, very well. I remember so clearly when I raised the question one time about— "Jeez, all of a sudden, you guys are calling yourselves black, and everyone else is calling you black. I would have been thrown out of my own home by my mother if I'd used that term instead of 'Negro' or 'colored.'"

Dennis said, "Jack, I'll say it to you, but I'll say it to anyone else too. I am not black, and I don't want to ever be called black." He felt very strongly on that subject. Some of the others, I think, just shrugged their shoulders and would just take it as a meaningless identification that the world, as it exists, suddenly had taken upon itself to use. Dennis Nelson was kind of a human spark plug. He was a man who activated things. Sometimes they led to dissension; sometimes they led to constructive criticisms, but almost always they were well brought up and disposed of.

The first reunion of the Golden Thirteen following World War II was at Monterey, California, in 1977. Left to right by rows, from top to bottom: Dalton Baugh and Jesse Arbor; John Reagan and Frank Sublett; Graham Martin and Syl White; Samuel Barnes, George Cooper, and Dennis Nelson.

Reginald Goodwin, of course, is gone now, and I was very sorry to lose contact with him. We kept in touch after the war for a while. Before the commissioning, probably I knew him better than any of the others, and on a number of occasions, since our homes were near each other, he came to my home in Highland Park and visited with me and my wife. He could have been a great politician, but I mean that in the nicest sense of the term. He had a natural affinity for people and related to people and sensed their relationship to him about as well as anybody I have known.

George Cooper is certainly one of the outstanding men of the group. His general demeanor, the grace with which he moves and conducts himself—I don't mean that entirely in a physical sense, but the role he plays as a man among men—is, to me, very impressive. I think he was destined to be a leader from childhood. I think anyone of balance would recognize in him the leadership qualities and the kind of personality which would attract you to him if you felt that you needed something done by him or needed his opinion on something.

Sam Barnes was and is a very active, very progressive, leadership type of individual. He showed that in the Navy, and he has shown it in private life. He's a good organizer, and he will participate in any activity that he thinks is good and wholesome and proper, and he'll do a good job of it. Dalton Baugh had a degree, or perhaps more than one, in engineering. Engineering was certainly his specialty in later life. He was obviously of leadership quality. He was able and willing to express himself at any time or on any occasion where he felt it appropriate, and yet had the grace and judgment not to press it unless it would serve a beneficial purpose.

Jim Hair I remember as being quiet but very warm and expressive about friendships. John Reagan I did not know as well as I knew some of them. He was a rather quiet member of the group. His physical stature was truly impressive. Frank Sublett has a very engaging personality, very good looking man, very articulate. He has always been willing and ready to participate in dialogue of any kind. Jesse Arbor is a gregarious individual. He was then, and he still is. He's fun to be with and quite loquacious. If you want to really get a subject exhausted or even well and thoroughly treated, you'd better stay right with it before Jesse brings some other subject into play. But anything

Dille, the chairman of Federated Media, Inc., poses with Samuel Gravely, the Navy's first black flag officer, during the 1970s.

he does, he'll do it with a laugh and always with great kindness.

Charles Lear I really didn't know well enough. He was physically a fine specimen, and he certainly had leadership qualities. I gathered from his being brought to the group without a college degree that he must have had superior leadership qualities that the Navy itself recognized in whatever assignments he had prior to that time. Phillip Barnes I knew much less well than the others. I really never spent enough time with him on a one-to-one basis to form much of an opinion, so I don't retain any particular impression of him.

Of the group, Syl White had perhaps the most prestigious career in terms of his academic background and his years since. He was a classmate of mine at the University of Chicago, the class of '35, although we did not know each other at that time. It's a big university. Both of us later did graduate work. I stopped after a master's degree; he went on and finished his law degree and has been in that field ever since. He is very analytical, certainly wanted always to keep things moving in his own career, but also in the Golden Thirteen. For example, he sometimes expressed the feeling that the Golden Thirteen ought to have something more purposeful to be doing than just having reunions. But I think this was simply meant as a constructive suggestion more than criticism, but typical of a searching mind. I think that's what brought him to his naval commission, and that's what has brought him to eminence in his professional career.

Graham Martin is extraordinary in the sense of a man whose background, only one generation back, went to the town of Tobacco Port, Tennessee. He came from the most rural and the most unrefined of backgrounds in terms of heredity and history, and yet he was an outstanding athlete. He played football as a tackle for Indiana University, an outstanding one, and he wasn't there on an athletic scholarship. He made good grades because he's the kind of a man who knew that that would be important to him later. He also played on the Great Lakes Naval Training Station football team. If you know anything about the World War II days of that football team, it was about as all-American, about as top-notch as you could get. They had some of the greatest stars of history on it, and he played on that team.

Graham is very quiet, devoted to his family. His wife is crippled, yet they came to our reunions as long as they were physically able. He's really in a wheelchair mostly now, but he's as attentive to her as can be. He does not speak much unless you let him know that you're interested in his opinion, and if you do, he'll give it, and it will be very logical; it will be very, very sound. I would say that Graham Martin was probably the most unusual of the Golden Thirteen, in the sense of what he started with and what he wound up with in the whole group.

As part of the process of getting back together with these men in the past fifteen years, we have formed friendships of the kind that were not possible in the training environment during World War II.

In fact, since they have gotten together, they have always made me welcome, and they've also honored me with their stationery. The design in the center of the paper is quite legible, although it doesn't spoil the stationery for typing. It says simply, "13 + 1," and they've designated me the one. I am very proud of that honor.

Chapter Six

A Naval Officer Instead of a Flier

John W. Reagan

Of the several athletes in the Golden Thirteen, John Reagan ranks with Graham Martin as having been the most spectacular. Martin was a small lineman; Reagan was a big back. In his oral history he mentions a few examples that provide a tip-off of his talent. In high school he wrestled on even terms with a man who was later a professional football player; after World War II Reagan was sought by two pro football teams and wound up playing in the Canadian Football League. He is still impressive physically, although years of smoking have taken their toll. He recently lost a lung and speaks with a weakened voice as a result. That is only part of the reason he is a quiet man. Even though he and Graham Martin starred in the most aggressive of sports, neither has an aggressive, pushy personality. Both are inclined to think before acting, to offer opinions when asked rather than volunteering them. The things they do say are the product of thoughtful reflection.

A number of these memoirs, including John Reagan's, convey the idea that the Navy didn't know what to do with its new black officers once they were commissioned. They were sent to essentially make-work jobs rather than filling the sort of billets that were available to white officers of comparable backgrounds and training. What distinguishes Reagan from the other members of the Golden Thirteen is that he was called back to active duty in the late 1940s and wound up serving during the Korean War. By that time, the armed forces had been integrated, and he got to serve in the fleet. He was thus able to fulfill a goal one war later than he expected.

In the various civilian careers John Reagan pursued after his naval service, he displayed a real bent for business, particularly in the real-estate field. His work took him to California, and his real-estate dealings enabled him to set up a delightful home for himself and his third wife, Dede. They live in a sun-drenched condominium in Encinitas, north of San Diego. Their apartment faces the rolling Pacific Ocean on which Reagan once served as a Navy enlisted man and officer. Down the hill from their place are coastline railroad tracks. From time to time the whistles of trains punctuate the tapes of his oral-history interviews.

Farther north is Beverly Hills, where Reagan's mother worked as a maid during the 1940s. One of her employers was a woman named Virginia Hill, who was the girlfriend of the notorious gangster Bugsy Siegel up to the time of his murder in 1947. (Hill was portrayed by Annette Bening in the 1991 film *Bugsy*.) Reagan's mother took such jobs because she wanted to make a better life for her children. John Reagan himself later made plans for the future of his son and namesake, John Reagan, Jr. The plans never came to fruition because after the young man did a hitch in the Navy, he was killed while serving with the Marine Corps in Vietnam. The memory of his son's loss is still a painful one for this man who was a pioneer in the big war a generation earlier.

My earliest memories go back to Shreveport, Louisiana, which is where our family moved soon after I was born in Texas in 1920. I guess we were in Shreveport until I was about five or six. I remember running around in the country all the time, climbing trees, riding horses. Our dad was a jack-of-all-trades, very mechanically inclined. He went north to Chicago to try and better himself, and we joined him there. Later, we moved on to Flint, Michigan, where he worked for Buick Company. One thing I especially remember from that time is laughing like hell at "Amos and Andy," a radio program with two white comedians playing black men. Many years later, when the "black is beautiful" era started coming along, there were criticisms about the show, but we didn't feel that way at the time.

My father and mother took different approaches in disciplining us. When I was in high school, for instance, I smoked occasionally. It was all right with my mother. She caught me in the bathroom a couple of times blowing smoke out the window. She said, "You don't have to sneak and smoke. If you're going to smoke, smoke." Dad was a lot more conservative. Once, a kid whose dad was an importer gave me a case of beer. I brought it home and put some in the refrigerator. Just before dinner one day I took a bottle out and asked my dad if he would have a bottle with me. He said he wouldn't. I don't think it was because he didn't drink beer; my perception is that he didn't want to appear to be condoning my drinking. On the other hand, in our younger years it was my mother, not my father, who did most of the spanking. Part of that could be traced to the fact that he wasn't always living with the family. Even when he was with us, we were more likely to be working together than playing. His attitude was, "I'm a father; I'm not a buddy."

During the Depression, my dad always worked. He was a dyed-in-the-wool Republican—a real conservative politically—and hated relief. I had a younger brother and younger sister, and he always cared for us well, but my parents were separated from time to time, mainly because my mother wanted to work too. She wanted to make a better life for us. Dad didn't want her to work, so that was a source of conflict off and on. My parents probably drifted apart and went back together three or four times. We children were bothered by this sort of arrangement and wanted desperately for them to stay together. Finally, however, we adjusted to the fact that our parents had to work out their own relationship; we couldn't do it for them.

Chicago was where I got most of my elementary education and high school. And I must say that both of my parents provided a lot of motivation for doing well in school. One of the real breaks in my life—though I didn't know it at the time—came when I was about eleven or twelve. My mother moved the family from the east side of the city to a neighborhood called Englewood. The kids there were more family oriented than where we came from. They were interested in athletics, Boy Scouts, and other wholesome things. I started being a better-than-average athlete and a pretty good student. I had a good chance of going pretty sour in our old neighborhood because a lot of the kids I knew and ran around with there were later involved with drugs (mostly marijuana) and crime. I was lucky enough to escape that. People like my scoutmaster and others out in Englewood became a good influence for me.

I especially recall an English teacher named Mrs. Edwards. She taught at Lindblom High School. She gave a number of students special attention, and we all profited. She frequently encouraged me to be a leader and set an example. There were not a lot of black students at Lindblom, but color didn't matter to her. She just wanted to get me to do my best. She was a very positive influence on my life. My mother had indirectly brought that situation about by moving the family to a school where I could benefit from the help of someone like Mrs. Edwards. Not every student is so fortunate.

For the most part, my upbringing in the North sheltered me from the kinds of unpleasant racial incidents that others in the Golden Thirteen experienced. I think the first time I encountered prejudice was when I visited relatives in Texas. I suppose I was ten or eleven years old. Some white kids pulled up in a car beside me once and used the word "nigger." The incidents after that were usually fairly isolated. When I first went to college up in Montana, the Chinese restaurant didn't want to serve me. But I happened to be going with some other football players, and there was no way they could avoid serving me. My school canceled Texas Tech from the schedule because they said I would have to stay with a black family, not in the team hotel, if we went to Texas to play a return game. It seems that I was almost always in some sort of protective situation.

Maybe that was why I never got involved with the members of the Communist Party, although it wasn't for lack of effort on their part. I remember they used to have nice-looking young men and women come around our neighborhood and say, "We're having a picnic and music and dancing over here at the park." A lot of the guys did go. That came to haunt them later because somehow it was found out that they had fooled around with these groups. I don't remember thinking, "Well, if I go get involved in this, some day I might want to go in the Navy and be an officer." I didn't have an idea of anything like that at the time. The group I was with just didn't happen to get involved in those things.

My college experience was at Montana State University in Missoula. I went there on a football scholarship in 1939. I'd had quite a successful time in athletics in high school in Chicago. I had earned twelve or thirteen letters: football, wrestling, boxing, track. I guess I would have played basketball, but they wouldn't let us play both football and basketball. I won city and state championships in wrestling. One of the students I wrestled was Lou Rymkus. He was about 6-6 and three hundred pounds; he later played and coached in professional football.

Our whole backfield in football was supposed to go to the University of Michigan and did have offers from most of the Big Ten schools. But my wrestling coach, Mr. Spade, was a good friend of the football coach, Doug Fessenden, at Montana State, and Spade talked me into going out there. I'll never know what I missed by not going to Michigan with the rest of the guys.

As a boy, I had aspired to be an entertainer. My goals had changed by the time I got to Montana State; then I got kind of serious about wanting to be a doctor. In fact, I took courses leading to premed. The thing that stopped me there was that I had a chemistry course that interfered with football practice. So that wasn't the strongest goal in the world. I switched to economics and sociology after not doing so well in chemistry, and my grades were good enough to get me designated as a scholar-athlete.

During my first year of varsity football, I made all-America honorable mention. That fall we played the Marines here in San Diego, and they had some really talented players. Even so, I just had one hell of a great day running off tackle, so I kept hearing, "Stop that nigger! Stop that nigger!"

In 1940, during that sophomore year, the Army Air Corps recruiting team came around to the campus and tried to sign me up. I was interested in football and my education, so I didn't sign up. In 1941, after the attack on Pearl Harbor, they came around again, and I did sign up. I dropped out of school at the end of the first semester of my junior year. I went home to live with my dad in Chicago and waited to be called up for pilot training. It didn't turn out that way, of course.

The draft board was interested in me, so I didn't have the luxury of waiting for the pilot training I really wanted. I had to enlist to avoid being drafted, and the idea of eventually being able to go aboard ship and travel just felt better to me at that point than becoming a foot soldier. There was never any question in my mind about whether I wanted to serve the country. I felt, and still do, that fighting for the country was a part of fighting for equality. So in July 1942 I went ahead and enlisted in the Navy since I still hadn't heard anything from the Army Air Forces, as the service was known by then. A week after I was in boot camp out at Great Lakes, I got orders to go down to Tuskegee, Alabama, where the Army was training the 99th Pursuit Squadron, which would be an all-black outfit. I went up to the boot-camp executive officer and said, "I've only been in the Navy a week, and I've got these orders where I can be a flier. Can't you let me out?" He said that the Navy orders took precedence, which made me pretty unhappy for a while.

One thing that helped make the Navy more palatable was that I got into a leadership role right away. I had had some ROTC training in college, and so I was chosen to be the apprentice chief petty officer in my company. The regular Navy chief petty officer evidently liked the way I was running things because he left a lot of it up to me. I remember I had this attitude that "I'm going to be the best

Prior to his officer training, Reagan served as an electrician's mate in small craft.

sailor I can be, and I want this company to be the best outfit it can be, and I want every colored guy in the Navy to be the best he can be." I wouldn't call it gung ho; it's just the way I felt. I suppose this attitude played a part in my being chosen as apprentice chief petty officer for the company.

Later, I went to service school at Hampton, Virginia. Frank Sub-lett was the battalion commander there, and I was the adjutant. I don't remember pushing for these things, necessarily. Apparently, the officers felt I could handle the jobs. During my time at service school I learned to be an electrician's mate, one of the many skills needed to operate Navy ships. Virginia, of course, was part of the old South, and a number of the racial attitudes from years ago were still in force when I was taking Navy training there.

In particular, I remember a time I got on a bus on the naval base in Norfolk and paid my fare in the front. It was really crowded, and the lady driver said she was not going to move unless I got off and went in the back door. One young white passenger said, "Let the guy stay on. The bus is crowded back there."

She said, "I'm not moving. I'll just have to wait here for the cops."

Finally, one of the city policemen arrived and said, "Well, you'll have to get off the bus." I just stood there, as I recall, for a while. Then he said, "Well, come on, son, you've got to get off. That's the law."

So I sat there a little while trying to be stubborn. I said, "I'm not getting off until she gives me my dime back." So she gave me my dime back, and I got off. That was one of the few times that I had to confront segregation by law. In other instances, it was mostly discrimination or prejudice on the part of individuals.

By late 1943 I had advanced to electrician's mate second class. In the meantime, I had served in the battery locker of an auxiliary minesweeper, the *Firefly,* around San Diego. We had some interesting missions looking for mines, and I enjoyed that duty immensely. While I was in that area, I spent quite a bit of time with another enlisted man, Sam Gravely, who later became the Navy's first black admiral. He was involved with the athletic program at the section base in San Diego, and we played a lot of softball. After my stint in the *Firefly,* I was ordered to go aboard a destroyer escort on the East Coast. This was a combatant ship—the type of assignment I'd really been looking forward to.

Commander Downes was the skipper of the training school at Hampton, and I'd gotten to know him well during my training as an electrician's mate. I developed a great deal of respect for him then because he worked hard to create good morale and to motivate people. I thought he was the epitome of a military officer. My image of good leadership was developed primarily from him. You don't have to be a screamer. You do need to be concerned about the people under you, and he always was. As for racial slurs, he was death on them, just wouldn't tolerate anything untoward.

One day in late 1943, when I was waiting for my new duty, Commander Downes just happened to be over at Norfolk, where I was stationed briefly. He saw me and asked me what I was doing there. I was really proud. I said, "Skipper, I'm going aboard this DE as an AC electrician's mate. I'm going to get a ship at last."

He said, "The hell you are! You come over to my quarters at the school this afternoon, and I'll tell you a little bit about what's going on." So I did, and he didn't tell me, actually, that it was officers' indoctrination. He said, "We're sending you up to Great Lakes for a special class, and it's something that you'll like. You'll be glad you're going. It might lead to something that you never suspected." He was certainly right about that because I hadn't had any inkling that the Navy was going to commission any black officers. His recommendation was undoubtedly a big factor in my being chosen for that first group. I was very unhappy about being deprived of that destroyer escort until I found out what I'd be doing instead. It was the most surprising thing in my life when I was ordered to go back to Great Lakes for this officers' class.

Even though I had known Frank Sublett from our time together at Hampton, I suppose the officer candidate that I was closest to was Dalton Baugh. Dalton had, in my estimation, a brilliant mind, but he was a "good old boy" type. He had a tremendous personality. He was not as outgoing as Dennis Nelson or Jesse Arbor—a little more serious, but definitely not a wallflower. I recall visiting him years later when he was doing research at MIT. Like a lot of those fellows from Arkansas, he had good, old, down-to-earth common sense. He was a solid man who took the time to think through a situation.

I'll always have fond memories about the guys who were going through training together. It was absolutely great the way everybody worked together, stuck together, and supported each other. We were very much aware of our role as pioneers. It was a part of everybody's motivation to do well because we had a sense that what we did would affect what other people had a chance to do after us.

During our training, the group was truly isolated in our barracks at Camp Robert Smalls. We had very little contact with anyone besides our instructors and officers, not even with the black enlisted

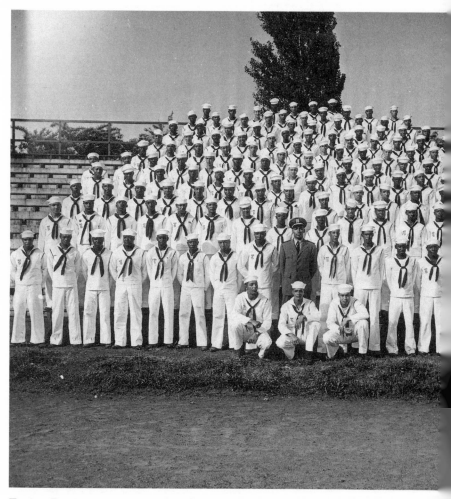

Ensign Reagan, center, poses with a company of enlisted men at the Naval Training School, Hampton, Virginia, shortly after his commissioning in 1944. His role was to be a role model.

Reagan at the time of his commissioning as an ensign in March 1944.

Commander E. Hall Downes of the Hampton Naval Training School congratulates Frank Sublett and John Reagan upon their return to the school following officer training at Great Lakes.

men in the camp. I didn't question the program. It could have been that the isolation was meant to keep us away from distractions during this period of intense, concentrated training; I accepted it for that, anyway. I thought that particular arrangement was possibly the best setting available for what the Navy was trying to do with us. The situation there did strike me as wasteful—the duplication of training facilities for whites and blacks. Camp Robert Smalls might have been the largest-scale segregated situation I ever encountered.

As for the academic part of the training, I don't recall having any great deal of pressure. I'd spent two and a half years in college by that point and another year and a half in the Navy, so I was able to take it all pretty well in stride. If there was a book on a particular subject, I didn't know everything about it, but I could pass tests. I'm usually pretty good at absorbing material quickly. Sometimes, though, you come across something that you don't understand right off the bat, and you have to struggle a little bit for. I think I learned a lot more that way, and, of course, the instructors were helpful in explaining things that we didn't understand. Our instructors were great. I think they were dedicated to doing a good job with us.

In March of 1944 the sixteen of us in training got to the end of our course. I remember the end of the examinations, and then we were notified one at a time whether we would be commissioned as officers. This tended to create some anxiety and tension. The guys that hadn't been informed were wondering whether they were going to make it or not. When I found out that I had been chosen, it was possibly the outstanding event in my life. It was sort of like a great dream coming true, a minor miracle or something. I had always hoped to be a chief petty officer, a chief electrician's mate, if I stayed in the Navy long enough. I never even thought of becoming an officer; before then it wasn't in the realm of possibility.

Naturally, all of us were very proud, and I guess I could say that Dennis Nelson was the epitome of pride. I don't know if this is a figment of my imagination or not, but it really seems to me that the first uniform Dennis bought was a formal one with a sword. At the time the rest of us were just trying to get grays and khakis. Dennis went to downtown Chicago, I believe, and he even got the naval officer's cape, which was optional. He had everything from the start. Even in non-Navy things he carried himself with an attitude and manner that were distinctive.

I remember him telling us about one particular experience. Soon after we got our officer uniforms, he went down to the Palmer House, a fine hotel in Chicago, and had a dinner with all the trimmings. He pulled out a cigar to add the finishing touch. A dowager lady was sitting over at the table next to him, and he said, "Excuse me, lady, do you mind if I smoke?"

She said, "I don't give a damn if you burn." It's one of the few times I ever heard when someone got the best of Dennis Nelson in a verbal exchange.

As our first assignments after graduation, Frank Sublett and I were sent back to Hampton, Virginia. My impression was that the Navy officials didn't really know quite what to do with us at first, so they said, "Well, Reagan and Sublett graduated from Hampton.

We'll send them back." I was made officer in charge of the electrical course, which fit in with my enlisted experience but wasn't very challenging. They had instructors to teach the courses themselves. I would show up in classes and try to give a little pep talk to the students and ask the instructor how they were coming along. I think my main job was to be a role model, to show these young black enlisted men that they did have something better to aspire to. The irony in all that, of course, was that I personally didn't have much of a job to go with my impressive new uniform and rank.

Fortunately, that situation lasted only about three months. Then I spent a couple more months as officer in charge of a patrol craft before I got transferred to a yard tugboat, known as a YTB, operating out of New York City. Jim Hair, another member of the Golden Thirteen, was the skipper, and I was aboard with him. He got the command because he had quite a bit more experience than I did in handling boats. Jim was just a great all-around individual. He had all the good qualities of all the guys in the group, a very good officer and shiphandler. He had a beautiful disposition, just beautiful. If necessary, he could be very stern and strict, but his predominant manner was one of calm deliberation, timely action, and a nice sense of humor.

Among other things, we used to help dock and undock ships at the Brooklyn Navy Yard, break up ice floes on the Hudson River in wintertime, put water on fires on ammunition piers in New Jersey, and just generally be on call. It was a versatile kind of vessel. I picked up the seamanship aspects fairly readily, especially because Jim knew so much already. He demonstrated his stern side once when the tugboat was ordered to fight a fire. A chief petty officer was kind of pleading with Jim for the boat not to go. Jim was so resolved to do his duty that he was about to pull out his .45 to enforce the order. That persuaded the chief to carry out his assignment in the fire-fighting detail.

I guess the biggest thing I remember about the tugboat was a tragic event. One time when Jim Hair wasn't aboard, we were helping a loaded-down amphibious ship, an LST, get away from the docks down at the ammunition pier in Bayonne, New Jersey. We were on the starboard side, and the pilot instructed us to let loose and go around to the port side and help him out because the current was heavier than we thought. At the time, it seemed like such an urgent order, so I tried to respond quickly. In doing so, I gave an order that caused the tugboat to heel over. Three men went over the side, none of them wearing life jackets. We recovered one of them, but the other two drowned. Losing those people was the worst thing that ever happened with me in the Navy. Afterward there was an investigation, and I got a letter of reprimand. That was a really down, down, down experience.

On the bright side, New York City was a wonderful place to be in wartime. Servicemen were treated like kings. The civilians just couldn't do enough for us. We hung around the Theresa Hotel, which was a big center of activity at that time. Generally, we'd stay over there when we were in town. We met a lot of the top celebrities there, particularly the black celebrities. For instance, I remember boxers such as Sugar Ray Robinson and Joe Louis, and we met a lot of the top musicians. I remember also seeing some veterans of the 99th Pursuit Squadron at the Theresa Hotel. These were the black airmen who had gone into combat. Some got shot down and were wounded or killed. As I thought about them and my earlier desire to join the Tuskegee airmen, I decided that maybe my service in the Navy was for the best.

My new wife was with me in New York; her real name was Lillian, but she was known as Tommie. I had met her during the time I was at Hampton as an enlisted man, and then we got married. After I reported to the tugboat, she got a job as a nurse at a hospital for maybe a month. Then she became ill with tuberculosis, and she was sick much of the time I was there. I was, however, able to take her out once in a while on a weekend, and, in fact, our son was conceived just before I left. When my time in the tugboat was up, I was ordered to Oxnard, California, prior to being sent overseas as part of a logistics-support company. Of course, I hated to leave her, but she had improved so much that I knew it was just a matter of time that she would be well. By the time I left the States, her health problem had pretty well gotten taken care of.

During that time in Oxnard, there were a great many sailors around, but black ensigns were very rare. Once I went into a restaurant, and the waiter did not want to seat me at a regular table. He said he would have to serve me in back, by the kitchen. I said, "No."

Finally, I called the base, which sent an officer over. When he arrived, he said, "You know, most of your business is with Navy people, and if you don't serve this gentleman, you're not going to serve anybody else. You're off-limits. Sorry." The almighty dollar is a very powerful persuader.

Once I got overseas, I was made an operations officer with a logistics-support company. I guess a lot of fellows had similar experiences. I think our pattern of assignments was pretty much the same, except for Hair, Baugh, and White. I went to Guam first and then Okinawa with this logistics-support company. There was not a lot to do on Okinawa. I don't recall for sure what they had me doing, but I know that morale was quite a problem at that time. The skipper called all the officers together to discuss the problem. The adjutant general was going around and inspecting all the bases, trying to find out why morale was so bad and what could be done.

One big problem was that the war was over, and men were eager to go back home, but they hadn't been released yet. Besides that, all the camps were muddy. When it rained, the result was a mess of mud and water. I recommended that they build a great big concrete slab, the size of a football field, and have a basketball court, badminton courts, shuffleboard, and things like that. I remember well the chaplain saying, "What we need is a chapel here, and that will take care of the morale." Somehow I won out. They built a slab.

When the inspector came through, nothing much was going on except in our specific camp. It had stopped raining, but everything was muddy and flooding. All our guys were out there playing basketball and shuffleboard, or just sitting around talking on a dry concrete slab. So the skipper got pretty high marks for that, and he was happy.

I don't remember anything else that was too remarkable about that tour over there. It came to an end, and I was released from the service right around the beginning of 1946. At the outset, I returned to New York and began working for sort of a boys' club in Harlem. About April or May of '46 Coach Doug Fessenden called from Montana State and asked me to come up for the summer. He wanted to get together with me on being his quarterback. Then the baby was born, and we decided that Lillian would go to Kentucky with her parents and then join me out in Montana that fall.

I finished my last year of football eligibility in the fall of that year.

Reagan was an outstanding back at Montana State University following World War II, then played professional football in Canada.

I was chosen for some all–Pacific Coast designation, which means that people who were following the game concluded I was a pretty fair football player. Before the war I had been a blocking back in the single wing formation. Once I got back, Coach Fessenden went to the T formation, and I was a quarterback, which was rare for a black player in that era. I could pass, but running and blocking were my strong points. I generally handled the ball on every play, either run or pass. I wouldn't say that I was a speed-burner like the guys are today, but I could run the 100-yard dash in 10 seconds. And at 6-1 and 195 pounds, I was big enough to out-muscle defensive men.

Even though my college work had been considerably interrupted by the war, I did better than before in my studies. I think a lot of the veterans did because we were more mature than we had been. I went ahead and continued with economics and sociology, and I liked Mike Mansfield, so I took his class in political science. He was later a U.S. Senator and ambassador.

In a year and a half I graduated. Then I had an offer to try out for a spot with the Chicago Rockets, a team in a new professional football league that later merged with the NFL. I also had an offer to play up in the Canadian Football League. That was an even better arrangement because it was a bona fide job, not just a tryout. So I reported to the Winnipeg Blue Bombers, the team coached some years later by Bud Grant before he went to the Minnesota Vikings. I got hurt in one game because our blocking wasn't as good as it should have been. I had a knee extended, and about half a ton of linemen landed on it during one tackle. Even so, we played for the Grey Cup and lost the league championship by only a rugby, one point. I threw the touchdown pass that should have won the game. The officials wouldn't allow it because they said I was over the line of scrimmage when I passed. The films after the game showed that the pass was legal, but this was before the days of instant replay, so the films didn't do us any good.

I had fun up in Canada, and I think I might have stayed up there longer, but my wife didn't like it. She had had a taste of California, and it was just too cold for her in Canada. Back in the States, I faced the real world. I worked in a liquor store for a while, then I worked in the insurance business. At some point we bought a home.

Then, in the fall of 1949, I got a call to go back on active duty with the Navy. I mentioned, before, Dennis Nelson's concern about style and wearing the uniform. But he was also a man of substance. He put himself on the line. It was his plan to call a number of veterans back in and use us as recruiters, to build up the strength of blacks in the naval service. I was assigned to duty at the headquarters of the Third Naval District, which was in my old stomping ground, New York City. I wound up spending about three years there. Even though the assignment was supposed to be temporary, I got extended when the Korean War broke out in the summer of 1950.

Our operation really became busy at that point because we were doing the paperwork to bring thousands of reservists back for wartime duty. We were also involved in going out to recruit prospects for the NROTC college-scholarship program. We gave our best pitch, and then we'd open it up for questions. More than once, even though I was wearing the uniform of a lieutenant, I was asked, "Can a Negro be anything other than a mess cook in the Navy?" Our status still hadn't sunk in, even at that time.

Finally, in 1953, I got a shot at a real operational assignment when I was ordered to an amphibious-boat unit that was stationed first in San Diego and later in Japan. That was a fulfilling job because at last I was involved in legitimate naval operations. Back in 1944 I had had the idea that we would finish the officer-candidate school, and then I expected to get on a big ship as a division junior officer and go that whole route. So I had a little disappointment about that. I was always asking to be transferred to an active theater, and that never came about.

With the boat unit, I got a satisfaction that went beyond being a division officer. We were due to get a new executive officer in the unit, and the skipper had to choose between me and a white lieutenant. There were about twenty officers, and I think most of them expected the white lieutenant to get the job, but I was chosen instead. Being an executive officer was both challenging and frustrating because of all the administrative requirements. But it was a great honor to get that position, especially since the unit was nearly all Caucasian. This was a positive step beyond 1945 when the black officers were in charge of segregated labor battalions. I no longer felt I was a token; now I felt part of the Navy—all of it.

After that second tour in the Navy, I went back to school. I took some courses at Southern Cal, and I took a job with the state of California in the employment service. I also got a real-estate license because I had a friend that was in the business. I was progressing really well with the state of California, and I got hold of a transaction in which an old man was losing some property. I started a relationship with him, seeing if I could help him save it in some way, if he wanted to try to sell it. It got to be a situation where every time I talked to him, he'd tell me about something else, some other piece of property. So there were a number of pieces of property. I got all involved in that deal, and so I resigned from the state, and I started working in real estate full time.

As it worked out, though, I had several interruptions in my career. After Skip, my only son, was killed while serving with the Marine

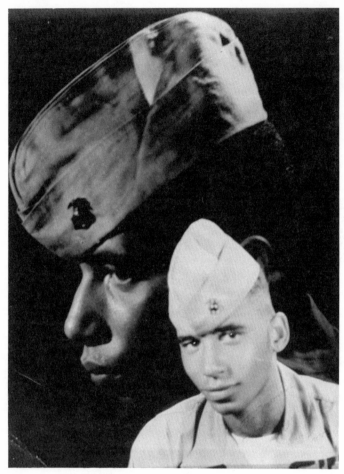

John W. "Skip" Reagan, Jr., was killed while serving with the Marine Corps in Vietnam. His name is among the more than fifty thousand inscribed on the Vietnam War Memorial in Washington, D.C.

Corps in Vietnam, I got depressed. After he had served a minority enlistment in the Navy, I think he might have gone into the Marines to show me what a man he was. I had planned to go into business with him, but we never got that chance. So that was a real blow. Also, about the same time, the riots and other racial disturbances were starting in Los Angeles, and the real estate in the area that I was working with was kind of dead. Dennis Nelson, my old friend from the Golden Thirteen, was with the National Urban League at that time. I was talking to Dennis about how I was feeling, and he said, "Why don't you take a job for a while? I think you'd do a good job for the Los Angeles Urban League."

I did so, and that work provided a great deal of satisfaction. For instance, we set up job fairs. We related to all types of industry and business people in developing jobs, and we started apprenticeship programs. I think we were at the forefront of the nontraditional jobs for women, to get them in "apprentice-able" trades. We did an educational project in Pasadena that resulted in substantially fewer dropouts than before in the school system. We ran a street-academy school which actually recruited dropouts and gave them remedial education in a storefront setting. We did a brochure for the school district so that the general public could understand the policies and rules and regulations and that type of thing because the rules hadn't really been spelled out except for insiders.

In the figurative sense, we put out a lot of fires at schools; we were able to negotiate things. For instance, one school had to break up a riot because they didn't have any black girls on the cheering squad. We were able to get in there and talk to the principal and negotiate a situation where they would go ahead. They had some sort of a competition or something like that, and no black girl was selected. We simply got them to increase the squad and include a black. On a more serious note, we were able to stop a lot of activity on the part of street gangs.

In the Watts riots of 1965, lives were lost and a great deal of property had been destroyed. In the aftermath, things were still hot and heavy. We got the Urban League to relate to the black militant groups and to work out effective alternative programs rather than just marching and picketing. We showed them that demonstrating was not the whole ball game. We could make progress by developing and submitting proposals for positive action in social programs, that is, fostering employment, education, and so forth. I had a great personal part in this particular thing, which helped to attract funding and people, not only to the Urban League but also to other community organizations.

At the same time, I continued working part-time in real estate. I

During the 1982 reunion of the Golden Thirteen on board the guided-missile destroyer USS *Kidd,* Reagan poses on the bridge with Commander William J. Flanagan, the ship's commanding officer.

got involved in a great big deal that was complicated and was able to pull it together. That's a satisfying feeling and explains why I've stayed with it. Except for the time after I lost Skip and went to work for the Urban League, that's what I've been doing and still do. I no longer do much in the way of commission sales. I've got some investments with a partner in several income units, and most of my time is in managing that. Just as in the Navy, the country has made progress in the real-estate area. I can easily remember a time when blacks couldn't be realtors.

While all this was going on, it's worth mentioning that Dennis Nelson introduced me to my second wife. After I split up with Lillian, I married a physician named Hazel Morse, and we were together for nearly twenty years, from 1960 to 1980. Later I married Dede, who is a few years younger than I. She's interested in her career with the telephone company, which involves a long commute. But we enjoy life here, and so I'll just keep on doing what I'm doing as long as I can.

The Golden Thirteen had its first reunion in 1977. Up to then, I'd seen maybe one or two black officers at a time. Then we walked into this auditorium up in Monterey, California, and we saw wall-to-wall black officers—admirals on down. That was a genuine thrill and was made even more special by the opportunity to meet and get to know members of today's generation of black officers. It was the most amazing thing for me to see so many of these bright, young, beautiful, clean people—all ranks, all types of assignments.

This group made us feel like we were high up on a pedestal. I guess I don't take myself that seriously, and I'm not sure any of the guys do. I know it was kind of a remarkable event that we were in the first group to be commissioned and all of that, but these new guys were astounding, these young captains coming up and telling us, "We owe it all to you. If it hadn't been for you guys, we wouldn't be here." They and their counterparts today don't know how awestruck I am about them.

Chapter Seven

Live and Let Live

Frank E. Sublett, Jr.

Those who believe in astrology can make a lot of points about the similarities in the lives of John Reagan and Frank Sublett. They were born on the same day of the same year, March 5, 1920. Both were born in the South but grew up in the Chicago area, participating in Boy Scouts and going to integrated schools. Both came from broken homes and had mothers who worked in domestic service. Both were football players and trackmen. Both began premed courses, played college football, then dropped out of school because of the onset of World War II. Both sought to be pilots in the Army Air Forces but enlisted in the Navy because the Air Forces didn't get to them in time. After boot camp they both served in small auxiliary vessels as enlisted men. The same Navy commander recommended both of them for officer training because of their demonstrated abilities as leaders. They served together at the Naval Training School at Hampton, Virginia, both before and after their training period as officer candidates. Both wound up on island duty in the Pacific after Hampton, although they would have preferred service in warships. Both left the Navy at war's end to enter civilian life. And both of them have been married three times.

There are many differences as well, including the fact that Reagan returned to naval service in 1949 and Sublett didn't. And, unlike his friend Reagan, Frank Sublett has returned to the Chicago area of his boyhood. His home is in a racially mixed neighborhood in the tony suburb of Glencoe in the North Shore region. It is a bedroom community for Chicago and has a lot of the charm that one associates with small-town living. It's only a short drive to the commuter trains and the corner drugstore.

Retirement suits Frank Sublett; he is comfortable in this home in which he has lived for many years. He has many friends, for he is a genuinely warm and outgoing individual. As the title of his memoir suggests, he is the kind of man who accepts people as they are and tries to work with them rather than change them. He is delighted to show visitors his memorabilia from the two principal interests of his life, his naval career and his work as a model. His scrapbooks attest to his success in both areas. Indeed, there is a considerable suggestion of glamour in the latter. It's a heady feeling to see oneself pictured in magazines, newspapers, catalogs, brochures, television, and films. And yet the experience has not gone to Frank Sublett's head. He is truly down-to-earth, the sort of individual whom anyone would enjoy having as a friend.

*E*ven though I was born in Murfrees-
boro, Tennessee, I spent most of my growing-up years in the Chicago
area. My parents moved to Highland Park, Illinois, in the mid-1920s,
when I was about five years old. After just about a year in Highland
Park, our family moved to Glencoe. As a matter of fact, I grew up in
the house right next door to this one.

My dad, for whom I was named, held a variety of jobs. He was a
milkman, a railroad porter, redcap, waiter, sold insurance, and I think
at one time he was a chauffeur. His last job, as I remember, was with
the Chicago and North Western Railway. He died in September 1956.
I heard a lot of people approach him and talk about how great he was
as a football player. I was proud of that and certainly wished I could
have seen his prowess on the athletic field. My mother did domestic
work, including cooking and cleaning. She worked here on Chicago's
North Shore, in Highland Park and in Glencoe. In her later years she
was a companion to a lady who just passed a while ago. Mom is not
working now, but she still lives and is doing pretty well.

My mother's father was a Scotch-Irish gentleman, so she was a
mixture of Scotch-Irish, what we then called Negro, and also a bit of
Cherokee Indian. Race was something that was never discussed in our
home—not at all. I was never race-conscious in any way. In our neighborhood, I remember the Jewish, the Italians, the Irish, and the
Negroes. The atmosphere was just very congenial and remains so to
this day. The neighborhood still contains a mix of ethnic backgrounds.

I had relatives down in Tennessee, but I was never aware of any
difficulties they faced. I understand now that some lived under sup-
pression, but there wasn't much talk about it. It was their way of life.
Any time I visited in Tennessee there was good feeling between
whites and blacks, as far as I could see. They spoke to each other

respectfully and did business together. Discrimination was essentially taken for granted.

In 1931, shortly before my teens, my mom and dad split up and divorced. I stayed with Mom and also spent some time with an aunt and uncle who lived here in Glencoe. During the Depression, I don't recall too many problems. I know I always had a lot of chores to do, whether it was stoking the furnace, polishing cars, raising chickens, mowing the lawn, helping to raise a garden, or capping the bottles when my uncle made home-brewed beer.

As for a more formal job, I used to go up to a tearoom where my uncle worked, and I did odd jobs there. I was a busboy, or a cleaner-upper, before going to school in the morning. It wasn't a necessity, but I suppose it was part of my upbringing. It helped to get to work early in the morning and sometimes on Sunday afternoon because I spent a lot of my other time down here at the beach, either swimming or fishing. And I used to go with my uncle on fishing trips to Wisconsin maybe once or twice during each summer. In effect, I suppose my uncle became something of a substitute father for me; it was a good relationship.

Another good experience was that of being in the Boy Scouts when I was young. Our sponsor was a wealthy man whose name was William Baehr. He was white, and the troop was integrated. He used to take us hiking; he'd take us to ball games at Wrigley Field, where the Chicago Cubs played, and other niceties. We learned knot tying, and we went out camping, cooking outside and sleeping in tents overnight—all the regular things that young Boy Scouts learn. We had to know the scout manual thoroughly so we could pass our tests and advance. I love the out-of-doors, so scouting was enjoyable, and I think it also helped instill in me some of the values of good citizenship. Mr. Baehr thought enough of my leadership qualities to make me junior-assistant scoutmaster.

After Dad left, my mom did not push me in any way. The environment here creates a situation where you just go to school; there is no thought of dropping out. I lived a good, clean life, growing up as a kid here, as most of us did. The boys and girls around here just lived that way as a matter of course. I was never involved in any activities that would be embarrassing to my family or to myself. Mom has always figured that I knew best, and she'd let it go at that. I never gave her any trouble, and she'll say so today. I'm proud of that.

I went to school here in Glencoe, first through eighth grades. I went to high school in Winnetka, which is about four miles away. All along I was involved in integrated situations. When I grew up here, there were very few black families. In high school there were only four blacks—three boys and one girl—in a class of 539. So I grew up in an atmosphere that didn't involve any overt prejudice. I don't know about the attitudes of all my classmates, but I didn't encounter any problems. I was accepted, and my attitude probably had a lot to do with it. I believe you should just live and let live. I wasn't looking for anybody to give me any trouble, and I wasn't giving anybody else any trouble. I was dark skinned and somebody else was white skinned; it didn't matter to me. We did things together.

I participated in all the athletic programs that were available in high school. I specialized in football and track and did pretty well in those. On a couple of occasions I received useful prods from coaches. My football coach, as a matter of fact, told me at that time I was lazy. And it helped because I graduated with an A in algebra. My track coach also advised me in that same area, that I could do better. I was doing all right, but they saw a potential for me to do even better, and I did. Coaches are used to giving that kind of guidance, and I appreciated it.

In 1938 I got some financial assistance through an alumnus to go to the University of Wisconsin. I played a little football up there as an end on both offense and defense. The head coach was Harry Stuhldreher, who had become famous a number of years earlier as one of the Four Horsemen of Notre Dame, the backfield that played for Knute Rockne. In track and field I was involved in the discus and the shot put. I had a little problem with grades, so I had to give up my participation in sports. I was able to pull my grades up slightly after I began concentrating on the academics, but then I left Wisconsin. I went down to Northwestern University for a couple of semesters in '39 and '40. Then in 1941 and '42 I went to George Williams College at East 51st Street on the south side of Chicago.

Perhaps part of the reason I kept moving around was that I didn't really have solid career goals at that point. At first I got involved in a

Sublett, who enjoyed working with automobiles as a young man, had the aptitude for service as an enlisted machinist's mate prior to undergoing officer training.

premed course. That was the only inkling of a future that I antici-pated. I was just average in mathematics at that time. I probably did better in physiology and anatomy. George Williams College was more or less a teachers' school, so I concentrated on YMCA work and edu-cation. As I look back now, I should have probably gotten into a busi-ness course; I would have fared much better in today's world. Another observation in retrospect is that it probably would have been better if I had been paying the full freight instead of getting financial aid. I think you appreciate things more if you have to pay for them yourself.

As it was, I went to college for a little better than three years but never did finish a degree because the war came along. I left school in 1942 in order to go into military service. My primary goal was to join the Army Air Forces and be a flier. When I had finished high school, I was 185 pounds and went up to about 220 while playing football my freshman year in college. I slimmed down quite a bit when I attempted to get into the Air Forces. Unfortunately, at that time there was not an opening because only one field was available for black pilots, the one at Tuskegee, Alabama.

I turned twenty-two in March of 1942 and was a prime candidate for the draft after I left school, but I didn't want to go into the Army. I've always loved water—fishing, swimming, and boating—so I enlisted in the Navy on July 7 of that year. The Navy had just opened up the general-service ratings for black sailors a month earlier, and that was also a big factor. I wasn't interested in being a cook or stew-ard's mate, and the change meant I would have a wide range of other opportunities.

I had a good tour of duty in my entire hitch in the Navy, starting out from boot camp on up. I was in one of the early companies at Camp Robert Smalls at Great Lakes. The naval training station was only a few miles north of my home, so I didn't have far to go. Once I was there, I had no trouble whatsoever adjusting to the Navy disci-pline and way of life. Part of that stemmed from the fact I went to Fort Riley, Kansas, for two weeks in the summer back when I was six-teen. It was called CMTC, Citizens Military Training Camp. We wore heavy woolen leggings, Smokey the Bear hats—the whole bit. I had some good military training there, including drilling, marksmanship, and hiking.

I've always been regimented and well-disciplined anyway, from the time I was a kid all the way up, so I had no trouble in that area. As a matter of fact, I became an apprentice CPO, one of the leaders in the company in boot camp. I was evidently singled out as having leadership qualities. That could have come from football, from track, general education, Fort Riley, or maybe inherited from Mom or Dad. Maybe it was a combination of all of those.

As part of my duties, I inspected both the recruits and the barracks. In the process, I encountered some young men whose backgrounds were far different from mine. I had to assist the men who did not know how to get clean. Some of those fellows came from places in the hills and didn't know what running water and good soap were. I helped teach the men about military bearing, general seamanship, and cleanliness. I knew about knots and so forth from my Boy Scout experience. I called cadence when we drilled and marched. Some of the men didn't know their right from their left. Some of the young men were illiterate. I was about the same age as most of the men in my company but definitely had more education; that was undoubtedly a factor in my being chosen to lead the group.

One of the interesting things about boot camp was that we slept in hammocks that were lashed up to vertical stanchions in our barracks. Men still slept in hammocks in many Navy ships at the time, and this was a way of preparing for shipboard duty. It took a little time to get used to sleeping that way. Every night somebody hit the deck. They were told to make the hammocks taut in the stays. A lot of fellows were afraid of falling on the deck, and they wanted to sleep with a sway in the hammock because they thought it was more comfortable. Sure enough, they'd flip out of it. They'd have sore backs, they'd urinate in the hammock. (Sleeping in that kind of position started the kidneys.) That took some getting used to for some.

After completing recruit training, I was assigned to what was essentially a Navy vocational-training school at Hampton, Virginia. My aptitude tests indicated that my talent was in machinery, probably from having a background of working with the automobiles. I was delighted to get the opportunity to become a machinist's mate because I was good at something which I truly enjoyed doing. The biggest adjustment I had to make in getting used to the Navy was in

E. Hall Downes, officer in charge of the training program at Hampton, Virginia, dictates to his secretary, Annette Hatton. Black enlisted men who went through the school at Hampton praised Downes highly for his leadership qualitites.

the racial area. Both my boot training and service school were all black. These were my first experiences with all black people. Some of the guys used to tease me about the way I talked because they came from areas in the South, and I grew up here on the North Shore with an accent that was different from everyone else's.

While at Hampton I developed an excellent relationship with Commander Downes, who was the officer in charge of the school. He gave me a wonderful compliment one day. I've forgotten exactly how he put it, but he told me that he wished one thing in life, and that would be that his son Hall would grow up to be as fine a gentleman as I. I thought that was the greatest thing I'd ever heard. He was a very fine gentleman himself. He contacted my mother personally and told her of my progress, and he kept tabs on everyone else in the company. He had a remarkable memory. When we first got there, he asked all of us where we came from and what our experiences had been. The next time I talked with Commander Downes, he knew my name, where I was from, and what schools I had attended—all that I had told him before—without hesitation. The fact that he would make the effort to learn so much about us and remember it indicated a genuine concern. He instilled pride and dignity, reminding us frequently that we were *men.* He was a fabulous guy.

I had a real feeling of satisfaction when I graduated from service school. On my uniform I got the two chevrons for second-class machinist's mate, and the insignia was a propeller. From Hampton I was shipped up to East Boston to work in a Navy machine shop. This was my first integrated Navy assignment. There were some much-older white fellows in that outfit who were experienced and probably came in the service after having been machinists in civilian life, so they were instructors too. At the outset I had menial jobs to do as a machinist, working on small craft.

My next assignment was to go aboard a converted fishing boat named the *Queen of Peace.* It had been equipped with sonar, so it could listen for submarines. I was far from being a machinist then. I recall listening to the clang of buoy bells, and once in a while I'd hear a big ship go by. We tried to distinguish which sound was which. It was just in the Boston Bay area. We didn't get out to open sea. It was a precautionary measure, I guess, to see if any submarines might slip through. That didn't last long, though, and I went back to the section base at East Boston. I learned a lot about being a machinist and also got some training in diesel engines. During the course of my time there, I was advanced to first-class petty officer.

I spent nearly all of 1943 in the Boston area. My time there was enjoyable, especially because I was able to get out on liberty much more than I had at Hampton; the racial climate was more hospitable. My assignment came to an abrupt end late in the year. I got orders one day to lash my hammock and seabag in seagoing fashion and ship out. I was gone the next day. My new assignment, of course, was officer training at Great Lakes. It came as a great surprise, and I'm sure the reason I was picked had to do with Commander Downes. I had

Four men of the Golden Thirteen, all rated as petty officer first class, pose together during the course of their officer training in early 1944. Charles Lear and Frank Sublett are in the front row, Syl White and James Hair in the back.

been a battalion commander during the time I was in service school at Hampton. I was an assistant to the commissioned officers, and I'm sure that Downes was impressed by my attitude and my know-how, so he recommended me.

I felt really honored about getting involved in something so glamorous as this new opportunity. I knew about some of the officer-training programs, like V-7 and V-12, at the civilian universities, but this was special. It was a course established solely for our group of sixteen enlisted men. As far as I can recall, the men in charge of this program told us why we were there, what we were up against, what we had to do to achieve our aims, and bang, there we were—books and studies. It was a cram course; we had a lot to learn in a relatively short time—only about two and a half months.

In our courses I would say that we had a good bunch of instructors. The course was demanding, and they were all very helpful and gave us all the attention that they should have. I don't know what their qualifications were, but I think they made a genuinely good, honest attempt to teach us what we needed to know. We studied such things as navigation, seamanship, gunnery, naval history, and Navy regulations. We were graded on our classroom work, but I don't recall having seen any of the grades until afterward—at the completion of our studies.

There was no feeling of competition among the members of the group. Instead, there was a sense of camaraderie. We became very close because we stayed in the same barracks and studied together. In fact, we did almost everything together. We pooled our knowledge. Some of the men hadn't had any sea duty, so the rest of us shared the things we had learned. I helped out, for example, in some of the mechanical areas. It was a full cooperative effort on everybody's part. The men in our group had the capacity and ability to grasp the information, and we just worked together.

One member of the group who made an especially strong impression was Dennis Nelson. He was the mouth of the group—good and bad—and he always loved being the center of things. In fact, he had a flair for calling attention to himself. Guys used to get pretty sore at him because he'd come up with the darnedest things, but we all loved him. From time to time, one of us would say, "Oh, shut up, Nelson," or something like that. But nothing serious. He was flamboyant, wild, and sometimes crude, but everybody loved him. I mean, you could be angry with him in one minute, and the next minute you just loved him, observing his misdemeanors and how sneakily he got out of them with a weak joke or some kind of a wisecrack. You couldn't get angry enough with him to battle him.

After our commissioning he was stationed at Great Lakes, and I guess he had problems with the skipper, Commander Armstrong, about wearing different types of uniforms. Dennis enjoyed the glamour of the Navy. He loved the Navy, he really did. He was a proud man until the day he died.

Sublett as a newly commissioned ensign in March 1944.

At the end of the training, three of the men in the program were dropped; I'll never know why. The rest of us had no graduation ceremonies whatsoever. We were probably the only group of officers that got commissions but had no graduation exercise of any sort. One interesting thing was that a photo of the group was taken for *Life,* which was then a very popular weekly magazine. We were pictured there because we were a novelty, and I would have to say that what we accomplished has achieved more importance in retrospect than we thought about at the time. It's only lately that I've realized what we went through and how valuable it was. I hear the kids next door say, "I see you in our history book," and it's a good feeling.

Actually, I don't think the white hierarchy at the time expected the group to make it. This was a new experience, to have all these black people in the Navy in the first place, other than being mess cooks and that sort of thing. So the Navy was taking a risk. It was a pressure thing on all sides, I'm sure. Certainly we were qualified; they must have thought that, or they wouldn't have recommended us. But still, the higher-ups might have been saying, "Oh, boy, look what we've got here. What are we going to do with them?"

When we got our orders as officers, we discovered that the Navy didn't really use us as well as they could have. To put it bluntly, we got menial jobs. We had to be open-minded about the whole thing. Other people were making the decisions; we had to go along with whatever they said. On the positive side, we did in fact get our commissions, and that was a source of great pride. It was a big step beyond what we'd been before. The Navy was at least willing to give us a chance.

Although I didn't have a choice of duty initially, my previous association with Commander Downes was useful. I know that he wanted John Reagan and me back at Hampton, so we were both assigned there. I was put in charge of a company of 250 students. It was similar to the group I had been a part of when I first went down there for service school. I instructed in small-boat handling, seamanship, military bearing, and that sort of thing. I executed the duties of a commanding officer for this company.

One completely new aspect of our status had to do with the relationship between black officers and white enlisted men. The students were all black, but a number of the others assigned to the school as instructors or clerical personnel were white. Obviously, there was no basis of experience, so I decided just to take it one day at a time. I will say that I was never involved in any maltreatment or disrespect. I know I didn't have the attitude that if somebody didn't salute me, that I was going to put him on report. That's just part of my live-and-let-live philosophy. Dennis Nelson probably put people on report for not saluting up at Great Lakes. His temperament was a good deal different from mine.

Actually, that assignment at Hampton didn't last too long. I wanted to serve in a warship, but what I got only resembled sea duty. I went to the 12th Naval District—Treasure Island in San Francisco Bay. I was put aboard the *YP-131,* which was a patrol craft, a converted yacht that had an all-black crew. Among other things, we took a bunch of nurses out for a ride up and down the bay. At other times we'd serve as an escort vessel, clearing the area so that submarines could make dummy torpedo runs. But we didn't do anything important ourselves—nothing involving warfare. This reinforced my idea that the Navy didn't know exactly what to do with this group of black ensigns who were qualified to be deck officers.

After that I went aboard a yard oiler, the *YO-106,* where I served with Graham Martin, another member of the Golden Thirteen. That YO could have been run by a first-class boatswain's mate. It didn't need one commissioned officer, let alone two, but that was a place to stick us. Still, it was good duty because the oiler had a legitimate role. Typically we went to an oil refinery, picked up oil, and went alongside battleships, aircraft carriers, cruisers, destroyers, and all sorts of ships to refuel them day and night.

I got considerable satisfaction from operating the YO because handling an oiler was a challenge. You went to a loading dock at one of the oil refineries to take on a load when the tanker was empty. When the currents were fast and the wind was strong, handling the vessel could be a problem. Many shiphandlers have crashed the docks, doing that. I had a commendation from the port director after a few months for my very good handling of that oiler. I had a good engine crew, a good helmsman. It was beautiful. That was the kind of experience for which I had joined the Navy.

Graham Martin and I would change watches sometimes so that he could go over to San Francisco to play semipro football under an

Because Navy policy prevented them from being assigned to combatant ships, early black officers wound up being detailed to run labor gangs ashore. Gathered here at Eniwetok in the Marshall Islands are Dennis Nelson, Frank Sublett, Graham Martin, and Sidney Smith, one of the earliest black warrant officers.

assumed name. We had a couple of white kids on that vessel. They were capable, and they respected us. Everybody got along together as a crew; there was teamwork. That was the only mixed crew that I was involved with as an officer.

When we served on the West Coast, we found a new reason for people failing to salute us, and it wasn't a matter of disrespect. The fact was that many people in California did not know that we were commissioned. Cooks and steward's mates wore uniforms similar to

ours, with a cap and so forth. A lot of people just didn't know the difference between a steward's mate and an ensign. They had not been
indoctrinated in it. There were some who knew and accepted us. A
few even praised us, but nothing big. They were respectful. I didn't
have any problems, perhaps because I didn't look for any.

In early 1945 I was called back to Great Lakes and given indoctrination in how to conduct training on the prevention of venereal dis-
ease. I did give a few lectures on the subject but was not really
involved in doing much training. Again, I suspect the Navy just
couldn't find anything better for me to do at the time. For my next
duty, again I had no choice, none at all. I went aboard a naval transport on July 18, 1945, to Pearl Harbor. One other officer was with
me. I was probably there for several days or a week while waiting for
an assignment. Then I went to Eniwetok in the Marshall Islands.

Several of the Golden Thirteen were reunited there when we were
assigned to Logistic Support Company 515, essentially a group of
about two hundred black stevedores. Unloading supplies from ships
was the main duty of this outfit; occasionally we loaded. We were
making preparations collectively for the invasion of Japan. There was
a huge setup at Eniwetok for the gathering of all types of ships and
weaponry for the invasion of Japan. We were quite busy there in that
area.

Lieutenant (j.g.) George Reed, a white Naval Reserve officer, was
the commanding officer. He was a real gentleman, very congenial. I
was the executive officer and supply officer. Dennis Nelson handled
personnel, and Graham Martin handled recreation. We had a nice
group over there. And even though it wasn't like San Francisco, it was
good duty, actually. The lagoon was beautiful; you could go swimming every day. The water was so clear that in twenty feet of water
you could see the bottom as if it were right below the surface. We
spent time looking for shells and that sort of thing. Obviously, we had
a fair amount of time for recreation.

As the time for the invasion of Japan drew closer, the buildup of
Navy ships in the Eniwetok lagoon was absolutely massive. I was
envious of the men serving in those ships. We were quite shocked
when the word came in early August that the Army Air Forces had
dropped atomic bombs on Japan. We were happy, of course, that we
didn't have to go and lose a lot of lives over there. The war was over,

and we had survived. I hadn't been exposed to the danger that a lot of people had, and yet I believe I did my share. I know that I helped to train some who did get involved in combat. I was never given a chance to do more. I don't say that defensively, merely as a statement of fact. I did enjoy my Navy time—from start to finish. As I've told many people, "If I could do it all over again, I would."

I would have liked to have stayed in the Navy, actually, and I could have gotten another half-stripe for staying longer. I was a lieutenant (j.g.) when the war ended and could have been promoted to lieutenant. But I had gotten married the day after I got my commission, and by late 1945 I had a young son also. The war was over, and my mother-in-law strongly advised me to come home. She was concerned that the marriage would not last if we remained separated, so she felt it was essential that I get home. So I responded.

I had met my future wife, whose maiden name was Eugenia Beck, when I was going to George Williams College. She was going to the YMCA school down in Chicago. My mother had moved to Evanston by that time, and Eugenia lived in Evanston with her family. We had gotten acquainted while we were commuting back and forth to school. We dated. Then, when I went in the Navy, we were still together and were dating, and we got married March 18, 1944, right after my commissioning. I took her on my assignments to Virginia and to California.

After Eniwetok I came back to Pearl Harbor on the USS *PC-813*; I arrived in late November and stayed about a week. Then I went back to San Diego in December on an aircraft carrier, the USS *Card,* and stayed there for a few days. Then from San Diego I went back to Great Lakes to the separation center. In February of 1946 I was terminated from active duty and assigned to the reserves. I liked the Navy. I had a good tour of duty all the way through, and I didn't want to terminate it.

When I got back to Illinois, I didn't know whether I should go back to school and get my degree or go to work. It turned out that I went to work to take care of my wife and child. So I missed out on a naval career, and later the marriage failed anyway. I was given the opportunity to return to active duty in the late 1940s but decided to remain in my civilian employment and support my family. That was the last chance I got. I wish things had wound up differently, but you can't turn back the clock.

After my return to civilian life, because of my interest in mechanical things, I went to work for a Buick dealership. I've done body work, I've been a mechanic, been in the parts department. I think I've been in about every department except sales. After being assistant service writer for a number of years, I became a service manager. I think I was the first black service manager for a GM dealership in the Chicago metropolitan area. I had a good experience. Altogether, I did that kind of work for thirty-four years.

I don't regret the fact that I didn't finish college because I enjoyed what I was doing all those years. I had a good work attitude and a good business going for me in the automobile industry. It was interesting. It used to be great. The reason I'm out of it now is that it has changed. It's not as interesting as it used to be because our domestic automobiles are not what they used to be. The Japanese and the German automobiles have just about taken over the industry. The prices are up, and the quality is down.

My attitude toward the work—and life in general—is probably what enabled me to get by without ulcers. Sometimes a customer would come to the service entrance. He was there for a reason, a problem with his automobile. He might, on top of that, have another problem at home or in his business. He might want to unleash that on you. But you just respect the fact that he has a problem and handle that individual diplomatically and you don't have to get ulcers. In some places I'm sure that approach would not work. But since I had lived for so long in this North Shore area, I knew that these people expected good service and were willing to pay for it, so I was able to give it to them. Chicago is totally different. In that city a guy may come into your shop with a long knife and shout, "Why isn't my car running?"

As the years passed, the family grew, but my first marriage finally came to an end after about fifteen years. We parted because we realized that we just had different personalities and different expectations in life. I married my second wife, Frances, in 1964 and had a little girl with her; we were married for about five years. Then I was a bachelor until 1975, when I married Karen. We share a happy, wholesome togetherness of love and trust.

After I had had enough of the automobile business, I retired at the end of 1979, and then I got into the modeling business because of a

FRANK SUBLETT

Height:	6'1"	Shirt:	17½–35
Weight:	205	Pants:	38–31
Suit:	48 L	Shoe:	11 C

Exclusively Represented by:

Emilia' Lorence Ltd.

619 North Wabash Avenue   Chicago, Illinois 60611
312-787-2033

One of the many portraits from Sublett's modeling portfolio.

young man who used to live across the street from me. He had been a model. He said, "Frank, you ought to be tired of getting up at 5:30 every morning, going to that place up there, listening to people scream about their cars. Why don't you give me a picture and let's go down to see my agent." So I did, and here I am. They don't use people like me every day, but the industry is not flooded with older models, so it has worked out very nicely. When you do work, it's good pay. You don't make a heck of a lot of money on it, but it's fun. It's a lot of fun.

My modeling work has been in print ads, television commercials, and some industrial films. In one local television commercial I portrayed former Mayor Harold Washington of Chicago. I was shown walking away from the camera in an ad for radio station WLAK; that ran for about a year or so. I was in a national TV commercial for Bud Light. It was filmed at the old Comiskey Park on Chicago's south side. I was sitting in the bleachers, and the shot showed the ballpark's exploding scoreboard in the background. The man next to me had some lines to say as part of Budweiser's advertising campaign suggesting that people should specify Bud Light, not just ask for a light beer.

Most of my work has been in print advertisements, including one for Pillsbury that showed just my hands as I broke open a hot biscuit. I did another with an orange in my hands. I've been a judge, I've been a doctor, I've been a pharmacist. I modeled preachers' robes for the catalog of a company that sells them. I've done cover flyers for automobiles, a cover for a telephone-company book. Though I am actually a great-grandfather, several people have been kind enough to tell me that I don't look old enough even to be a grandfather. I have some gray hair, but I don't fit the image of the white-haired old man, stooped over with arthritis and limping along with a cane. So I can play middle-aged roles, as I did when I was a computer instructor, vice president of a corporation, and a member of a board.

At this stage in life, I feel very comfortable. Karen and I enjoy puttering around in the garden, so we raise both flowers and vegetables. It's outside work, and that's what I like most. I walk a lot and ride my bike a lot. I belong to a health and swim club. I haven't used it as much as I should have, but I'll get back to it. I also keep in mind my obligations as a citizen because I think that comes first. We can gripe and groan about our personal problems, not having everything we want in life. But you can do without and still be a first-class citizen by taking care of your own business, your own home, and your own surroundings. You shouldn't waste time worrying about the other person, what he has or doesn't have.

As for the Golden Thirteen, I've looked forward every year to our reunion, our mini-conferences that we have. It's good to see the guys again since we've gotten back to know each other a little better and

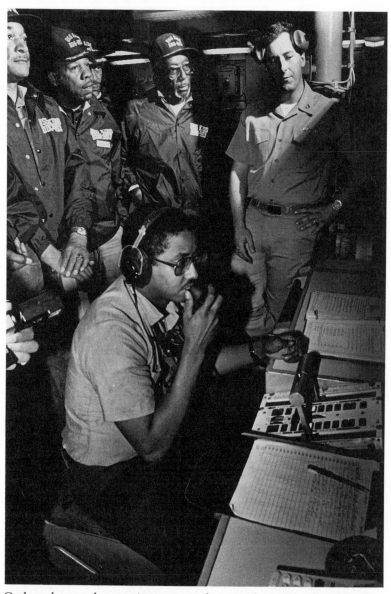

Gathered around an engine-room technician during the Golden Thirteen's reunion on board the destroyer *Kidd* in 1982 are Sublett, first black Naval Academy graduate Wesley Brown, John Reagan, Dalton Baugh, and one of the ship's officers.

we communicate. It's interesting to grow old together and laugh, have a few drinks. We are definitely involved as a unit in recruiting. The price of an education in the civilian world today is unaffordable, but you can go into the service, particularly the Navy, get a good education, and make a career of it. If you learn a trade in the Navy, you can come out later and, if you desire, go into business.

I certainly would like to see more of our young men get into it and learn to be good citizens, which is first. A lot of people are complaining about what society doesn't do for blacks and this sort of thing, but blacks have to do for themselves too. You can make it, no matter who you are. Learn to discard all those unpleasantries that are available in anybody's life.

Three of us from the Golden Thirteen live in the Chicago area, and we try to get people from this area to go into the Navy. I try to pass on to young people the good experiences that I had and an idea about the even better opportunities that exist today. I get mail regularly from the Navy Recruiting Command to keep updated. As a matter of fact, the Navy Recruiting Command sponsors our get-together every year. They also sponsored our return to sea in 1982, when we went aboard the USS *Kidd,* one of our newer combat ships, a beautiful piece of machinery, beautiful, absolutely wonderful. I liked that. I wanted badly to serve in a fighting ship during World War II and didn't get to. But we all have unfulfilled wishes. All in all, I have no complaints. It's been a good life. Looking back on it—being in the Navy was the outstanding thing that happened to me in my lifetime.

Chapter Eight

Run My Mouth and Boss Like Hell

Jesse W. Arbor

The title of this memoir comes from a listing of his job skills that Arbor provided to a prospective employer in the late 1960s. It could apply as well to his naval career and was perhaps a factor in his selection as one of the sixteen black officer candidates in late 1943. Even in his seventies, Jesse Arbor is a bull of a man—large but not fat. He is muscular, as he was when he played right tackle for a small segregated college in Arkansas in the early 1930s. He talks a lot, as others in the Golden Thirteen have made clear. He is also given at times to the tall tale, the humorous story, and the wisecrack. He frequently provided remarks that lightened the atmosphere during the pressure-filled time in early 1944 when sixteen men were seeking commissions in the Navy. He was a relief valve for the tension, although sometimes his talkativeness reached such a degree that the others had to employ mock threats to get him to be quiet. The combination of his loquacious nature, outgoing personality, and imposing physique is probably what led to his selection as an officer candidate. He is the kind of individual who commands attention by his very presence and manner.

The tall tales in Arbor's repertoire are at times a handicap in trying to get at the real truth through the medium of oral history. As
soon as the tape recorder went on for the first interview session,
Arbor began, tongue in cheek, by saying, "This tape should have
been taken as far back as, I'll say, 1948 or '49. Now, since that time,
you know, I'm an old man now, and senility has set in." One example
of the exaggerated truth is a story of Arbor's college days in the
memoir that follows. He describes the process of copying a fellow
student's test paper during trigonometry class. Few readers will fail
to smile at his narrative. Sometimes the tongue-in-cheek is obvious in
his recollections, sometimes not. And memory obviously is a variable
thing, subject to erosion with the passing of time.

Arbor has a good heart; he is a kind and generous individual. He
and his wife still live in the same place they have for many years
while they worked in Chicago. They are enjoying their retirement
years in a brick house in a comfortable neighborhood on the city's
south side. Wisecracks abound, as when the dog barks at a visitor.
Arbor calms it down with an admonition that the guest is not an
insurance collector but a friend. On another occasion, when walking
proves painful, he quips, "My feet are so bad they carry guns."

Jesse Arbor remains active in the work of the Golden Thirteen,
seeking to pass the word of opportunity on to prospective Navy
recruits and studying the overall history of blacks in America so that
he can put the achievements of the group into appropriate context.
In his basement, set up as a family room and office, is a desk at
which he works on correspondence and maintains the records of his
naval career. Nearby is a television set so that he can keep up with
Chicago's sports teams. And there are photos of his children and
grandchildren, an obvious source of pride for a man who recalls
growing up as a member of a large family in Arkansas in the second
and third decades of the century.

*I*was born on December 26, 1914, the day after Christmas. It was in a little place that only me and the Good Lord knows—Cotton Plant, Arkansas. The land was deeded to my ancestors after slavery ended. I remember my grandmother on my mother's side. She was eighteen years old when slavery was abolished, because I was thirty-five years old when she passed at the age of one hundred and five. The population of Cotton Plant was 1,661 up until the day we left, and there's never been that many since.

My dad was a carpenter, and he could make about anything. We never had a toy for Christmas that he didn't make. If we had a little old cap pistol or a wagon or something like that, he made it. Mama weighed about 200 pounds, but Papa never did weigh any more than about 150 to 160. Every time one of his sons got to be twelve years old, he was larger than Papa. The old man was soft-spoken, never used a word of profane language in his life, but he was a disciplinarian. Boy, he was rough on us boys. For instance, you couldn't play ball or shoot marbles on Sundays. He wouldn't whip you on Sundays, but if you had one coming, you got it before breakfast Monday morning. The oldest boys got whipped for smoking on every Monday morning that the Good Lord sent.

All of us had to go to church every Sunday. We'd all sit in line in the pew. Papa would sit on one end, and Mama would sit over on the corner—she always had a baby—watching the rest of us. You'd better not go to sleep or punch anybody while you were in church. Maybe it's that upbringing that stuck with us because not one of us was ever in trouble of any kind, unless someone got caught in a poker game. But all of us went to school, and all of us who have children always swore that there wouldn't be as many around the breakfast table when we got grown as there were when we were kids. Out of ten boys and two girls in the family, there are seven grandchildren, and three of those are my own children. All three of them are out of college now and working.

At night, when we were growing up, everybody had to sit down around the fireplace and take turns reading out loud from a book. We didn't know for a long time that Papa couldn't read seventh- and eighth-grade work. He was in the first generation of children to go to school after slavery and made it only to the fourth grade. But he wanted us to have the opportunity to go to high school. He wanted us to learn. He would sit there listening to us, and every once in a while he would tell you to read something again. If you stumbled over a word, he didn't know whether it was right or wrong, but you didn't say it smoothly enough, so you had to repeat it. So we learned to improve our reading there in the living room.

We didn't encounter any prejudice there in Arkansas because all around us in that entire country there just weren't that many white people. The blacks owned all the surrounding land, so Cotton Plant was essentially an all-black town. When I was almost sixteen we moved to Chicago, and I've been here, off and on, ever since. We came because my mother's brothers had settled here, and they insisted it was the place for us.

None of my brothers and sisters attended public schools a day in our lives. In Arkansas we went to Presbyterian Academy, and then when we came here we went to Catholic schools. The main thing I remember is that I never was in a library until the first day I went to college. Now they have libraries in all these schools. But you couldn't beat the academic training and the discipline. You didn't hear of anybody who couldn't read or didn't know spelling or math.

Altogether I had three years and six months of college. The colleges were looking for football players the same as they do now, but they didn't pay as much back then. I was offered six or seven scholarships altogether, to places like Clark College in Atlanta and Wilberforce in Ohio. The problem was that they were all some distance away, and I couldn't afford the fare for the railroad or bus to get there. I finally got lucky when the coach from Arkansas A M & N, which is now Arkansas State, was over in Gary, Indiana, to do some recruiting. Somehow he heard about me, so he came over and found me and took me back with him when he went home. That's how I got to college. I was a pretty good right tackle, if I do say so

Arbor played right tackle for a small college in Arkansas in the early 1930s.

myself. Some of the reports of my games were in the *Chicago Defender,* a black newspaper that my parents read. That was rough play because you were in the whole game—sixty minutes. I was strong and good at putting out punishment on opposing linemen.

I was a fair student at Arkansas. I was a good C or B- in everything but math. In the social sciences, where you could theorize, I made A- or something like that. One man's theory is no better than the other's; only the results are going to matter. Initially, I had in mind to become a minister. Then I switched to biology, but that stuff was almost like taking medicine. If I had been better in the hard sciences, like chemistry or physics, I might have done all right because the practical work in biology was interesting. But I really didn't know how to study, to tell the truth, and the school didn't even have a chemistry laboratory.

I'll never forget my first exam in trig. We were seated alphabetically, and this old girl next to me had a name that began with a B. She was so homely that nobody would dance with her, but she knew her math. When we had our first exam, the professor put the problem up on the board, and it was all full of sines and cosines and so forth. I don't even know if there was a number in it. Then he said, "I'm going down the hall a few minutes. Don't you all disturb each other." When the grades came out, there was one A, one B, one C, and all the rest flunked. I made the B. I had copied just about everything off that girl's paper but her name. If the professor hadn't come in when he did, I probably would have copied that too. The prof knew something must be wrong if I could pass a test, so he gave another one. This time the best I could do was copy off somebody who made a D. From then on, I started dancing with this girl at the football dances, hoping she'd hold her paper so I could see it. I would sure like to know where that girl is now. She helped me through school—until I left, that is. I quit school and went home after I ran out of football eligibility, even though I hadn't completed my degree.

In 1935, about the time of my twenty-first birthday, I began working as a doorman and receiving clerk at the Chicago Beach Hotel, at 51st and Lake. That was a pretty typical job for a black man in those days, and it paid better than the type of job that a college graduate was getting then. At that time teachers were making maybe $90.00 or $100.00 a month. I was pulling down $60.00 a month plus tips, so I did all right. I stayed on that door until 1939, when a vice president from the Pullman Company came along one day and recognized me because I had been in high school with his son. He said, "What are you doing standing up on this door? Why don't you do something commensurate with your education?"

I said, "Mr. McMannen, I need not tell you why I'm on this door. The jobs that I can get commensurate with my education do not pay as much as this."

He said, "Well, why don't you go out here and get on the railroad then?

I said, "They are not hiring anybody. They posted a list three weeks ago that they would not hire any more in five years." He gave me his card and told me to go see someone with the railroad about being a Pullman porter. But I didn't do it because I was concerned about what kind of job I'd get with no seniority. I might not be able to work steadily. He came back a few weeks later and told me that if I didn't go work for Pullman, he'd see to it that I couldn't work for the hotel any longer. So I worked as a Pullman car porter for two years, and actually it was a kind of honor because at that time nobody worked for the Pullman Company but the cream of the crop. This was before we had many airplanes, and all the celebrities traveled by train. I followed the actress Helen Hayes for one entire summer. But I still wasn't comfortable, so when this vice president left Chicago, I came back.

For a while I was at the hotel again, and then I began making clothes at Kuppenheimer's. It turned out I was pretty good at it, and I never made so much money in my life. Some weeks I'd make $150.00; I didn't know there was that much money in the world. Nobody I knew had a salary like that back then. In 1940 I opened up my own shop and pretty soon had ten people working for me. Then the war came along.

My choice of the Navy was an easy one; I was ducking the Army. I had three brothers that were already in the Army. They told me, "Go anywhere you can go other than this place. Don't come." I also remembered my mother's brothers coming home from World War I. They talked about how rough it was in France. In September 1942 I found out that the papers were in the works for me to be drafted. The Army was after me, so I went down to the Navy recruiting station on Plymouth Court in Chicago and signed up.

I reported to Camp Robert Smalls at Great Lakes that same month. The Navy routine took some adjustment after this high life I'd been leading. For instance, I'd been wearing Thom McAn shoes, and they put me in these thick-soled things that wore blisters on my feet and made them swell up. So I sat down with my little old pocketknife and cut those shoes up. I was standing there in line at muster the next morning. A little chief petty officer named Ross, a black man, came up in front of me and said, "What's the matter with your shoes there, Mac?"

I said, "Sir, they hurt my feet."

He said, "You're in the Navy now, boy. Didn't anybody send for you; you volunteered. When you're in the Navy, you do what you're

Arbor as a quartermaster while undergoing officer training.

told, when you're told, and how you're told." He walked up and hit me in the chest and said, "Now, get out of that line." He took me out and walked me all the way back over to main side, got me another pair of shoes. He threw them at me, and they hit me in the chest. Fortunately, the second pair fit, but I still wasn't happy. I had missed chow for one thing. So I went back to our barracks and just sat down and cried. We didn't have bunks in the barracks, so I just sat up in my hammock all night long and wondered what I'd gotten into.

Gradually, though, I got the hang of it, especially with some coaching from a little fellow named Arthur Collins, who had had some ROTC training in high school. He was known as Duck because of his small size, and he was afraid that the other recruits would pick on him. I was big enough to protect him, and in return he taught me how to give commands and call cadence for marching. He taught me by saying things like, "Dummy, don't you know how to give a command to keep them from walking into the wall?" After a while I got to be an apprentice company commander and was teaching other people how to drill. But Duck was never far away from me, making sure I got it right.

After boot camp I went to service school at Great Lakes. I studied navigation, flashing-light communication, sextants, compasses, steering, and so forth. I came out as a quartermaster third class, among the earliest blacks to get rated in that specialty. Then the Navy shipped me to Boston, first to the receiving station, which was a catchall for transient personnel, and then to Pier One in East Boston. Those of us who were rated as petty officers posed a problem for the people making assignments. They couldn't put us in the kitchen, so they didn't know what to do with us. After they found out that I was good at reading semaphore and flashing-light signals, they began using me as a signalman on the docks, so I could direct incoming ships to their berths.

I was called off the docks one day to go aboard a minesweeper for duty as a quartermaster third class. After being out there about six weeks or two months, I was transferred ashore for a course in navigation being taught by the Navy at Harvard. Once I had finished that course, I became a quartermaster second class, and then I was assigned to a larger minesweeper than the first one.

By then it was late 1943. In November of that year the destroyer escort *Mason* was launched at the Boston Navy Yard, and the Navy announced it was going to have an all-colored crew. That was the term they used in those days. They didn't use the word "black"; it was "colored." They announced that I was going to be in the crew, and, boy, my chest flew wide open because I was so proud. I had truly enjoyed my time in the minesweepers, and this would be even better. It would be real shipboard duty, not just operating off the coast. I lashed up my seabag, and I was ready to go aboard, but then they put one of my buddies on in my place. They said, "No, Arbor, you can't go." They said they were going to send me to another navigation course, starting in January. I was so mad I didn't know what to do. All I could do was follow orders, but at least they gave me some Christmas leave.

I came home to Chicago on leave and ran around during the holidays, then headed back to Boston to be in time for this course. When I got back there, I checked in at the commanding officer's office, then went to the barracks. All my uniforms were dirty, so I threw them in the washing machine. While the stuff was washing, I got involved in a little poker game that was going on in the barracks. You've got to do something to pass the time. While I was sitting there in my skivvies, someone came in and said, "Jesse Arbor, quartermaster second class, report to the officer of the deck."

Without looking, I said, "Hell, I just left there." Then I looked up and saw that this was an officer standing there. So I stood up and said, "Sir, I don't have anything to put on. In a few minutes, it will all be out of the washing machine, and then I've got to dry something."

So he said, "I'll go back over and tell them."

Before I could get my hand dealt out, somebody else ran up the steps and said, "Jesse Arbor, you're wanted by the officer of the deck on the double." I looked up, and this was another officer. He didn't seem to have any patience about my laundry, so I starting borrowing pieces of uniform so I could get dressed and see what it was all about. I started down the steps of the barracks, and there was a captain holding a brown envelope for me. He said, "You have ten minutes to get your seabag lashed up. There's a car sitting down below to take you to the Back Bay Station. In thirty-five minutes you're going back to Chicago."

I didn't have time to get my uniforms and seabag. I just had on the few things that the other guys gave me—bell-bottom trousers, an undress blue jumper, and a peacoat that wasn't quite my size. Nothing fit except the shoes and socks, which were mine. As I was leaving, all sorts of thoughts went through my mind. For example, I remembered that I had wrecked a Packard for a doctor right on the corner of 51st and South Park when I was driving an old Pontiac. I thought, "They're sending me back there for that accident." But I jumped in the car, went to the station, and got on the train to Chicago. The brown envelope was sealed and had my orders in it, but I didn't know what they were for at the time.

Once I got to Chicago, a sailor in Union Station was looking for me, and he helped me get up to Great Lakes. I was taken to a barracks and saw two or three guys sitting around. By that night all sixteen of us were there for what turned out to be officer training. On the top deck were sixteen bunks, two long chow tables drawn together, and sixteen chairs. On the first deck it looked like an improvised library. I thought I was just back in another service school because I had been in and out of several service schools by that time.

This was a different setup. We were kept void of contact from anyone, excepting ourselves, all day long. We had to go to the chow hall, march by ourselves and go before anybody else ate. Then we were right back in that barracks, where we were getting eight hours of classroom work a day. It was a lot like college, but there was none of the college social life. We had no weekend leaves or anything.

We had 100 percent cooperation in that course because we were all trying to make it. In every course we had, we had an expert among our group of students. For example, Reggie Goodwin and George Cooper were good at math. Frank Sublett and Dalton Baugh knew about boilers. Alves had a lot of experience in seamanship, one of the few who really knew about that area, so it's surprising he wasn't one of the final thirteen. From looking at the capabilities of the people and comparing them with the curriculum, it looked like they designed those courses just to fit us. As for the instructors, I don't know how the Navy picked them. We didn't go to class; they came to us because everything was conducted right there in our barracks building. We never left that building for anything but to eat.

We went along for a number of weeks in this officer-type training, and none of us were really sure what was going to happen to us. Then one Saturday Phil Barnes—Big Barnes, we called him, because he was chubbier than Sam Barnes—got a card from his baby sister. She was working out in Washington, D.C., as a chambermaid or something for James Forrestal, the Undersecretary of the Navy. She said she would call him a week later, and she did. She said, "Don't tell anybody because it's top secret and it's not supposed to be on this desk. I can't pick it up, but I can read. It doesn't say what date it's going to be, but they're going to make the first colored officers." She read him the list of names, and we were on it.

I remember how it was when we finally got commissioned. They sent us to the officer in charge, Commander Armstrong, and one by one he gave us our commissions. There was no formal graduation

Arbor at the time of his commissioning as an ensign in March 1944.

exercise, no anything. We just got our commissions and were told to go over to main side and get fitted for uniforms. I shall never forget Armstrong. I really couldn't stand him because he was so condescending. His father opened the Hampton Institute, so he thought that made him an authority on anything black—black people, black shoes, black birds. Anyway, he said, "You're Arbor."

"Yes, sir."

"Now that you're an officer, how do you feel?"

I said, "Sir, having never been an officer before, I will first have to be one for a day or two before I know how I feel."

He said, "I understand all of you made good grades over there, and that's commendable. Now, you know, you will have to make choices as an officer instead of an enlisted man."

"Yes, sir."

"Now, in the event that you would be in a position where there was a colored sailor and a white sailor in a fight, whose side would you take?"

I said, "Sir, I have to wait until that occasion arises." He looked at me, and then I said, "The first thing I would think of to do is to approach it as an officer, as has been taught to me. It's the only thing I could rely on. My personal feelings would not enter into the case."

He reared back and said, "Well, that sounds pretty good. Now, you know there are no quarters for you in the BOQ. And the second thing, I don't want any of you fellows going to the officers' club."

One of the first things that happened after I became an ensign was that I ran into Duck Collins, the little fellow who had helped me through boot camp. He hadn't heard about any black officers being commissioned, so he was really surprised when he saw me in my new uniform. He just stood there and cried. Then he said, "Son, I'm proud of you. How did you get this and you didn't tell me about it?" I told him that it had just happened a little while before, and then he said, "You wouldn't have been a damn thing if it hadn't been for me." He was right; I probably wouldn't have.

My first orders as an officer were right there at Great Lakes. After a while there, Charles Lear and I were shipped out to Hawaii. He was a boatswain, the only warrant officer in that group of thirteen, and he was a sweet guy. He and his wife were very devoted; they wrote letters to each other every day. I was really sorry when he died right after the war.

Soon after we got to Pearl Harbor, one of the white officers slipped me a copy of a memo from the executive officer of the supply depot at Pearl. It explained that two Negro officers would be attached to the command and really spelled out clearly that we were to be treated with the respect that was due to officers in the Navy. I still have a copy of it. The last paragraph said, "No discrimination of any kind will be shown these officers, and they will be treated equally with all other officers. Any officer violating this order will be sternly dealt with."

Actually, when we got to Hawaii we were curiosities more than anything else. I wish I'd had some kind of videotape or recording device back then to tape some of the conversations we had with people. They wanted to know why you were born, where, and what you were there for. Some were sincere, and some were patronizing, but I answered all their questions. There were some who evidently didn't get the word that we were coming because they were really surprised to see us. At least we weren't prohibited from officers' clubs after we got away from Great Lakes. I can remember walking into some clubs and seeing guys just turn around in amazement. As a matter of fact, it was a great setup because all the whiskey was free out there. All you'd have to do was set your glass down, and it would be filled up. That led to another source of curiosity. Some of these men wondered how I could drink so much whiskey and never get drunk.

While we were at Pearl, I had an experience that demonstrated how the tables had turned now that I was an officer. One day I went down to meet an incoming ship and welcome people to the island. I was wearing khaki shorts and had a big .45 strapped on my hip. Off the ship walked the same chief petty officer who threw the new shoes in my chest at boot camp two years earlier. Back then I'd had some other run-ins with him as well because he didn't think I was pulling my load on guard duty. There in Hawaii he resisted when I tried to take his orders for processing. I said, "That's all right. Forget about everything." I took him in my car so he didn't have to ride with the rest of the people on a bus. I wanted to bite him back so bad for what he had done earlier that I didn't know what to do. Fortunately, I didn't take any revenge, and I'm glad I didn't. I think I

As an officer in charge of shore patrol during duty on the island of
Oahu, Hawaii, in the summer of 1944, Arbor wears a .45-caliber auto-
matic pistol on his hip as a badge of authority.

demonstrated that I was a bigger man than he was, but that was
quite a temptation.

One of the things we did for entertainment in the evenings when
we were stationed there was play poker. Our skipper, Lieutenant
Commander Grady Avant, was a fine man from New Orleans, and
somehow I always seemed to beat him. One particular night I figured I should let him win if there was any way I could because he
had been awfully nice to me. I figured he would take the pot because
he had three jacks showing, and I had three deuces. Somehow, I got

Warrant Officer Charles Lear and Arbor relax in their room in the bachelor officers' quarters in Hawaii in the summer of 1944.

the fourth jack and the fourth deuce, and I beat him. While I was raking in the money, he unconsciously said, "I should have known there was a goddamned nigger in the woodpile." The game broke up pretty soon, and I went back to my room in the BOQ.

After a while I heard a knock on the door, and there was the captain with a fifth of brandy in his hand. He said, "I came down here to apologize."

I said, "For what? For losing the pot? I wouldn't apologize to you if I lost."

He said, "No, didn't you hear that expression I made?"

I answered, "You said you had a full house, didn't you?"

He said, "That's all you heard?"

I said, "That's all I was supposed to hear."

He said, "My executive officer said I made another expression there that might have insulted you."

I said, "No, the only thing that insulted me was that we didn't have some more money in the pot." He knew I was lying, so it hurt him worse than it hurt me because he had to live with it.

From Hawaii, Lear and I went on out to Guam; we were sort of troubleshooters in the area of supply and logistics. By then I was a lieutenant (j.g.). Since I was the senior black naval officer in the area, I became sort of an unofficial adviser for the black sailors. I tried to provide the kind of help that any officer should for his men. I will never forget one day when a boy walked up to me and said, "Pardon me, Lieutenant."

I put my arm around his shoulder and said, "What is it?"

"Are you married?"

"No."

"Oh, hell, you can't help no damned body if you're not married."

"What are you talking about, son?"

"Here, read this letter."

"Son, that's to you. Who is this lady?"

"That's my wife."

"I don't want to read your personal mail, son."

"Go ahead and read it."

It said, "Dear John, I hope you take this the way it is. I don't love you anymore. Don't worry about the baby. I'm taking it down to your mother's house, and I am cutting out. Good-bye."

Then he said, "Now, if this was your wife, and you loved her, and she was getting your allotment and wrote this to you, what would you do?"

I said, "Son, I'm going to tell you the truth. You know how far you are from home."

"Yes, sir."

"One good thing she said is that she has taken your baby down to your mother's house. You don't have to get out; you're already out. All you've got to do is just cut loose. You take this letter and take it over to the Red Cross. Cut that allotment off from her and send it to your mama. That's all you need. Come on and get in the jeep."

So I helped the boys when I could, and that included the white ones as well as the black ones. In a way, I felt I accomplished more with what I did than if I had been out killing Japanese. If I'd killed Japanese, it could have been necessary or unnecessary, depending on whose side you're on. But when you see a guy in need and you can save him with a word or a pat on the back, you get a lot of gratification.

That time I spent on Guam was the closest I got to the realities of warfare because I never did get into combat. But the U.S. forces had invaded the island several months earlier, and it hadn't really been secured all that long. I saw a lot of bodies that hadn't been completely buried, and I saw the condition of the children and other natives who were there. Seeing something like that just makes you hard. You get to the place where you don't feel any compassion for anybody. Then, later, you get off in retrospect and think about it. You say, "But for the grace of God, this could be my mama or sister or little child lying there." Seeing things like that was what made some people drink and other people crazy.

There on Guam we were supporting preparations for the invasion of Japan, which turned out to be unnecessary. When the war ended, I was still there. One of the captains wanted me to stay with him on the island after the war. But then I came home on leave in early 1946 and decided I didn't really want to go back out there. I had gotten back here and got tied up with one of those old big-leg gals. After running around, I decided to stay where I was and opened up my own business. I remember thinking to myself at the time, "I have served my country well. With the little salary rate they pay, I can't stay in there for that." Now, 20/20 hindsight is the best thing I've ever known. Had I known the potentials at that time, I would have stayed because I think I could have done more in the Navy than I did out. But knowledge only comes with age and experience. I only regret that I didn't stay in longer.

The only one of our group of thirteen who stayed in the Navy was Dennis Nelson—Dennis the Menace. He was forthright, but he was egotistical, and he was a character. He loved to show off. Nelson had a 1940 convertible Mercury, and he washed that car 365 days a year. If it was twenty below zero, he'd wash that car, and he wouldn't let anybody else wash it. After Commander Armstrong left Great Lakes, Commander Ludwig Gumz came in and took his place. One day Nelson was driving back from somewhere on the main side of the base. He had the top of the car pushed back, and his naval cape was flying in the wind one wintry morning. He stopped and offered Commander Gumz's wife a ride, and the next thing Nelson knew, he was shipped right out to one of the Marshall Islands. He turned right

around and wrote them a nice letter, thanking them for sending him
to such a nice place.

Well, after he came back from the Pacific, Nelson asked for a
commission in the regular Navy because we had been commissioned
as reserve officers. And actually he didn't know anything about seamanship and that sort of thing; his specialties were public relations
and training. But he didn't let that stop him. When I saw him after
the war, I said to him, "Nelson, when you applied for the regular
Navy, what was the extent of the conversation?"

He said, "Jess, they asked me, 'What reason do you think that we
should accept your application for the regular Navy—on what
basis?'" Nelson told me he said, "I'm going to just reverse it. What
reason would you deny my application?" And that's the reason that
Dennis Nelson was one of the earliest black officers with a regular
commission.

When I came out of the service after the war, I never gave any
thought to going back to college and finishing my degree. Now, Dalton Baugh did go back. He had been with me in college in Arkansas
before the war. Afterward, he got his bachelor's degree, and then he
went to MIT and got his master's in engineering. I was more interested in getting back to the kind of money I'd been making before
the war. I didn't see any point in going to school again for a few
months just so I could say I had a degree.

I went back in my clothing business, but it wasn't easy. You
couldn't buy material then. Everything was in short supply. You
couldn't get any help, and you couldn't get any equipment for cleaning and pressing. Gradually, I got things built back up again, but I
was a real workaholic at that job. I hardly ever took a day off, and I
wound up with a light heart attack. Then in the late 1960s urban
renewal came through, and they tore down everything just about
from 39th Street to 61st Street. My business went to pot. That's
when I went looking for another job. I was married by then and had
three kids. One was finishing high school. I had to get something
steady to be sure that they could go to college. My wife was teaching,
but I didn't want to do that myself.

I went down to the board of education, and as luck would have it,
I ran into the brother of Reggie Goodwin, one of the men who was
commissioned with me. He was quite helpful and put me in touch

Dalton Baugh went to college in Arkansas with Arbor, then went through officer training with him in 1944.

In his later years, Dalton Baugh headed an engineering firm in the Boston area.

with a man he said could get me a job. He showed me all sorts of jobs available, certified public accountants and stuff like that. I said to him, "I don't see anything I would want to do."

He said, "What can you do?"

I said, "Run my mouth and boss like hell." That's exactly what I told him. The outcome was that he put me in touch with a woman who had the specific jobs. She wouldn't see me at first, then she saw the name of Goodwin's brother on his card. It turned out he was the civil-service commissioner for Chicago, and that's what got me a job running steam boilers, because I was familiar with them from the cleaning and pressing business. I had run the little ones, and then I learned to operate the bigger ones they had in schools. I spent a little time at night boning up on the boilers, and then I just applied a little common sense and practical experience. If something big broke down, you'd call the district office anyway. I had to do a little paper-work in that job, make out the payroll for the janitor, and see that the

Arbor at work in his tailor shop in 1957.

work was being done. I took that job in 1968 at one of the elementary schools and stayed there until the school closed in 1984. They found out I was seventy years old, and they kicked me out.

Before that, in 1977, we had the first reunion of the Golden Thirteen, and that was really the doing of Dennis Nelson. He told the Navy that since it hadn't given us any recognition when we were commissioned, it could at least do something all those years later. If it hadn't been for Nelson, we probably never would have gotten together again. So I always have a lot of love for Dennis the Menace. Some people aren't good at coordinating and administrative angles.

But you have to have some tree-shakers, and then some others come along and pick up the fruit from the man who shakes it down. Nelson was a tree-shaker. Everybody has the highest respect for Nelson.

We've met every year since then, and our meetings have included John Dille too. He was our battalion commander at Great Lakes and always checked on us to see how we were doing. His daddy's newspaper also gave us some nice publicity after we became officers. The greatest laugh we had with Dille was in 1979, when we had the reunion at Treasure Island in San Francisco. He flew out there in his own jet, but he forgot his ID card and wasn't permitted past the gate. Here was a man who could almost buy Treasure Island, and he couldn't get in. Baugh, Nelson, or somebody had to go down and vouch for him. I saw him and said, "Now, don't you feel bad, with all your money and can't even get inside without us black boys?" He just about died laughing and said that, of course, he didn't. That's the way he carries himself—that money isn't everything. He still keeps in touch with us.

I make all the conventions of the National Naval Officers Association, which is really the professional association for black naval officers. I run into all these officers who have done ten, twelve, maybe eighteen years, and the way I see it, the Navy is programming them for defeat. Too many times they get settled into comfortable jobs, but they don't take enough of the sea duty they really need in order to make them eligible for promotion and for full careers. The best of them frequently get recruited by big companies like Borg-Warner, General Motors, or U.S. Steel. These companies can offer much better salaries than the Navy pays, and they know they're getting top-flight black talent. In the short term, it's great for the guys who accept these offers, but they're throwing away all that potential in retirement pay and other things if they go for a full career in the service. And maybe the company will keep them only for a short time because of a merger or acquisition, and all those golden promises go down the drain. They need to stay on active duty, put in their sea time, go to the schools, and prepare themselves for promotion to higher rank. I really admire the top-notch officers who are willing to give the Navy their best and stick with it.

As I mentioned, we get smarter with hindsight. As I look back on my own career, I can truthfully say as I look at myself in the mirror that I did the very best I could. I'm not ashamed of anything I did as an officer. But I wish I had been a little bit wiser at the time and stuck with it longer because I was strictly dedicated to the service at the time. Having been one of the guinea pigs, I'm glad I had the endurance and fortitude to withstand the challenges we faced. Fate has been kind to me and the rest of the group—because we learned to walk so that the ones behind us could run. The black officers today express their appreciation when they see us. That's my reward.

Chapter Nine

James Hair and the USS *Mason*

Commander Norman H. Meyer, U.S. Naval Reserve (Retired)

Of the narrators included in this volume, only Norman Meyer was not connected with the officer training at Great Lakes, Illinois, in early 1944. That year was, however, an important one for him in terms of racial awareness because it was then that he decided to seek command of a ship with an all-black crew. And during the following year Meyer recruited a member of the Golden Thirteen, James Hair, as the first black officer in his ship.

One of Meyer's Naval Academy classmates, the noted submariner Slade Cutter, unwittingly sowed the seed for this recollection during the course of his own oral history. While mentioning some of the top-notch men out of the class of 1935, Cutter recalled Meyer's duty in command of black sailors. That, in turn, led to a request for Meyer himself to record his memories as part of the oral-history program. In so doing, he showed himself to be a man of extremely high principles, conscientious enough to seek command of the USS *Mason* at a time when most academy men would have strenuously avoided such duty.

One benefit of these recollections is the insight Meyer provides into the Naval Academy mentality of the 1930s, and doubtless it was a way of thinking that had stretched back for decades previously. Because of the attitudes and prejudices that were passed down at Annapolis from one generation of officers to the next, the service needed some external stimulus toward integration. It was unlikely to move in that direction on its own. The reluctant Navy was forced to accept black officers and to give enlisted men a much wider range of occupational opportunities than had previously been available. Even so, the Navy had integrated on only a limited basis by the end of World War II, as demonstrated by the collection in one ship, the *Mason,* of an all-black crew.

During his visit to the Naval Institute to be interviewed, Meyer reported on a reunion he had had just a few weeks earlier with his former shipmate at Hair's home in New York. It was a joyous occasion for both of them. Meyer recalled that they had gone together for lunch to a restaurant in which Meyer was the only white person; the customers and the people running the place were all black. The interviewer had the same experience a few weeks later when he also went to see James Hair. It produced an unusual feeling. Perhaps if more white people had the experience of being in the minority, even temporarily, their attitudes would be different.

Now in his late seventies, Norman Meyer is tall, slim, and still vigorous physically. A friendly man, he has a nice sense of humor and an almost compulsive nature when it comes to trying to do the right thing. He enjoys the outdoor life and the taking on of physical challenges. He already demonstrated years ago an eagerness to take on moral challenges. Commanding the USS *Mason* was one such challenge.

When I was growing up in the twenties and thirties, our family lived in southern Minnesota, and we never had much money around. I'm the seventh of thirteen children; all my older brothers and sisters had to work to help the family survive. Both of my parents were, in a quiet way, religious—good, solid Lutherans but tolerant. My mother had this absolute faith in the Protestant ethic: God was in charge, and ultimately things would work out right. That faith was tested sorely because we had some bad times, including bankruptcy.

My father was a man of great integrity. When he was a councilman once, he had a sign that said, "I've accepted a public trust, and I will keep the faith." If you accept a job, you do it. That's it. It wasn't easy being honest, what with having to borrow money and to move in search of work. Day by day, it was touch and go in our family. The bad times became worse when one of my little sisters died of scarlet fever. Then, in 1931, as a result of a friendship I had developed through Boy Scouts, I got picked to go to the Naval Academy. That was just like going to heaven in those days, and it was a great boost in morale for my parents. Their faith had been justified.

As a midshipman, I ate the Naval Academy up. I think the second month I got a 4.0 in a calculus monthly exam. The next month it was another 4.0. I was off and running. From then on, I got top grades, and it was easy. During part of my last year in Annapolis, 1934–35, I served as the regimental commander, or five-striper, as they called it. I was the top-ranking midshipman in the Naval Academy, which also made my parents very proud of their son.

At graduation in June of 1935 I got a conditional appointment as an ensign in the Navy because my eyesight was marginal. I had an enjoyable time as a junior officer, spending one year in the aircraft carrier *Lexington* and one in the destroyer *Barry*. But that active ser-

At the Naval Academy in 1935, Meyer commanded the entire regiment of midshipmen as a five-striper.

vice came to an end when my appointment was revoked after two years because I had 14/20 vision in my right eye, and it needed to be 15/20. I was disappointed but not bitter because those were the rules. In any event, I was far ahead of where I would have been without the Navy because I had gotten a fine college education that just wouldn't have been available otherwise.

The Naval Academy experience was helpful when I got a job in industry. I began working for a company called Bakelite. My boss was a man named Rupe Lowe, who had spent a couple of years as a midshipman at the academy in the early twenties before resigning. We had a nice relationship, and I enjoyed the work. I was a factory supervisor at the Bakelite plant in Bound Brook, New Jersey. They were bringing out a new type of plastics raw material. I was young enough so that I could walk into hot ovens and do some experiments, and I also had a college education. I was what you'd call today a process-development engineer, sort of an efficiency expert working out the bugs in new products. I lived an hour from New York City, and I remember sitting in Carnegie Hall on a Sunday afternoon. I would spend part of my time listening to the New York Philharmonic and part of it working out in my head the problems that I'd deal with at the plant on Monday.

At the time I was a young bachelor and lived in a crazy boarding house for a year. The food was so wretched that I used to join one of the other guys in his room before each meal. We'd each have a belt or two of bourbon in order to put the food down. Finally, he said, "I wish I knew somebody who could cook so we could rent an apartment."

I piped up and said, "I got the cooking merit badge in Boy Scouts. I know how to fry pancakes." So, with three other guys, we rented a place up in the hills of New Jersey and lived in something like an adult fraternity house. Of course, the word was that we had naked women at the spring. We didn't have a spring, and we didn't have any naked women, but we thought about them.

The war in Europe had started in 1939, and by the following spring the news was all bad. France had fallen, and it was obvious that we were going to get into the war. In the fall of 1940 I got a letter from one of my Naval Academy roommates, Dick McGowan, who was then on duty as a naval aviator in Pensacola, Florida. He said, "Norm, we need guys like you to teach these smart-ass college kids how to be officers. I wish you'd come to Pensacola and teach these aviation cadets and be their duty officer."

As a result of that, I volunteered and went back into the Navy in March 1941, well before Pearl Harbor. In the last month before leaving civilian life I met a redhead named Barbara Allen on a blind date in New York. Within ten days we were engaged; it was a whirlwind courtship. Then I was off to Pensacola. Three months later I drove up to Rockford, Illinois, and married this woman that I hardly knew. We celebrated our fiftieth wedding anniversary in the summer of 1991.

The Navy brought me back on duty as a lieutenant (j.g.) in the Naval Reserve. I well remember the pay I received as a young married officer: $196.00 a month, every month. I was at Pensacola for about a year, and then I got orders to report to New York, where the Navy was assembling convoys for the protection of ships crossing the Atlantic. In the early part of the war the Navy was trying to guard the East Coast of the United States with clearly inadequate forces, and the German submarines were having a field day. So the British gave us ten corvettes to serve as antisubmarine vessels. I was assigned as executive officer of one of these corvettes, the USS *Saucy*, and sent over to Ireland to join the crew that would bring her to the United States.

As I once told one of my Naval Academy classmates, "My life has had many bright spots. It's had some rather dark spots too." During that time in the *Saucy* I went through a period of depression. I had come out of Annapolis filled with illusions about perfection and duty and performance. Those ideas had reinforced the things I had learned at home about integrity and the Protestant ethic and so forth. Being second in command of the *Saucy* was a real jolt because the skipper of the ship just didn't fit my ideas of what a naval officer should be. I couldn't abide the way he did things, and he didn't think much of me either. There was no meeting of the minds.

When the *Saucy* got to Boston after crossing the ocean, I finally just threw up my hands, left the ship, and said, "I can't do this anymore." I went out to Beacon Hill, where we had rented an apartment, and said to Barbara, "I'm done. I quit. I quit." Fortunately, we got help from Captain Wilder Baker, a destroyer-squadron commander based in Boston. I had known him from the time he was a destroyer-division commander in the *Barry* when I was right out of Annapolis. He got me into the naval hospital in Chelsea, Massachusetts, and there I got into the hands of a wonderful civilian doctor, Bob Schwab, who'd become a naval psychiatrist.

Schwab invited Barbara and me to spend a weekend with him on Cape Cod. When I got back to his office on Monday, he said, "You know, there's nothing wrong with you. You just set your standards too high. Why don't you come on down to the earth with the rest of us human beings? As far as the captain is concerned, learn to swear like he does. Then go back to your ship. You and your wife have a life to lead."

That was good advice because an officer just doesn't desert his ship in wartime. But I must say that the longest hundred yards I ever walked in my life were down the dock at Guantanamo Bay, Cuba, to rejoin my ship. I resumed my duties and learned to swear. One day the captain heard me say, "Goddamn," and he said, "Meyer's a pretty good officer now." That was his standard.

Eventually, I got to be captain of the *Saucy,* and then I could run her according to my own standards. It makes an enormous difference when you're the boss. In the spring of 1943, when I was the skipper, one of our actions was to rescue a torpedoed tanker that displaced ten times as much as we did. The corvette towed her 125 miles to the shore of Brazil and safety. Another time we had been convoying some ships, and one day we spotted a periscope just off the Amazon River at about 4:00 P.M. We stayed with the submarine through the night and just kept dropping depth charges on it. The water was so shallow that the explosions impacted on us and did more damage to the *Saucy* than to the sub. Early the next morning we sighted the bubbles of a torpedo fired right at us. Even before I could order, "Hard right rudder," helmsman Bud Morgan had the ship swinging. That probably saved us because the torpedo went whistling by, close aboard. Two more were fired at us before we lost contact with the submarine.

Among the things I did as skipper was give the men ice cream, a hand-crank phonograph and records, and a bulletin board. I said, "You can put anything you want on it as long as it's not obscene or unpatriotic." They'd write letters and poems, and I enjoyed seeing them because enlisted men have a lot of talent; they're great guys. On one Friday inspection I looked at the bulletin board and saw a cartoon drawn on rough paper. It was a picture of the ship with all the armament going off at the same time, and underneath was the caption, "The Mighty Battleship *Saucy.*" In other words, this sailor was saying, "The captain thinks he's in charge of a battleship. We're nothing but a little corvette."

I could tell by the writing who had made the drawing, so I called him up to my cabin. He was scared when he got there, but I said, "Don't be afraid. Just two things. Could you draw a smooth copy for me? And this time something else. You think you've got all the guns going off at once, but you forgot the captain's .45." So he drew another picture, putting me in there with my .45. That picture is framed and now hangs in my study.

Even though I felt the *Saucy* was making a useful contribution to the war, the real action for the Navy was in the Pacific. I had a good exec who could take over for me, so I requested a transfer. I was assigned to the staff of Commander Cruisers and Destroyers Pacific Fleet. My job was as a training officer for ships passing through Hawaii on their way to combat. I was preparing the officers and men who would soon be facing the enemy. After a while I got so I could tell within my first five minutes aboard how well a ship would be able to shoot. I noticed whether the gangway watch was sharp and well dressed, whether there was dirt in the corners, and how well informed people were. The correlation was high; the smart-looking ships operated well also.

It was an interesting job, but then some of my classmates would say to me, "Norm, your lectures would have more of a tinge of authority if you'd ever been out to the Western Pacific." So I got a chance to go out on a destroyer for the invasion of Peleliu in September 1944. Then I ran into my old friend Wilder Baker, who was by now a rear admiral and chief of staff for Vice Admiral John McCain. McCain was running a fast carrier task group, so I was taken aboard the flagship and got to see carrier operations during the early strikes against Okinawa and Formosa.

After that, it was back to Pearl Harbor for more training—this time with some solid experience under my belt. In Hawaii I lived in the bachelor officers' quarters, but I wasn't a geographical bachelor.

In other words, I didn't chase around with women, so I had a lot of nights free. I read a great deal, including a *Time* magazine review of *An American Dilemma: The Negro in America*. It was the result of an extensive study by Gunnar Myrdal, a Swedish writer. The review piqued my interest, so I sent away for the book. It was in two big volumes, and it really opened my eyes.

Up to then, my experience with black people was just sort of blank. We didn't have many blacks in Minnesota. When I entered the Naval Academy in 1931, I had three roommates. Jack O'Handley was from New Jersey, and the other two were from Georgia and Florida. Of course, we all opened up our high school annuals, and Jack's had black classmates in it. One of these kids from the South said, "My God, you mean you went to school with these people?" I didn't know anything on the subject, so I just listened as these fellows said things like, "Well, niggers can't think; their heads are just solid unless they have some white blood." They hit me with all the clichés and vile names and then said, "We know, because we've lived with them all our lives. You Northerners don't know because you've never had niggers around you."

The only blacks I had seen at Annapolis were the janitors that cleaned the corridors and the rooms of the first-class midshipmen. I didn't see any bright, educated Negroes. I just saw the lower end of the spectrum, so that reinforced what my Southern friends had said, that they were inferior—hardly human beings. Now, after reading Myrdal's work, I felt so strongly that I wanted to do something about it. I wrote to Eddie Fahy, who was a detail officer at the Bureau of Personnel in Washington. I said, "Eddie, I'm due to go to sea and take command of a destroyer escort. While I'm doing that, since I am a layperson in the Navy, anyhow, I volunteer to be captain of one of these Negro ships." I sensed that it was probably not a job that many people would go for.

Eddie wrote back and said, "We've got one, and it's a mess. If you want it, you can have it." Quickly, people warned me that it was a national disgrace, one of Eleanor Roosevelt's crazy ideas. Some of my contemporaries said, "It'll ruin your professional reputation."

I answered by saying, "My reputation's back at a factory in New Jersey. I'm just trying to get this war over with and get back with my wife and baby."

By then I was confident enough of my ability as an officer that I wrote back and said, "I think I can swing it. I'll take it." That was a real watershed experience for me. In mid-June of 1945 I reported to the USS *Mason* in Brooklyn. As soon as I got aboard and took command, it was obvious that this was a poorly performing ship. As I said, in that job in Pearl Harbor I could walk on board and tell in five minutes whether a ship could shoot. The *Mason* was simply not a good ship. For instance, we'd be ready to get under way, and the exec was supposed to come up and say, "Captain, ship's ready to get under way." But it wasn't. There was always something holding us up because somebody hadn't finished some requirement.

Right away, I saw I had work to do, so I called the crew together and said, "You are not Negro sailors. You are American fighting men. I'll expect the same from you as from anybody else who's ever served under me. And I'll fight for you, the same way that I have fought for others who have served under me." It was apparent that these men had not experienced good leadership previously. I told the men that I believed in their potential, and I was damn well going to make sure that they lived up to that potential.

Then I began inviting individual officers and chief petty officers to my cabin to have coffee and get acquainted. The ship still had all white officers at that point. I remember one who was from Texas. He said, "Captain, I've been on this ship for eighteen months, and I know what you're going to do. You're going to get colored officers on board. I'm all for it. I'd like to stay, but my dad is a politician in Texas, and if they ever heard down there that I eat at the same table with colored people, my dad would be dead." He had done his tour of duty, so I got him transferred.

I talked also with the exec and the gunnery officer, and they just verbally fenced with me. Finally, I met with John Phillips, who was the fourth-ranking officer, and he exploded all of a sudden. He said, "Oh, Captain, I couldn't stand to be in the same room with your predecessor. He's such a repulsive, alcoholic, incompetent officer. I've been trying desperately to get off this ship." I was smart enough to recognize his ability, so I called Eddie Fahy in the Navy Department the next day. I said, "Eddie, I want John Phillips to be exec, and transfer these other two off the ship." So I had a fairly junior exec, but he had a law degree from Penn State and later became a

Commander Meyer as commanding officer of the USS *Mason* in 1945.

very successful executive in the insurance field. He was just a hell of a bright guy and a man of integrity. He and I made a good team. He liked me, I liked him, and we worked things out together. Every once in a while, I'd get a wild hair up my ass, and he'd say, "Captain, I don't really think that's a good idea. Let's not push things too far, too fast." He was a steadying influence.

Soon after I got John to be my exec, the *Mason* got its first black officer. One day we were putting in at the ammunition depot at Earle, New Jersey, near Sandy Hook. The tugboat that was helping us dock was very sharp. The brass literally shone and sparkled; the shiphandling and everything else were smartly done. Everybody on board was black, and the skipper was an officer named Jim Hair. It was obvious to me that he knew his business. I was so impressed by his tugboat that I invited him over to lunch on the *Mason,* and I had the Myrdal book handy when he got there. The next day I called Eddie Fahy to say I wanted Jim to be my first lieutenant.

That was great for the *Mason,* but his tugboat crew wasn't so happy because I was stealing their nice skipper. Jim was a very intelligent guy and intensely patriotic. He felt, and rightly so, that it was a real honor to have come to the ship. It was a reward for good performance, and I'm sure he communicated that to the crew. If the enlisted men had some doubts about this honkie Meyer, he could tell them I was sincere. I was really interested in performance but also in the men's concerns. You know, Norwegians can probably communicate with Norwegians better than anybody else. As much as I liked and respected blacks, I never could quite communicate with them as well as a black man could. Jim Hair was the communications

The destroyer escort *Mason* (DE-529) was commissioned in March 1944, then decommissioned in October 1945 following wartime service. She was the largest ship to have a black crew during World War II.

medium. He believed in me and what I was trying to do, and that was very helpful. The great thing about Jim Hair was that he had a real, real sense of humor and no bitterness. He was very conscious of the fact that blacks have been pushed around, but he didn't brood on it. Inasmuch as a black man and a white man could, he and I communed about the unfair treatment of American blacks.

Once we had the turnover in officers, the *Mason* took off and really excelled. Good leadership can make a difference. We had three busy months. We went through tests and drills, and we worked hard. Most of the men were eager to do what they could to win the war. The fighting in Europe had just ended, and the Navy was getting ready for the rest of the war in the Pacific. The first assignment we got was to test some brand-new depth charges that would be set off by the sound of a submarine's propellers. The Navy wanted to determine whether the depth charges would be set off by the destroyer escort's propellers as they were sinking down to the submarine. At the time I just carried out the orders; since then I have reflected on that situation. If one of the weapons we were testing had failed and gone off prematurely, I wouldn't be here talking to you. The whole ship could have sunk.

With the attitude that the Navy had back then, I wouldn't be surprised if they said, "Oh, that Negro ship isn't worth a damn anyway. If we blow it up, what have we lost? Let's let them test these things." These were 300-pound depth charges. That's a lot of weight for a crew to manhandle on deck. In two days, operating off Atlantic City, we dropped more than four hundred of these at depths that ranged from fifty feet—which is mighty shallow—to fourteen hundred feet. They did considerable superficial damage to the ship, and we killed fish by the thousands and thousands. But we did it successfully and received a letter of commendation for our performance. I think that began to open some people's eyes.

After that, we went for a period of training in Casco Bay, Maine, to prepare us for a possible mission in the Pacific. During my time on the staff in Hawaii, I had been much involved in training ships to provide gunfire support to Marines and Army people as they assaulted the Jap-held islands. I got the idea to do something of the same training on an uninhabited island up in Maine. I was going to put some people ashore to direct the gunfire. Of course, it would have been a very foolish and hazardous thing to do. John Phillips wisely said, "Captain, I don't think this is a good idea." I was in charge, but fortunately I had people who would speak up, and I listened to them.

John gave me some useful advice on another occasion. After we had been running the ship for a while I said, "John, let's write an article for *The Saturday Evening Post*." At that time, white people "knew" that black people had unusual body odor—one of the many myths that have somehow been perpetuated. I was going to say in the article that it just isn't so. The quarters were clean, and the men were clean, and I wanted to make a point of telling people what I had learned by living with these men. John said, "Captain, you're going to write an article about body odor?" So he talked me out of that one.

Actually, a number of white officers learned some useful things, even without any magazine article. For a while we had visiting officers from the subchaser school at Miami, Florida. We took them to sea, a week at a time, to give them antisubmarine training. We cleared out one compartment of the crew's quarters, and the officers lived there. There were no incidents. At the end of one of these training periods, the visitors were filing off the ship, and an officer with a very deep Georgia accent came over to me. He said, "Captain, when they assigned me to this ship, I almost refused to go. I wasn't going to go on any black ship. But I realized in wartime you just don't do that. I want you to know how much I appreciate this week. It's a revelation. Your gunner's mates and others gave us lectures. They knew their jobs, they spoke very clearly, they were good instructors. The men had a good time, and we visited."

Another one of our missions was to track submarines so they could try out evasive maneuvers that they would use against Japanese submarines. The officer explaining the ship's role to me said, "We need some fresh bait that hasn't been subjected to these evasions, to see how effective they are." We were going down the East Coast at the time, and we were diverted to be a target ship. The first day the submarine was ten miles away and told that it had to constrain its movements within, say, a two-mile-wide corridor so we could try to find it. Our sonar crew was superb, and we found the submarine. The next day the submarine had more latitude, but we found it again. The *Mason*'s men felt a justifiable pride in their accomplishments. On the final day the submarine skipper was free of any restrictions in movement. This time he eventually succeeded with his evasion tactics. I went ashore to talk to the captain in charge of the operation, and I said, "Well, Captain, I'm sorry that we goofed up, that the sub got away from us."

He said, "It's a Goddamned good thing. You had his morale down at the bottom of the ocean. He couldn't get away from your crew."

The morale of our crew was high because they were succeeding and because they knew that the officers were working on their behalf. They had noticed when I got rid of those officers whom I didn't feel were very good, and they adjusted their performance to meet my standards. The men particularly liked one program that I used. Whenever one of them got advanced in rating, I'd write a letter to his parents or his wife. Under wartime censorship, I couldn't say too much about what the ship and the men had been doing, but I'd write something like, "Dear Mrs. Jones, Your son Johnny serves on my ship. He has been promoted to signalman third class, and I want to congratulate him." In the second paragraph I would sort of outline his duties, and in the third I would say, "I am proud to have him serve underneath me, and you can be proud of his contribution to the war effort." I don't think anything else I did was so gratifying and brought such good rewards because I got nice letters back from those families.

In terms of native ability, I can look back and say that the *Mason's* sailors were probably about as capable as their white counterparts in any destroyer escort, although they didn't have as much experience because the general-service ratings had only recently been opened up to blacks. They fit the classic bell curve, a few at the top and bottom and most of the men in between.

At the time, I never stopped to question whether they were a typical DE crew or not. They were my crew, and there were enough of them. I don't go about wearing it on my sleeve, but Albert Schweitzer's "reverence for life" idea expresses my attitude toward the people who work for me, whether sailors, factory workers, or supervisors. They put forth their time, effort, and their souls working for me. I should care enough to help them develop to the maximum, and caring takes many forms. In addition to being nice and thoughtful, I believe in being pretty firm when necessary. I mentioned I had some crazy ideas sometimes. For example, I didn't like people going around with their shirttails out. So I had scissors with me, and for a while I was snipping them off square. That earned me the nickname of "Warden," which is really not a term of endearment among black people.

Liberty presented some interesting challenges when the men of the *Mason* had a chance to go ashore. In the North things were fine. A lot of the crew seemed to have come from New York City or had families there. I saw white women come down and meet their husbands, and they seemed just as happy as the blacks I saw. Things were much less pleasant when we moved south for training. We had one incident in which we were scrimmaging with a submarine on evasive tactics near Port Everglades, which is right at Fort Lauderdale. Hell, a Jew in those days had better not be overnight in Fort Lauderdale, much less a black man.

In every Southern port we went to, the minute the mooring lines were tied up, I'd jump ashore and go to the police department. Back then white policemen down South were a pretty scruffy, prejudiced lot, so I needed to talk on the sailors' behalf. I'd say, "Look, I'm in here with this crew. They're not just steward's mates; they're not servants. They've been out fighting the war for you guys, and I expect them to be treated like American sailors. On the other hand, if any of them get out of line and commit crimes, I'll back you up."

Well, one night about 2:00 A.M. some of the crew woke me up, saying, "Captain, Captain, Willie's going to get lynched. He's down at the police station. They're going to lynch him." So I went to the police station, and they had Willie there. It turned out that at one in the morning a group of sailors had been coming from a black section of town in a cab. There were about eight of them, and Willie was at the bottom of the pile, hardly able to breathe, much less talk. A white woman walked across the street, and that by itself is curious. What kind of a woman except perhaps a whore would be walking around by herself at that time of night? But the policeman said Willie had insulted her. I got him back to the ship, and the next day I called the crew together and talked to them. I said, "This happened. I think it's unfair. But we're in Southern territory. We're just going to have to be more pure than pure. If we have any incidents where anybody steps out of line, I'll have to restrict the whole damn ship, and you won't have any liberty." I suspect that incident also had something to do with my nickname of "Warden," but there were no more incidents.

VJ Day—the end of the war against Japan—came in mid-August. We were in Miami at the time, and even before the actual surrender there was a false report that the war was over. Somehow the jubilation in Miami got out of hand; a mob started to attack four white

Meyer as an executive during his civilian career following World War II.

Navy shore patrolmen and was beating up on two of them. The other two escaped, running to save themselves. Two of the *Mason's* black shore patrolmen waded in and rescued the two white men under attack. They did their duty well and got a letter commending them for their actions. In all, that was one of four letters of commendation for the ship in three months. It was quite a change from the state of affairs I found when I stepped aboard.

In September, with the Japanese beaten, our destroyer escort was one of hundreds of warships suddenly considered unnecessary. The Navy directed us to go to the navy yard at Charleston, South Carolina, and put her into mothballs. By now I had become something of a crusader in this business of integration. Once we got to Charleston, I called in the ship's two Negro officers, Jim Hair and Ensign John McIntosh, who had reported during my time in command. (McIntosh had recently reported in a group of four new ensigns. Three were white, one was black, and all were green.) I told the two black officers that I wanted to take them to the officers' club at the navy yard. Jim spoke up and said, "Aw, we don't want to go to the officers' club, Captain. It will get you in trouble."

I said, "Goddamnit, you're officers, and you have a right to go to the club. I insist." So we went to the club and sat in very conspicuous seats. Service just about stopped because this was a startling development. The waiters and other service people in the club were black, and they were amazed.

After we'd had one drink, Jim Hair said, "Well, Captain, you've had your fun now. Could we please excuse ourselves and go to our part of town, where we can have some fun, and you stay here?" They left then to pursue their own kind of recreation, but I think I made a useful point.

Soon after we got into the routine at the navy yard, some of the enlisted men came to me and said, "Captain, we're being 'Jim Crowed' at the movie theater in the navy yard." It turns out that one of the petty officers at the door had said, "You colored men sit in the last row of the balcony."

So I went to the officer in charge of the theater and insisted on their rights, which I thought was their due. The officer said, "That's wrong. Your men have been out there. They should sit where they want, anywhere." So that was another obstacle overcome. On the other hand, the navy yard swimming pool was integrated with no fuss at all. To my surprise, I found out that my men had been swimming in the same pool with whites, and no one complained.

The *Mason* was decommissioned on October 12, 1945, and disposed of by the Navy within a few weeks. The war was over, and so was my time in the Navy. Even before the decommissioning, I turned the ship over to John Phillips and went home to New Jersey. I returned to Bakelite, which had been bought by Union Carbide. As a civilian, I got involved in civil rights because the experience with the *Mason* and its men had truly changed my way of thinking. I got to

Former crew members of the USS *Mason* gather for a reunion in New York in 1990. Meyer is second from the right in the rear row. Next to him, capless, is his fellow officer James Hair.

know Duke Ellington and worked with him on a benefit concert that raised $7,500 in one night for our church. When I met Ellington the first time, he kissed me four times. I said, "Why four times?"

He said, "Once for each cheek."

Union Carbide decided to set up a factory in Mexico and sent me down there to establish and run it. There I got to know Mexicans who had been subject to discrimination, and I worked on their behalf. I had a great deal of autonomy as general manager of that company and really enjoyed the job. I loved the Mexicans. My wife and I both learned the language. We were Protestant Americans in a Catholic country, but after a while the Mexicans sensed that we liked them. We were invited to parties and social functions that other Americans didn't even know existed.

Still later I worked for ITT in Peru for a while, for Roosevelt Hospital in New York City, and eventually settled in New Mexico, where I was involved in hospital administration. In Union Carbide, I think

I was viewed as a crusader, missionary, whatever you want to call it. I tried to get jobs for black secretaries and to see that Jews got a fair break. I undertook to do what I thought was decent and right. I took the Declaration of Independence seriously.

There have been setbacks along the way when I have several times encountered situations that didn't live up to the high expectations I had. In a number of ways, including the *Mason,* I believe I've had a hand in making things better than they were. In recent years I had the pleasure of being reunited with Jim Hair and the other men who served with me in the ship. The sense of delight we had in renewing acquaintances will always be a great source of satisfaction.

My experience in command of that ship reminds me of something I heard from Rupe Lowe, the old Naval Academy man I worked with at Bakelite before the war. One of his great sayings was, "People will fly up to meet your expectations." If you think well of people's potential, they'll do their damndest to be sure you're not disappointed in the faith you've had in them. Dozens of those fine black sailors sprouted wings when we served together in the USS *Mason.* I only wish I'd had more time than I did to help them develop their potential.

Chapter Ten

Son of a Slave

James E. Hair

During his final years of life, James Hair lived alone in his brick home in a quiet neighborhood in Hollis, New York, a municipality on the western edge of the borough of Queens on Long Island. His three children were grown up and had moved away to families of their own. He and his wife had been divorced, but he was still there, living with the memories of all the times the family had shared when it was together in that same house. Around him were the pictures of those people he loved, and there were the papers and photos collected during a lifetime. He had hoped to put the whole story together in book form, but the heart that had given him so much courage over the years finally stopped on January 3, 1992. The book was never written, but, fortunately, Hair had completed an oral history.

It is a remarkable oral history, for James Hair was one of the few men of the Golden Thirteen who grew up in the deep South. He lived with more racial prejudice than most of his brother officers in that first group to be commissioned. He was present one terrible day in the 1930s when his sister's husband, a man he idolized, was lynched because he had the courage to challenge prejudice and hatred. As he described those awful experiences of so many years ago, James Hair was overcome with emotion. The memory of that pain left him in tears, unable for a while even to speak. Hair acquired from his brother-in-law both his love for the water and his sense of courage. Though small in physical stature, Hair was not afraid to confront danger.

James Hair did not harbor a sense of bitterness, although it would have been perfectly understandable if he had. Instead, he had a sunny disposition and an outgoing nature. These traits well suited him for dealing with people in his chosen field of social work. Furthermore, even though he had grown up in a society that had made life difficult for him, Hair loved his country. He especially loved the Navy and served in it with an immense amount of pride. When he first visited the Naval Academy in 1987 to speak at a history symposium, his eyes glistened with excitement. He had finally reached the center of the universe as far as the United States Navy was concerned. The honor of his commission probably meant the most to James Hair, of all the men who constituted the Golden Thirteen. He advertised his pride every time he drove his car because its New York State license plate read, "GOLDEN13."

*M*y grandparents were slaves. One of the interesting things about them was that they were sold into slavery after the birth of my father. The slave master kept my father to raise him, so in a sense that makes me the son of a slave as well. Through some sort of fortune, my grandparents were able to be reunited after the emancipation of the slaves, and my father went back to live with them.

My birthplace was a little place called Blackville, South Carolina. Both of my parents were wonderful. My father, Reverend Alfred Hair, was minister and moderator for the local Baptist church and also moderator for the Baptist Church of South Carolina. I took a picture of his tombstone. He was born in 1851, so he was in his mid-sixties when I was born in 1915. We had twenty-one brothers and sisters in the family because both my parents had been married previously and widowed. I am the next-to-youngest child in the family. Some of my brothers and sisters were grown even before I was born. In fact, today I have some nieces and nephews who are older than I am. Of course, I keep my tongue in my cheek when I demand that they call me "Uncle Jim" with respect.

With that large a family to support, my father owned a big farm in addition to being a minister. We grew cotton, corn, peas, rice, sugar cane, and other vegetables. The children were there to help with the jobs that needed to be done. I started picking cotton at a very young age, with the goal of being able to pick one hundred pounds a day. In addition to these jobs, my parents were both very educationally motivated, which they passed on to the children. In South Carolina were several black colleges that my parents often talked about. I believe most of these colleges were started by missionaries or were strongly supported by churches. Naturally, with a minister as a father, I had a religious upbringing, although he taught us more by example than a lot of preaching.

There were two Hair families in this little town of Blackville—one black and one white. The white Hairs were relatives of ours. The father was an undertaker, and he took both blacks and whites. As young children, many of us used to play together when we weren't in school or working. With this kind of background, I did not know about racism until I was in my teens. There was physical integration in Blackville at that time; black and white homes were next to one another. But the thing that was most meaningful about this was the communication. There was always conversation between the people in the town. When someone got sick, people of all colors came to see the person, bringing food and good wishes. It was a good beginning for a child.

I think I was a teenager when I first became aware of the difference in races. We moved to Fort Pierce, Florida, in 1925, after my father died. After much thought, my mother realized that she could not keep the farm going because many of the older children had moved away. Some relatives had already moved to Florida, so we joined them. After being in our new home for a while, I became aware that there were no whites living in the neighborhood. Fort Pierce had a line of demarcation, and we were in the ghetto. It didn't bother me that much at the time, but the white politicians certainly emphasized the separation in their efforts to be reelected.

My mother died in 1933—which was a real blow because I had felt very close to both of my parents. Fortunately, I had an older sister named Margaret, and she was married to a wonderful man, a most industrious guy named Estes Wright. He was a fruit picker by trade, but he was the type of guy that never had to look for a job. He could go out and create a job. I had such high regard for him that I became his shadow. I'd follow him everywhere because he was really a dynamic individual, very strong. He wasn't afraid of anyone or anything. It was a wonderful family, especially because Margaret was one of the greatest Christians I've ever met. She practiced her religion in a quiet way, none of this emotional stuff.

Estes was a member of the church but not as religious as Margaret. His great strength was his character; he believed very strongly in the dignity and integrity of each individual. He didn't care what color you were. For instance, I was his shadow when the government was giving out surplus food during the Depression. They had two lines, one for whites and one for Negroes. But the Negroes had to wait until all the whites got their share. Then if anything was left, then you would come in and get it. But Estes would never wait. He and I would walk in right away and fill up our burlap bags from the stuff on the shelves, put them on our shoulders, and walk away. Usually the sheriff was right there, but he would say nothing. He and other people throughout the town knew that Estes always carried a gun with him, and they didn't mess with him.

Unfortunately, he finally pushed things too far. There was a law back then—and I don't know whether it was written or unwritten—that no Negro could go down and fish from a certain bridge at night. It went across the Indian River and right to the ocean—a beautiful location. Finally, Estes decided that he was going to do something about it. One night he and I went down to the bridge for some fishing. We both had guns with us. We hadn't been there for an hour when three white guys came up to us. I was a kid then, so they looked at Estes first. One of them said to him, "What in the hell are you niggers doing down here fishing at night?"

Just as soon as he had said it, Estes whipped out the .38 and stuck it in his face and said, "Because we want to. I'll give you ten seconds to get off this bridge. If I ever see you again, I'll kill you." All three of them took off because they were bullies, and he stood up to them. They knew he meant business, and we never saw them again. In addition to my great admiration for his character, I liked all the other things that Estes did for me, including teaching me about swimming and boats and water, about winds and currents and the other things that go into seamanship. I carried that knowledge with me when I later went into the Navy.

Above all, Estes taught me to be a man, but the courage that I so admired eventually proved to be his undoing. He was lynched in 1935. It all started innocently. One day Estes was walking to town, and a friend of his gave him a lift in his car. As soon as they got to the white section, about six white guys came out and ran up to the car. Estes was dragged out of that car and taken away. My sister Carrie lived only two or three blocks away from where the incident started, and she came running to where I lived. She was yelling, "James!

James! They're killing Estes. They're killing him." I took her on my bicycle, and we rode downtown, where they were taking his body to the jail house after hanging him.

There must have been about five or six hundred people gathered around the jail—all white, all white. We were the only black people in sight because it was a frightening thing, but they didn't recognize us. I have fairly light skin, so I think that kept the people there from knowing who we were. We walked through the fire station at the front of the building to get to the jail, and they had Estes lying on an old wooden bench. All he could do was give these death sounds, the death rattle in his throat—what a hurting sound. His heart was still beating, and he had just a little breath left in him. He had evidently been beaten badly before he was lynched because his head was as soft as cotton. We started wiping the blood off his face until we were chased out by the sheriff. Carrie turned to me and said, "Look like they would let us do something for him."

The sheriff ran over and grabbed her by the shoulder and yanked her around. He said, "What in the hell did you say?" I was so upset by what he had done that I hauled off and ran into him with my shoulder and knocked him back. I didn't knock him down, just back. He was shocked by that. Then he came up and patted me on the head and said, "Son, go on about your business." My sister and I walked back through the crowd to get our bicycle and go home. That taught me something. It taught me that courage can overcome any kind of fear that you might have.

Estes was only in his early thirties at the time he died, and his wife, Margaret, was expecting their sixth child at the time. As terrible as the killing itself was, the aftermath was worse because the police came to our house night after night. We were essentially ostracized in the black community because the Negroes around us were afraid to have anything to do with us. My poor older brother Sam, who was the oldest one in the house at the time, was taken out of the house at night. Sometimes he would be taken on trips, shifted from one car to another, or maybe put into the jail for "safekeeping." After he had been mistreated for months, he had a nervous breakdown and had to go to South Carolina to recuperate. I think the white people were trying to intimidate him and the rest of the family as a means of alleviating their own fears. If we could be kept in our place, then we would be perceived as less of a threat. The authorities kept us under surveillance for months. That's what can happen when a small number of guys with warped minds have some power.

I didn't leave Fort Pierce because of that situation. Fort Pierce actually was a good town. My education there in the Lincoln Park Academy was excellent. Part of it was founded by a grant from Sears-Roebuck, and the school had some outstanding teachers. Education was seen there as a means of improving yourself and through this process being able to go out and help others.

Besides the studies, we had a terrific athletic program at Lincoln Park. Basketball was our main thing, and then we got into tennis. In 1936, my senior year, I was a forward on the varsity basketball team. We went to play in an all-Southern tournament because they chose the best two teams in the state. That year Ocala was number one, and Lincoln Park Academy was number two. For the tournament we went to Tuskegee Institute in Alabama, the school founded by Booker T. Washington, and that was really fabulous. We got up to about the semifinals before we got eliminated by a team from Bluefield, West Virginia. We gave them quite a battle in the game, and the whole experience was really exciting. It was almost like going from Hollis, New York, where I live now, to Madison Square Garden, to see a big game. Tuskegee was a real mecca in those days.

Despite the glamour of going to the tournament, the trip itself was something else. The trip by car took a day and a night almost, and we had to drive right on through. There was no place you could stop off—no motels or anything in those days—because of the discrimination. We also had difficulties during trips inside the state of Florida. One time we were going to a game in Tallahassee, the state capital, and the car broke down just as we got there. We managed to get the car to the front door of a big old garage that looked a lot like a barn. It was wintertime, and I mention this because we all had on hats and coats. The owner of the garage was inside having a conversation with another white guy. He just left us there for a good forty-five minutes, standing and waiting. Finally, he came over and said to us, "Look, what are you boys doing in here?"

Our school principal, who was with us on the trip, was the type of individual who was easily scared, and I guess in a way you could say it was understandable. In those days, you know, some principals felt

James Hair is third from the right in the back row of this photo of the championship Lincoln Park Academy basketball team of Fort Pierce, Florida, in the mid-1930s.

that they had to bow down, or else they might lose their jobs. So when the garageman came over, the principal very hesitatingly addressed him, "Sir . . . ," and the owner recognized that this guy was scared. He said, "Oh, sir, our car is just broke down out here, and we wondered if you would be so kind as to come out and fix it." He was shaking, and he was really pleading with this white man.

Well, then the guy looked at him and said, "What in the hell you niggers doing in here with your hats on?" This was a big, old, greasy garage, but the principal got so frightened that before we could take our hats off, which we knew we were going to have to do, he went around and knocked each one of our hats off—bump, bump, bump. And he said, "I'm very sorry. I'm very sorry, sir, very sorry."

All of a sudden, this guy looked at him and said, "What are you doing with your own hat on?" He forgot he still had his own hat on, so he knocked that off too. The garage man finally repaired the car, but not until after he had thoroughly humiliated all of us. I relate this to show that there were many things like that, but it didn't leave a very good impression on me about this principal. He was terrific in terms of education and whatnot, but as an example, he just didn't work too well for me.

Eventually, I finished up high school and looked for an opportunity to go to college. I had saved up some money for my education from such things as being a soda jerk, digging ditches, and working as a chauffeur. The chauffeur for the family next door was a real ally because he helped put the bite on the family he worked for. He talked his employer into giving me $50.00, which was a heck of a lot of money in 1936.

Another thing that happened about that time was that I started spelling my name differently. I was working with this family in a drugstore, and they insisted that I change my name. They knew of a white tennis player who spelled his name H-A-R-E. They apparently had the feeling that a white spelling was better. Through their persistence, and because jobs were very difficult to get in those days, I began putting it down as H-A-R-E, even though I didn't get it changed legally. I finally went back to H-A-I-R after my Navy time.

After finishing at Lincoln Park Academy, I enrolled in Bethune-Cookman, a junior college in Daytona Beach, Florida. It was led by Dr. Mary McLeod Bethune, an outstanding black leader and later a consultant to three presidents of the United States. She was a very dynamic person, and like my brother-in-law Estes, she believed strongly in the dignity and integrity of the individual. I got to know her by being her office boy, which was part of the scholarship arrangement I had for going to that school. She had that marvelous quality that when you were talking with her, she could make you feel like you were the only other person in the world.

Bethune-Cookman was one of the greatest times of my life. It was a wonderful educational opportunity because the teachers were really dedicated. Out of that experience I decided to go into the field of social work. Having seen so many rough things in my life—my thinking was shaped toward extending services to people in a way that they could improve themselves.

Hair during the mid-1930s.

After I finished there I worked in the summer for one of the Bethune-Cookman teachers when she went away. She tried to get me to stay there because she liked the job I'd done, but I said I wanted to go to Florida A & M. She refused to pay me. I enrolled at A & M anyway, hoping that I could somehow scrape up the money. Each day the president called me into his office to find out whether I could pay. After six weeks I sort of gave up and went home to Fort Pierce. I must have walked out two pairs of shoes trying to find a job because the Depression was still in full swing. After doing a number of odd jobs, I finally fell into some wonderful good fortune in a most unexpected way.

Hair at Bethune-Cookman College, Daytona Beach, Florida, in 1938.

One day I was driving a car from up north to Florida for the lady who had reluctantly given me the $50.00 at the urging of her chauffeur. When I was in Georgia, I had a flat tire and managed to hitch a ride with a Catholic priest. He took me to the next town so I could get the tire repaired. While we were riding, I told him I was trying to get into a college but wasn't meeting with any success. So he very generously wrote a letter on my behalf to Xavier University in New Orleans, and I was accepted there and even managed to get a scholarship.

All through school I worked hard, so when I got my degree in June of 1942, I must have had at least 145 credits (including the ones from Bethune-Cookman) when 130 were required to graduate. I would have been drafted the year before, but I was able to avoid that because of an educational deferment. I got a letter telling me to report for duty on July 1, but I never wanted to go into the Army. Part of it stemmed from all that I had learned from my brother-in-law Estes back in Florida. I knew a lot about the water, and I loved it. I went back to Florida and got involved in an open-enlistment program being offered by a Navy recruiter who was very honest and open, very candid. I took the oath on July 1, 1942, and was sent to Camp Robert Smalls at Great Lakes.

The boot-camp training was terrific and really rather easy for me because of my athletic background. Going through the obstacle course was no problem at all because I was in great shape physically. I adapted well also to the military discipline and to the Navy curriculum, which was fairly easy after graduating from college. Then I went into quartermaster school. That appealed to me because of the idea of being topside on a ship rather than down in the engine room, and it also tied in with the navigation and seamanship things I'd learned from my brother-in-law.

After I finished that school, I came out as a quartermaster third class, and then I was sent to the Third Naval District, here in New York. I was ordered to a harbor tugboat called the USS *Penobscot*. It had an integrated crew of perhaps twenty-five or thirty men who all lived together on board. One of the jobs was to help set up antisubmarine nets in connection with the engineers. We had them on both sides of Ambrose Channel. I did most of the steering, which I was good at because of my previous experience. That was an important consideration because we were working fairly close to a minefield.

Sometimes we operated around the Navy ammunition depot at Earle, New Jersey. Once we had to assist in putting out a fire down there. We also did a fair amount of towing and assisted large ships in docking at the nearby Brooklyn Navy Yard. One that I remember in particular was the battleship *South Dakota* that arrived in early 1943 for repair of battle damage received at Guadalcanal in the South Pacific. After going through a number of operations of this sort successfully, you develop a real bond with the other members of the crew.

To this day I don't really know how I came to be picked for officer training. I do remember something that happened during the time I was an enlisted man at Great Lakes. I had to go over to Commander Armstrong's office for something, and while I was there I saw a Navy newspaper. It said that the recruiting office was looking for more officers. So, when no one was looking, I tore the thing out and put it in my pocket. I filled it out and sent it in; I told them I was at Camp Robert Smalls, so I certainly wasn't trying to deceive anyone as to who I was. Whether that had anything to do with my later selection or not, I don't know.

The call came one day in late 1943 when the *Penobscot* was out working on the antisubmarine nets. A message came in by radio: "Transfer James Hare to 90 Church Street immediately upon docking." That was the headquarters for the Third Naval District, so I packed my seabag and was all ready to go when the boat came in. At the headquarters in Manhattan I was given a large brown envelope that was sealed with a blob of red wax. Those were my orders, telling me to report to Commander Armstrong at Great Lakes. I was so tired after our time at sea that I fell asleep at Penn Station and almost missed the train to Illinois. I finally got to Great Lakes at one in the morning and wound up spending my first night in a bunk in sick bay because they hadn't been expecting me and didn't have any other place ready. The next day is when I met Sam Barnes, Charles Lear, and some of the other guys who wound up in the Golden Thirteen.

Reginald Goodwin, one of the officer candidates, did a terrific service during the time we were going through the training. You have to picture how the country was in those days in terms of race. Commander Armstrong and the white officers there needed a link with

Hair as a quartermaster first class in 1943. He served in a tugboat before reporting for officer training.

the black sailors, and Goodwin supplied this link. Because he served in that role, I'm sure there were a lot of people around the camp who didn't think too highly of him. They felt that he was too close to Armstrong, and certainly he was close, almost like an aide when it came to racial matters. Goodwin himself even used to talk about it; he said that he wasn't going to have to go to the Pacific because Commander Armstrong couldn't do without him. We realized that this link was something that Armstrong needed, so we didn't blame Goodwin for it.

Another thing he did was correct the rest of us if he thought we were out of line. That course was just study, study, study, study, you know. In everything there's got to be some relaxation or tranquillity, so one night I suggested a little break from our work. I said, "Hey, let's shoot some dice." So we got down on the floor and were shooting for pennies—not really gambling, just something to break the monotony and ease the pressure. Goodwin was in the head when we got this game together. When he came out and saw what we were doing, he reacted immediately: "Fellows, fellows, what's going on here? You're supposed to be officers soon, and here you are down on your knees, shooting dice. I cannot take this. Stop it, or I will report you." We knew he wasn't kidding, so we placated him. And I guess he was right. We knew we were on trial, so we had to walk the line, but we were still human.

We were under a lot of pressure during that training. We were cooped up in that barracks almost all the time, and we knew we had to make it. Our goal in this class took precedence over Jim Crowism, racism, harassment, and insults. We had to operate as controlled individuals. We would get many insults, many insults. To illustrate a little bit—I remember the time we had to go over for a physical exam to the medical building, which was over on the main side with the white sailors. The medical people who were running it were all white, and one of these sailors came out and said, "All right, you boys, strip down. Everything off. Strip down." So we did. "Stand over there. Stand at attention." So we did.

I'm not going to call any names, but it just so happened that one of the guys in our group had a pigmentation problem. It was on his penis, which was half white and half black. One of these white sailors spotted it, and he went over and got a ruler and began hitting the man's penis with it. He was saying, "Hey, fellows, come here. Look at this. Look at this." In the meantime, this brother was standing there and flinching with this thing because, you know, that's painful. While we were standing there at attention, I thought to myself, "Oh, my God. This is the end right here. This is going to be the end." Any little thing, and we could have blown it.

Pretty soon this whole group of white sailors gathered around, and they were all laughing and carrying on about it. They were saying things like, "Here's this Negro here. Look at this, man, half white and half black." I was standing there, wondering how this thing was going to end, when the sailor finally stopped hitting his penis and said, "Hey, boy, where did you get this from?"

The officer candidate said, "Well, I was raised in a white neighborhood." In a sense, that broke the tension for us, our group, although it was all we could do to stifle our laughter. On the other hand, that remark made the sailors very angry. They didn't know how to deal with it, so they went back to their work. I guess they finally realized that if they started an incident that they might get into trouble over it. Under the military setup, they didn't want that. Anything might have happened. They might have gotten disciplined, but the chances are that we would have been out.

One of the officer candidates that I especially remember was Charles Lear. He'd been in boot camp, and I think he had been an assistant to one of the company commanders or something like that before our class started. Whenever I think of Charles Lear, the image that comes to mind is a statue of a soldier. He was just a real military man in every sense of the word. At reveille he would be the first man to be on deck. When an order came, you could count on him to obey it, and he was the kind of leader who inspires confidence in his men. He was an outstanding individual and always ready and willing to help somebody else. He and I got to be very close friends during the short time we were there together. He was really a fine citizen, and it came as a great shock to me when I later learned that he had died. I think it really broke his heart when he left the Navy after the war because he was 100 percent Navy all the way.

Another man for whom I have the highest admiration is Graham Martin. I won't say too much about him because he has told you his own story, but I feel particularly close to Graham after all these years. While the sixteen of us were going through the course there, we had the feeling that not all of us were going to make it and become officers. Of course, all of us wanted to be. He was, and is, a man of great dignity and integrity. He tried as hard as he could to excel, but it was never at the expense of anyone else. He wouldn't knock down James Hair or anybody else to get ahead; he was determined to make it strictly on ability and hard work. The way he has taken care of his wife, Alma, in recent years shows the kind of man he is.

In March 1944 this period of training came to an end. It was a great feeling, but at the same time it was a mixed feeling. We knew that we had accomplished something, simply being the first black line officers of the Navy. At the same time, we knew that just getting these commissions wasn't the end of it. There was a big job ahead of us now. This was a step in breaking down a Navy that had had all white officers. We were encouraged by the fact that we were a strong, dynamic group of individuals. We had also demonstrated an ability for self-control, to withstand insults and harassment. That, in itself, demonstrated a lot of strength. The picture of us that appeared in *Life* magazine could give you a tip-off on the way we were perceived by the country at large. There was that wonderful picture of us but no names. We were just thirteen colored guys in a group; they didn't think of us as individuals.

Since I'd come from the Third Naval District in New York, that's where I went back to once I was an ensign. I was assigned as skipper of the *YTB-215,* another harbor tugboat. I had an integrated crew, so I certainly must have been one of the first black officers with white enlisted men working for him. Whereas the *Penobscot* had an old steam reciprocating engine, this one had an electrical power plant, and it was beautiful. As for our work, it was fairly similar to what I'd known before: a lot of towing and a lot of assistance to ships that were docking. I remember we had a role in the winter of 1944–45 when we had to serve as an icebreaker to enable ships to get up the Hudson River to reach an ammunition dump near West Point. And I'll never forget a night when we had to go out into a hurricane to assist a ship that was in trouble. Tons of water were coming at us, so you couldn't see but a few feet in front of you. That was a real test of seamanship.

The crew was great. For instance, I had a boatswain who had been in sailing ships in the Swedish Navy or one of them. He could run up that pole mast like a monkey. The cook, a fellow by the name of Blake, had previously worked for admirals, and the only reason I got him was because of his age. He wanted to stay in the Navy, and so they decided that even if he was too old for a battleship or a destroyer, he would be okay in a smaller craft. We ate the best of foods. The junior fellows were very cooperative, and they worked hard. All in all, my relationship with the men was very harmonious. Since the crew respected me professionally, they also respected me as a man.

Eventually, I came to be transferred to the USS *Mason,* a destroyer escort. After seeing me operate the tugboat around Sandy Hook, New Jersey, in the spring of 1945, the *Mason's* skipper, Commander Norman Meyer, called me aboard to have lunch with him one day. That was unusual in those days because most white officers wanted to have very little or nothing to do with black officers. When the invitation came, my crew members all had question marks over their heads: "Look at our skipper. What do you think is happening?" When I got aboard, I was pleased to see that Meyer was carrying a copy of Myrdal's book, *An American Dilemma.* He was very candid. He said he had observed my tugboat and was impressed. He wanted me to come aboard because this was a new assignment for him, and he didn't know anything about blacks. I was struck by the fact that he showed no prejudice whatever and was completely open. The whole meeting was very pleasant, and I agreed to join him in his ship.

Moving to the *Mason* was another one of those cases of mixed feelings. I was going to a bigger ship, one that was part of the fighting Navy, but I was sorry to lose the satisfaction of having my own command. I know the men of the tugboat were sorry to see me go, and I felt a sense of regret about that, but they realized this was a step upward. On board the *Mason,* the enlisted crew was all black, and the officers were all white until I got there. I was the first lieutenant, in charge of all deck operations and the topside appearance of the ship. Everything had to be shipshape, including the boats, the hatches, portholes, rigging, anchors, and so forth. We had a very fine crew in the destroyer escort, although I have to admit that there

Hair as an ensign.

wasn't as much closeness and feeling of family as there had been in the tugboat. That's one of the things you lose when you go to a larger ship.

We were in training to take the *Mason* out to be part of the Pacific War, along with doing some tests while we were in the Atlantic. But then came the end of the war and the order to decommission the ship. I know that Norman Meyer has told you about the time he took me and John McIntosh to the officers' club for dinner. It was an uncomfortable situation, but Commander Meyer's presence kept us from getting any direct heat. On the other hand, if we had gone there without him, just the two of us, the whole thing might have been okay because it would have been less ostentatious. He was deliberately putting us on display. He strongly believed in doing the right thing, no matter what the consequences were.

When the *Mason* was decommissioned, I really hated to leave. You get on a ship for a while, and you get attached to it. At the same time, though, I recognized that this was part of military life. You get your orders, and you just have to go. That's the way I accepted it. I was ordered to go out and join the Seventh Fleet in the Western Pacific. When we got out to China, I was assigned to the *LST-1026*, a ship designed for amphibious landings. She had bow doors that opened up so a ramp could drop down directly onto the beach.

I was a deck officer in that LST, and we wound up doing a lot of work for Chiang Kai-shek, who was the premier of China. We were providing training for the Chinese and also supporting them directly by transporting their tanks and troops to various places, such as Manchuria and French Indochina. We also took food supplies for the relief of the Chinese; we went five hundred miles up the Yangtze River, as far as Hankow. The fact that I was a black officer wasn't an issue at all on board that LST. The skipper was strictly military. I was one of his officers, and he treated me like the rest of them.

Eventually, that duty came to an end. I had gone into the Navy during the war because I wanted to serve my country as best I could, but I never had a thought of making it a career. In late 1946 I'd gotten enough points to be discharged from active duty, so I left the service on what was still called Armistice Day at that time, November 11. The LST had been decommissioned at Subic Bay in the Philippines, and then I rode back to the States in another troop ship.

That's when my life took a new direction. I returned to Florida and had a wonderful reunion with my family. But things didn't work out so well in terms of finding work. About the only opportunities for blacks there at that time were in the field of education, and I didn't have an education degree. So I went to New York. That's where my future wife was, and I knew the job opportunities would be better.

In 1947 we got married and eventually had three wonderful children. I held a variety of jobs for a while and then decided to matriculate at Fordham University because you had to have a master's degree to do much in the field of social work. In 1950 I got my degree; I later took some advanced courses, but I never did finish a doctorate. Once I got the master's, I spent nearly all of my professional life after that in the field of social work, ending up as director of the social-service agency in Brooklyn.

Among other things, I became quite an expert in the field of adoptions, and I was also heavily involved in child welfare, family counseling, and child guidance. It's a very satisfying type of field because you have the opportunity to help so many different people work out their problems. Adoption is a beautiful thing if you do it right. I was always a proponent of involving the biological parents and the adoptive parents in an open process. If you do it that way and do it right, you seldom have problems. There have been cases, for instance, in which we have sent the children each year to have a visit with their biological parents. It really helps the child with his own identity, and I've never had one backfire yet. In recent years it has become an accepted procedure, but I was doing it years ago on the QT because I thought it was the right thing to do.

In watching the developments in recent years I have developed a real concern about where our families are going, particularly in the middle class. Affordable housing is difficult, so couples work to make ends meet. That leaves the child to day care in many cases. So much of our service today is child-centered, as though the child exists in a vacuum. The family is the strongest unit, and in order for the child to develop and mature in a normal way, the child should be nurtured by the mother, and there also needs to be strong involvement by the father as well.

I have had an enormous amount of satisfaction being involved in so many cases in which I was able to deal with a difficult situation and get a youngster headed down the right path for later life. For instance, I remember a young black man I met for the first time when he was in jail for some minor infraction. He was about 6 feet, 6 inches tall. I worked with him and his family for about two years while I was with the social-service agency. Several years later, as I was leaving work one night, I felt a rather imposing figure close behind me. The person behind me was saying, "Sir, sir." He was coming so quickly that I wondered if I was going to be robbed. Then this tall black fellow said, "Pardon me, but are you Mr. Hair?" I told him I was, so he said, "I owe you so much, plus I owe you five dollars." He reminded me how I had worked with him and his family and then about going on to finish high school and the University of Minnesota. Now he was employed with the city planning department. He told me how thankful he was for being helped and how happy his family was for his turnaround. The visit I had with the young man that night is a wonderful memory.

In the broader context of the place of black Americans in our society, I think affirmative action is a good thing. For so many years we have been denied the rights of other citizens in our country. Our ancestors were brought here in slavery to be exploited while we labored to build America. We were not given the rights under the Constitution that other citizens had. During my early college days, there was a saying, "Teach or preach." Fortunately, there were leaders who did not hold to this and believed that we should shoot for the moon. It is good that things began to open up, and affirmative action has helped them to do so. It is a step in the right direction. I feel confident that once all the facts are in, the finding will be for us as a country to continue to an affirmative way and not down the dark road that has held us back for so many years.

When I think of all the changes that I have seen and have experienced personally over the course of my lifetime, I can count so many highlights. One of the most fantastic of all was my reunion with the other members of the Golden Thirteen. It was just unbelievable. I was sitting at home on Wednesday, the 14th of April 1982—I remember it so well—reading *The New York Times.* In the paper I saw a picture of all these buddies of mine, most of whom I hadn't seen in years, out to sea on a cruise. The headline said,

Sam Barnes joyously hugs Hair upon his arrival aboard the destroyer *Kidd* in 1982—the first time Hair had been with the rest of the group since 1944. At left is Graham Martin. At right is Dalton Baugh.

"First Black Navy Officers Hold Reunion." It said there were only eight surviving members, and they were all at the reunion. So I pinched myself and said, "I know damn well I'm alive."

Right away I tried to call the guy at the *Times*. But then I thought, "I'm going to call the Navy. Not just the Navy, but Navy intelligence." So I did, and I told them about the article in the paper and how I wasn't with the rest of the group. They questioned me for a little bit, then took my name and address and all that. I guess they did some checking to make sure I wasn't a crackpot.

After that, I must have gotten fifteen or twenty calls, each wanting to know the same things: where I was born, where I entered the Navy, what ships I had served in. It turned out that I came to be "lost" from the group because I was still spelling my name as "H-A-R-E" when I

Dr. Gerald Deas, a New York physician, introduces Hair at a meeting in May 1988 of the New York chapter of the Bethune-Cookman College alumni association.

was in the Navy. After all these calls, I got one from someone who said, "By golly, you are James Hair, aren't you?" And then, "Can you travel? Can you be ready in three hours? We'll have someone there to pick you up." Sure enough, within three hours a Navy car pulled up and took me to La Guardia Airport. I flew down to Norfolk late that night, and they put me up in a motel. The next morning I was flown out to meet my buddies in the destroyer *Kidd* at sea.

They had just told the guys I was coming, and there weren't many serious moments after that. Syl White had already prepared some legal document for my burial at sea. When the helicopter landed on deck, I was sort of looking around for the captain to request permission to come aboard, but I couldn't find him. One of the guys later joked that the captain got sick when he saw me coming. The *Kidd* was originally built for the Shah of Iran, and when the skipper saw me, he kiddingly said that I was the Shah, come to take back his ship.

Anyway, as soon as I left the helicopter, my buddies started hugging and backslapping and all that stuff. You just couldn't believe it. I hadn't seen most of these guys since 1944. It was really enjoyable; we had a grand time. That moment captured the thrill I have long felt over being part of the first group of black officers in the United States.

I would like to close with two things. First, I would like to dedicate this oral history to the people who made it all possible and to my three children—Danita, James, Jr., and Susan—and their mother. Second, I would like to quote from "The Warrior's Prayer," a poem by that famous black poet Paul Laurence Dunbar:

> I do not ask that thou shalt front the fray,
> And drive the warring foeman from my sight;
> I only ask, O Lord, by night, by day,
> Strength for the fight.

Chapter Eleven

A More Democratic Navy Than the Nation It Serves

Justice William S. White

Whereas some members of the Golden Thirteen are quite talkative, an obvious advantage in oral history, Justice White is economical in his use of words. His transcript is the shortest of the group, but filled with a great deal of substance nonetheless. When asked a question, he often doesn't respond immediately. In fact, he sits and contemplates for so long at times that it is almost disconcerting. Then, slowly, he spells out what he has to say. One is tempted to typecast him because he surely strikes one as judicial. He is analytical, and he carries with him the healthy sense of skepticism that is undoubtedly the product of the years he has spent in courtrooms. In effect, he says, "Don't just tell me something, show me. Prove it to me." And there is at times a bite to his answers. Asked how he first got headed toward a course of study in the law, White responded with a question of his own, "I know you're going to say I couldn't stand the sight of blood, aren't you?" That was his sardonic way of saying that medicine and law were among the very few career choices available for black professionals when he was a university student in the 1930s.

In both a figurative and literal sense, White reached lofty heights in his professional career. As American society assesses such things, he probably achieved the highest position of all the men who were commissioned as part of the Golden Thirteen. Until his retirement in 1991, he served as a justice of the Illinois Appellate Court, which is one step below the state supreme court, and he was at one time considered for the state's highest court. With his status as justice went the trappings of the position, including thirtieth-floor chambers at the top of the Richard J. Daley Center in Chicago. Through the picture windows in his office he could see Lake Michigan shimmering in the distance on sunny days. It was a lofty position indeed.

As John Dille has observed in his chapter, Justice White is a man of purpose. He frequently conveys a sense of impatience to those around him because he is eager to get on with things, to be doing something. Thus it is that he has sought to establish goals for the Golden Thirteen, to make them something more than a collection of old sailors. Together, they must have meaning for the Navy and society of tomorrow, even as the days allotted to the individual members of the group dwindle. Perhaps that sense of impatience comes from a realization that whatever the group is to accomplish must be done quickly. As White jokes, "I don't have time for long-range plans. I don't even buy green bananas anymore."

*N*early all of my life has been spent in and around Chicago. I was born there on July 27, 1914. I attended the public schools in Chicago, going to James McCosh Grammar School and Hyde Park High School. Then I went to the University of Chicago, getting my bachelor's degree in 1935 and my law degree in 1937.

My father was a chemist and a pharmacist, a graduate of Fisk University and the University of Illinois. My mother was a public-school teacher, a graduate of Fisk University and the University of Chicago. During the Depression they sacrificed and sent their only child to college and law school.

I knew that the opportunity to go to school was a precious opportunity which should not be wasted. Civil servants and small-business people don't live so high on the hog that they can afford to waste a chance for their son to go to school. My father used to tell me that his mother told him that almost anything you get, the white folks can take away from you—except learning.

Few professional fields were open to blacks when I was going to school. The choices were essentially law, medicine, religion, and education. Early on I found that law depended more on the powers of reasoning rather than memorization, so I preferred it to medicine, where you call a certain bone the tibia simply because that is its name. Of course, I came along when I could read the exploits of somebody like Clarence Darrow, the great lawyer who was involved in the famous "Monkey Trial" evolution case in the 1920s. Then, too, there were legendary giants here in the black community, like Earl B. Dickerson, for whom I later went to work. Then there were some guys who came down the pike just ahead of me.

Reality hit when I finished the University of Chicago. I graduated from law school when I was twenty-two, small of stature, and black.

So there was no thought of me earning a living except on a governmental job or out of the black community. I first set up shop where I acted as law clerk, really, for a very successful criminal lawyer, Joseph Clayton, a marvelous lawyer. He had his office in a run-down building in the ghetto on Chicago's south side. The toilet was down the hall and was not locked, and it was dirty. It wasn't really the kind of life I wanted. After a few months working for a Depression relief agency, an opportunity came for me to join one of the few black attorneys who had an office in the Loop, so I left Clayton, and I came downtown, and I officed with Earl B. Dickerson, who was general counsel for a black insurance company.

In 1939 a friend of mine who had gone both to Hyde Park High School and to the University of Chicago asked me how I would like to be an assistant United States attorney. I said, "I'd like it very much. I'd like to be a United States senator. I'd like to be President of the United States. What else is new?"

He said, "No, no kidding." It developed that he had worked with a man who was about to be appointed the United States attorney, and he was going to clean the office and put in new people. He asked this friend of mine, Charles Browning, to suggest who should be the token black. Almost everything good that has happened to me since then has happened as the result of that chance conversation I had with Charles Browning. I was appointed assistant United States attorney, and it was from that position that I entered the Navy.

For the most part, the people in charge of the U.S. attorney's office thought it was safer to have me handling civil rather than criminal cases. Any jury selected in those days in the northern district of Illinois was predominantly white. There might have been some thought that I would not be able to convince a white jury to sentence a white man for breaking the law. I doubt if that was true, but there might have been that thought. In any event, I think my chances of becoming a supervisor in that office were probably minimal, but I enjoyed it. I didn't concentrate on the hole; I concentrated on the doughnut.

When World War II began, I kind of thought that my work with the Department of Justice was almost as important as that of FBI men, and I felt perhaps that it might be of some interest to my draft board that I was working for the United States Department of Justice. In fact, I had already asked to get into the FBI, but at that time the director, J. Edgar Hoover, was not permitting blacks to become agents. It used to disgust me that whenever they had some under-cover work to do, they would take on a smart black detective from a local police force and have him work with them, thereby eliminating the necessity of having black agents.

As the draft board looked at me with more and more interest, I turned to Lewis Reginald Williams, a friend who was in the Navy. Williams, whose nickname is "Mummy," was one of the first blacks admitted into the Navy under the new policy in 1942 that permitted them to be assigned to general service rather than as cooks and ser-vants. He was in the selection office at Great Lakes Naval Training Station, so he said, "You ought to do well on the tests that they give you, and that ought to give you the preferment of getting into the service school of your choice." So I enlisted in October 1943 and went to boot training.

Recruit training was my first experience with enforced segrega-tion. Even before we got to Camp Robert Smalls, the people in charge divided the incoming men into black recruits and white recruits. I remember they had a double-level chow hall. All the white recruits were marched upstairs, and the black recruits were marched down in the basement. That hit me. But I was an aware person. I was quite mature, and I knew what I was in for.

I enjoyed boot training. It sounds crazy, but I did. And I don't think I'm looking at it through rose-colored glasses, either, because of the distance now from that period. The barracks were warm and comfortable. They looked like the barracks at every other camp up there. Everything looked about the same. It was kind of a world by itself. The camps were pretty nearly self-contained units with their own barber shop, with their own drill hall, and so forth.

The experience to some extent followed the pattern of the outside world, in that blacks did play on the Great Lakes football team because in those days there were a few blacks playing on college football teams. It sounds ridiculous now, but blacks could not play on the Great Lakes basketball team. You wonder now how they could get ten white guys who knew how to play basketball, don't you? But they did. Imagine, blacks played football but not basket-ball. Prejudice is not a logical thing. So why was it all right for them to play football? I guess because they had more clothes on. I don't know.

I think the reason I was picked for officer training was that I fooled the Navy. When I was working in the U.S. attorney's office, I got to know all the guys of the press. When my time came to go away to boot camp, I called up Bob Lougran, a reporter for United Press. I said, "I wish you'd kind of take special effort. You are doing it regularly anyhow, but be sure you don't miss when I'm leaving for the service. Get it into the paper and say I'm going into the Navy." So by the time I hit Great Lakes, they knew that William Sylvester White, Negro, Assistant United States Attorney, was coming into the Navy. That extra notice probably brought me to the attention of those who were picking the officer candidates.

I had intended to go to quartermaster school. A quartermaster deals with navigation and is in one of the most intellectual of the Navy's enlisted ratings. But the officer school came up so quickly that I never got a chance to be a quartermaster. I recall being summoned to Camp Lawrence, which was one of the Negro camps, and told that I was wanted on the main side. When I got there, a half dozen officers were waiting for me. I remember that they invited me in, and I stood at attention, as I had learned to do as a recruit. Although they talked to me for what seemed to be an interminable time, nobody told me, "At ease." So there I stood at attention. In substance what they said was this: "The Navy is contemplating commissioning a small number of Negroes, and your name has been submitted as one of the potential officers."

I don't know what other preliminary information they gave me, but they finally got down to saying, "It was thought that you might serve in the capacity of a public-relations officer." I had had no experience in writing a newspaper or doing anything else in the way of public relations, but I, at least as a lawyer, thought I was a pretty good generalist and could do most anything that required reading and writing. They asked me if I thought I could do the job, and I answered, quickly, "Yes."

One part of the interview I well remember is that one of them said, "Now, the policy of the Navy regarding the utilization of Negro personnel is being attacked by some Negroes. The Negro newspapers have been particularly vigorous in their attacks upon the Navy's policy. If the Navy makes decisions regarding the utilization of Negroes and that decision comes under attack by Negro leaders and Negro writers in the press, would you be able, still, to carry out the Navy policy?"

I said, "Well, we are at war and men are dying in following orders. And if men can die to follow orders, I guess I can follow orders." That's about all I remember. I don't know whether my being chosen for the program depended on my answer to that question. It was a question I was not prepared for, but, mind you, this was 1943. I was very conscious of the fact that this is still a democracy. I lauded the efforts of the black newspapers to change the policy through mass pressure. But I thought my duty on the inside was to follow orders, so although I wasn't prepared for the question, my answer was forthcoming.

Going through that officer training was kind of like fighting in the dark. It was demanding, I thought. I thought they worked us pretty hard. I thought they didn't know what they were going to do with us. It seemed to me that they were trying hard to make us prepare for any eventuality. I didn't really desire to go to sea at that point. If they had started me down a different path, yes, I would have. But I was totally unequipped. I had had this officer training thing, but I didn't feel I knew enough. If they had let me go to quartermaster school, I would have wanted to go. But I didn't think I had learned enough signaling and navigation to put me aboard a ship. Maybe I did. I just wouldn't know because that was never an option.

I don't know how our instructors regarded their assignment, but they were not condescending to us. I think most of them, like teachers everywhere that are good, want the people to learn. And I don't think they ever, in their demeanor, talked to us like they thought that we couldn't learn it or that they were impatient with our slowness in learning it. I never got that feeling.

On the other hand, we didn't really get to know these men all that well in the course of our two and a half months of training. We didn't have too much personal contact with them. We still lived our day-to-day lives. We got up, we shaved, we showered, and so forth; we didn't always think of this as history-making. We knew it was, but in some sense we might be more concerned with what we were going to do on liberty next weekend. In fact, I had a pair of twin daughters who were born just about nine months after we were commissioned.

One of the aspects of the training dealt with leadership and aptitude for the service. All of us were sent out to drill some recruits. Like the old Uncle Remus story, that was throwing me in the briar patch because I'd just come out of boots, where I was recruit chief petty officer of my company. Earlier, I'd had three years of Army ROTC in high school.

I don't know what grade I got in aptitude for the service, although one of the situations I remember wasn't exactly by the book. I was marching a company of men into a drill hall, and some of the companies were already there. I had been allotted the position between two companies, standing at what was called to be a company front. I marched them in there nicely, until I realized I had the head of the line in the wrong direction. Now, how did I solve that? I don't know whether I said, "Fall out and fall back in" or not, but I remember that was a little exercise that caused me some concern.

Of our group undergoing the training, Reginald Goodwin had been in the Navy longest and had the ear of those in power. He was probably closest to the principal Annapolis graduate associated with the Negro program, Commander Daniel Armstrong. I spoke at Goodwin's funeral. I said then that he played a difficult role. I believe that the white power structure would make known their desires to him, believing that he would transmit those desires to us. And we did the same thing in the other direction. He also carried information back and forth. His role was one that really I didn't appreciate too much while he was performing it because it smacked of being an Uncle Tom. From the vantage point of more than forty years, I can say what he did was useful for both sides. He did it in a way that he held our respect because he was smart, and his information and assistance were accurate.

Looking back over those years, I can tell you now I resented it some, but I never resented it so much that I would say, "Goody, I don't like what you're doing." Just down deep, I guess my resentment was part of not liking the position I was in, where having such a courier and such an emissary was necessary.

I remember Armstrong as being Southern, aristocratic, egotistical, and sincerely interested in advancing the status of Negroes in the Navy—according to his viewpoint. I think he was sincere when he

Ensign Reginald Goodwin is shown at the time of his commissioning in 1944. While the Golden Thirteen were going through officer training, Goodwin was the communications conduit with Commander Daniel Armstrong, officer in charge of Camp Robert Smalls.

told us that we were officers, but we should remember we were colored officers and not do all the things that white officers do. In particular we were not supposed to go to the officers' club. He thought by that course we would ensure the success of the program. We hated it, but I'm sure he thought it best. I guess, in a sense, it was rather like Branch Rickey in talking with Jackie Robinson, the first black player in major league baseball. Robinson was feisty by nature, so Rickey told him, "Don't let that show. You're a pioneer, and that might hamper others coming along."

At the time, we complained about Armstrong. Dennis Nelson was the most vocal about him, but who else could have been there during that transition? Here's a man who had ties to the antebellum South, who was a graduate of Annapolis. The Navy could have picked a do-gooder from the North, but instead it got Armstrong, who was from Virginia. He could sell the program to the Southern mentality of the Navy. "Don't tell me about the South. I'm from the South," Armstrong could say. "Don't tell me about Annapolis. I went there." And so, although Nelson hated it, I can see now that Armstrong was pretty good.

A college classmate of mine named John Dille was one of Armstrong's principal assistants, though I didn't learn until later that we had been in school together. Much of Armstrong's official communication and policy came through Dille. He also provided a good deal of moral support to the group. Dille always exhibited a compassion and an understanding of how the black guys felt. Then, too, he was closer to us in age. Armstrong was older, and Armstrong had more rank, too, so that there was no communication with him.

There was one sad aspect to the program. The man who urged me to get into the Navy, Mummy Williams, was also selected as an officer candidate. He went through the training with us, and then at the very end, although he had passing grades, he was not commissioned. I don't know why, but he wasn't. Three people did not get commissioned; my friend was one of the three, and he was crushed.

After the other thirteen of us were commissioned, I was made a public-relations officer at Great Lakes. The Navy at that time wanted to service the Negro press, so my staff and I ground out press releases. There was also a CBS radio show called "Men of War, brought to you by the men of the Negro regiments at Great Lakes." Then they eliminated the Negro regiments, so we proudly went on with our radio show "brought to you by the men of the Negro companies at Great Lakes." Then pretty soon you had no more Negro companies as the integration went on, and we had no radio show either.

I had some capable enlisted men who knew more about that kind of thing than I did, but I got pretty good myself. My staff could

Ensign White, seated, poses with Ensign Phillip Barnes, another member of the Golden Thirteen, at Great Lakes shortly after their commissioning in 1944.

make good reading out of stories that really weren't all that great. I chose as my task to give recognition to the individual blacks who were achieving in the Navy and to publicize the breakthroughs in Navy policy.

For example, the first black physician that the Navy commissioned was assigned to Great Lakes before he went out to Guam. While he was in Great Lakes, he was in charge of the sick bay. This sick bay had the usual table of petty officers and men. And I put out a press release saying, "This Negro doctor has been in charge of this sick bay, over twenty petty officers, two of whom are black." That's the way the Navy wanted me to put it out.

So what used to kick me, they wouldn't ever turn my lines around.

White in his Chicago apartment in early 1945 with his father, William S. White, Sr.; wife, George; and twin daughters, Marilyn and Carolyn.

They would just print it as I put it out. Stupid. See, I couldn't be there preaching integration; just give the facts. I was supposed to publicize black accomplishment, and it was an accomplishment that two of the people were Navy corpsmen who were black. That's all right, but the real story is that eighteen were white and under this black commanding officer. But be that as it may, we thought we did a good job.

The newspapers were receptive to our efforts; we got linage in the black press. It was not equal to the amount of space given the Army. Of course not, because the Army had generals and whatnot that were black, and the Navy only had us. I remember a paper in New York. In a political cartoon that characterized the Navy, it showed the Navy a proud ship going through the waves, and a towline out pulling a little rowboat. It had, under the big ship, "The Navy," and it had under the rowboat, "Negro programs." So 99 percent of the blacks coming through the selection process would pick the Army. They did not want the Navy because the Navy had a history of mistreating blacks. I don't know that the Navy is yet the preferred service.

In one sense, it is not entirely admirable that we black officers got along so well with the white power structure at Great Lakes. Maybe I should have been more feisty. For instance, I remember a time after I had been commissioned when Commander Armstrong came in to me, and he said, "Did you hear what happened up at Hastings?" That was the site of an ammunition depot.

I'd heard two things happened up at Hastings. I heard there had been an explosion there. I had also heard that there had been a near mutiny. I said, "Are you referring to the explosion, sir?"

"No, I'm referring to that ruckus up there." I had heard a little bit about the meeting up there, but I didn't become a naval officer to become a stool pigeon. What I heard was thirdhand, anyhow. If there had been some real insurrection there, I would have reported it. I don't hang my head in shame about my relations with the white officers, although I don't go around and boast about them either.

An incident one night remains as a vivid memory of the racial situation at Great Lakes. On this night the word came to me that company so-and-so, an outgoing unit of black sailors, was not going to obey when they got orders to shove off for duty. From a public-relations point of view, I knew hell was going to break loose. So I went over to the barracks, even though I had no authority to be there. I guess I went with the petty officer who told me about this. Everything in the barracks was quiet and orderly, so quiet and orderly I was suspicious.

So I asked to speak to the petty officers there, and they said they had been introduced to a white officer who was going to take them overseas as a logistics-support company. And this guy, in introducing himself, had acquainted the company with some of his philosophy—something to the effect that the only good nigger was an obedient nigger, and they ought to know that. If those weren't his words, "nigger" was in them or something equally derogatory. He let them know how tough he was and how he wasn't going to take any crap.

These men in the barracks weren't a bunch of Ph.D.s that I was talking to. But they were guys who had feelings and who could reason—and they had discipline. They had some petty officers that really had their men under control. They weren't being disorderly. They had made up their minds. They were not going to be disorderly. But if they were ordered to go with this officer who had talked the way he did, they weren't going to go.

In trying to respond to all this, I said to the guys, "Cool it. Right now, if we let things stand as they are, the fault's entirely on him. If you guys disobey the orders, they'll forget why you're doing it, and the fault will be on you, and they'll never get to what is the real cause of it. So please, cool it. Let me get this information into the right hands."

After leaving the barracks, I sought out somebody in authority, and I may not have been the only person to report this incident to the appropriate officer. What happened? The officer who made these remarks did not go with that company. I've long wondered— did he do that on purpose? Maybe he didn't want to go to Manus. Maybe he didn't want to go to New Guinea. One way of getting out of it was to do that.

In the summer of 1944 two ammunition ships blew up in Port Chicago, California. The cargo handlers were mostly black sailors, and the horrible explosion blew away many a black man. That had a chilling effect, as you can imagine. I think they put out a rule that no more than such and such a percent of any shore installation should be black. I think from that and from the experience with the *PC-1264* and the *Mason,* two ships with black crews, the Navy became integration-minded. At the end of the war I received a letter from one of the enlisted men who worked under me in public relations. He had later gone out to the Pacific, and he wrote, "I'm coming back to the States as a part of the Navy that's much more democratic than the nation it serves." That was a far cry from the beginning of our story, when I was going down into the basement to eat, while the white boys were eating upstairs.

In 1945 I was transferred to Washington, D.C., where I was put in the press section of the public-information office and had a desk with other lieutenants. I had no staff. I was staff then to the commanding officer, and we were doing stories. In that job I was more conscious of myself as a lawyer than I had been at Great Lakes because I had to do the writing of the stories myself and not direct that they be done. Newsmen can sit down and think into a type-writer, but I can't.

I recall the officer in charge of this section said, "White, you pick up the phone too. Don't you wait for something on Negroes to turn up." So I thought that that was the ultimate of the integration. Admittedly, when there was something with a racial angle to it, they would call upon me to give such expertise as I had.

I enjoyed my stay down there. There's a newsman here in Chicago who was in the press section with me, and we talk about old times, talk about the time when a hush fell over the press section when I walked in for the first time, wearing an officer's uniform. In fact, as a black naval officer I was still so rare that I got a lot of attention wherever I went in uniform. You won't believe it now, but my head wasn't always bald, and I even had girls whistle at me. It was a heady experience.

During my time there I had a visit from Dan Armstrong, who was by then a captain. I congratulated him on the fourth stripe, and he said, "Yes, too bad I couldn't have gotten it earlier during the war because there's so much more I could have done if I'd had the power of the fourth stripe." He was absolutely sincere in that. He would have done more for the blacks in the Navy, as he saw it from his Southern aristocratic background.

I remember one story in particular that I was supposed to work on as part of that job. The war was over, and I was given an assignment to write the story of a black Navy pilot who downed I don't know how many Japanese planes. I read over the information they had on him, and it seemed he was a member of a civilian flight group, and a whole bunch of them went over and joined the Navy.

Apparently, he was light of complexion, and he thought he was passing for white. However, intrepid Navy intelligence found out he was truly black. But I guess so long as he kept shooting down Japanese planes, they didn't care whether he was black or white. So did I cover that story? I went to New York, to the address they gave me, and looked around and saw that this was—what we had in those days—a white neighborhood. I said, "Well, damn if I'm going to pull the cover off of him just for the sake of a story." So I might have lied and said I couldn't find him.

One of our biggest battles during that period was against the formation of the Defense Department. We in the Navy didn't want that. I even convinced people that, from a black perspective, there should be competition among the services as to who could do the best job in the utilization of black personnel. Because everything I was doing was from the point of view of utilization, not necessarily because it's good and fair and integration, but because that's the most efficient way to use your personnel. I guess I was closer to administration than a public-relations officer should be, but I was involved in it.

The Secretary of the Navy was James Forrestal by this time, and he had picked an old Dartmouth chum, Lester Granger, who was black, to make the rounds of the shore installations that had goodly numbers of blacks, to see to what extent the Navy's integration policy was being implemented. We first made some trips around the United States. I know we went to New Orleans, among other places. We visited a shore installation down that way. I said to the commanding officer, "Do you ever get any people here from the Negro press? Do you ever release anything to the Negro press?"

His answer was, "No, we don't send anything to the Jewish press, the German press, the Japanese press. We just send it to the general press."

"Then, too," he would say, "the only time they come over here is when they hear that something is wrong."

"Did you ever ask them to come see something right?"

"No, I don't do that."

So you go talk to the black newsmen, and they'd say, "We have a lot of things to do and a lot of places to go. If he's got something good there, I presume he'll call us and tell us so we'll take a look."

So part of my bringing these things together was trying to talk a language that would be understandable by both sides.

To sum up the substance of Lester Granger's trip, the purpose of it was to see whether the Navy, in its remote places, was taking advantage of the opportunity to utilize fully Negro personnel, or were people restricting them to the more traditional roles. Lester Granger's findings, as I remember, were the farther you got from Washington, the less impact the words of the Secretary of the Navy had in affording Negroes an opportunity to make a useful contribution to the war effort. Once again, you see how public relations and

Lester Granger of the National Urban League visited a number of naval installations in 1945 at the behest of his friend, Secretary of the Navy James Forrestal, to see how well black personnel were being utilized. Here Granger talks with two black sailors.

personnel kind of get mixed up. That's a trip that Goodwin, with his personnel expertise, could well have taken, but they did it the other way around.

When it came time for me to leave active duty, the commander who was in charge of the press section sent me a nice letter. He said, "Judge Hastie is being considered by the Senate for appointment as governor of the Virgin Islands. He will be entitled to have on his staff a naval aide, and that position carries with it the rank of lieu-

Warrant Boatswain Charles Lear talks with a sailor during the course of his duty in Hawaii in 1944. Following his release from naval service at the end of World War II, Lear apparently killed himself because of difficulty readjusting to the civilian world.

tenant commander." At that time I was a lieutenant (j.g.). He said, "Why don't you go see him? Maybe you'll get a chance to make the step and become his naval aide." William Hastie was the first black federal judge. He later became judge of the Second Circuit Court of Appeals, but at that time he had been a district court federal judge and was being considered for this spot.

When I went to see him, he said, "Number one, I'm just being considered by the Senate, and I make it a point I don't count something before it hatches. But then if they do approve of my appointment and if I do have a naval aide, the one thing I don't need is another lawyer. So I wouldn't be interested in appointing you to the task."

My thought of spending more time in the Navy ended with that conversation. At that time I could get another half-stripe on my sleeve if I shipped over. But I didn't stay. I had my job as assistant U.S. attorney waiting for me, and I returned to that.

After I left the service, I ran into Charles Lear, one of the men who went through training with us and was made a warrant officer. In fact, I saw him the day of the night he killed himself. He and I were both living in Lake Forest, which is a nice suburb of Chicago, not too far from Great Lakes.

He had stayed in the Navy a bit longer than I had. I think he was unhappy over the fact that he was no longer in the Navy, and he was feeling uneasy since he hadn't picked up a job yet. I assured him that a man of his talents could certainly get one because he had what the world needs. I think he made some mention of perhaps going back in the Navy. As I remember, he was a farm boy from Iowa, and he probably never had a chance to command people before. As he looked at returning to civilian life, he couldn't see himself having the kind of power he had in the Navy, nor that kind of status either.

In the years since then I've played back that conversation in my mind and asked myself, "Was there something that I could have said?" You know, that's kind of a fruitless effort, but it's made me conscious of the fact that people can be walking around with things on their minds that aren't apparent to others. I've tried to be more alert to unspoken feelings than I was then, although I haven't criticized myself too much for not saying anything.

After being a lawyer a number of years, I received an appointment from Otto Kerner, who had been my boss when he was U.S. attorney. When he became governor of Illinois in 1961, he asked me to join him in the cabinet. I was director of the Department of Registration and Education, and in that I was the licensing officer of the state. I also directed the state's research in the fields of water and oil and natural history. I was also chairman of the board of the state museum. I did all that for $15,000, but I enjoyed it very much.

Then I was elevated to the bench in 1964. I spent some time as a judge in juvenile court. In that job I was amazed at the number of people who are conscientiously interested in trying to do something

The Great Lakes Naval Training Center honors the Golden Thirteen through this building that processes newly arriving enlisted men as they prepare to undergo recruit training.

for kids. The people trying to do something are not always on the right track, but, by golly, they're really trying—often when nobody else cares.

It's difficult to imagine how alone someone feels when there's nothing for support. I heard of one case when a mother standing in court said that she did not want to take her daughter back home. Now, there'd been a history in which the mother had said, "For my sanity and for the sanity and the safety of the other five kids at home, I can't take her back." And the girl wheeled around and jumped out of a plate-glass window.

In 1980 I was appointed to the Illinois Appellate Court, where I sat until retirement as a presiding judge of the Third Division. A few years after my appointment, I was the judge who was author of the opinion that settled legally and judicially the fact that Harold Washington's forces were in control of the city council. Washington was

Chicago's first black mayor and had established a very sound principle that majority rules. Isn't that profound? I took about twenty pages to say it, but it boiled down to that.

In looking at the group that came to be known as the Golden Thirteen, I've always said that we were lucky. The Navy reached down into a group of over one hundred thousand black enlisted men and picked up thirteen of us to be trained as officers. They could easily have dipped this hand into that pool and come up with thirteen more and thirteen more and thirteen more. We were not unique. There was a lot of talent to choose from.

As the years passed and the original black officers got together again, some people suggested that a ship might be named for us. Nothing ever came of it. I think that I'm one of those who came up with the idea that "since we can't get a ship named after us, why not a building?" Some other people came up with the idea, too, but I

Rear Admiral Roberta Hazard, herself a pioneer as one of the early women line officers to make flag rank, speaks during the June 1987 dedication ceremonies for the Golden Thirteen Recruit In-processing Facility.

This plaque was installed as part of the dedication ceremonies in June 1987.

know that I advanced it. In June 1987 the in-processing facility at the Great Lakes Naval Training Center was named for the Golden Thirteen. I think it's appropriate because most of us were not on ships, and this will reach a whole lot more people than a ship would.

The admiral at Great Lakes then was a woman named Roberta Hazard. As one of the Navy's early woman admirals, she explained to us, "I, too, am a pioneer. And I want to be part of the celebration, where we're celebrating your pioneering efforts." She did a great job with that dedication. It's ironic that we are now revered because back in 1944 we were reviled. There were articles in the newspapers and *Life* magazine. People intelligent enough to read *Life* decried the fact that the Navy was lowering its standards to admitting blacks to the officer ranks.

Much progress has been made since 1944. Sam Gravely was commissioned shortly after we were and eventually became a vice admiral in the 1970s. Certainly a vice admiral is the equivalent of a president of a corporation. I don't think General Motors or United States Steel has made the progress that the Navy has. Going back to the letter I received from one of my enlisted men at the end of World War II, I still think, on the whole, that the Navy is more democratic than the country it serves.

The Golden Thirteen reunion that drew the most publicity, by far, was the one on board the guided-missile destroyer *Kidd* in April 1982. Front row, left to right, are Syl White, Dalton Baugh, George Cooper, and Sam Barnes. Standing are Jesse Arbor, James Hair, John Reagan, Graham Martin, the first black Naval Academy graduate Wesley Brown, and Frank Sublett.

Chapter Twelve

Legacy of the Thirteen

After the commissioning of the men who would later come to be known as the Golden Thirteen, the opportunities available to blacks in the Navy increased. In part the atmosphere changed because of the death of Secretary of the Navy Frank Knox in April 1944, a month after the commissioning of the first black officers. President Roosevelt had had to prod Knox repeatedly to get more blacks into the service and open up more types of jobs. Knox shared a view that was prevalent among white naval officers of the time, that having blacks and whites serve together would be disruptive. Knox's successor, James V. Forrestal, not only accepted the idea of increased opportunity, he embraced it eagerly. As Justice White pointed out in his oral history, Forrestal sent Lester Granger of the National Urban League out on a fact-finding tour to determine how well black personnel were being utilized in the service.

In 1944 Forrestal also began a program of sending black enlisted men to serve in a limited number of fleet auxiliaries. These were still not warships, but they were seagoing vessels and closer to the fighting Navy than the small harbor-defense craft and harbor auxiliaries that had initially been open to black crews. Also, of course, it meant at least a limited degree of integration because the additional black sailors going to the fleet auxiliaries would be in general service, supplementing the stewards and messmen already there. Blacks worked with whites on board ship but still often had essentially segregated berthing. By the spring of 1945 black sailors began going to fleet auxiliaries in larger and larger numbers. In June of that year recruit training was integrated.

The steps toward integration, such as the opening of the general-service ratings and the commissioning of a token group of black officers, had been taken as a result of political pressure from the President, not from initiatives originated within the Navy itself. The acceptance of black women into the service followed the same pattern. In this case the impetus came from Thomas Dewey, the Republican candidate in the 1944 presidential election. During his campaign he accused Roosevelt of discrimination for not permitting black women to join the Navy. Shortly thereafter the Navy announced that it would begin allowing black women to enlist and to become officer candidates. Secretary Forrestal directed that the training would be integrated because the small numbers of black women in the service did not make segregated training practicable.

In his superb study of the integration of the armed forces between 1940 and 1965, Morris MacGregor reported that on VJ Day, at war's end, the Navy had 164,942 black enlisted men, 5.37 percent of the total. About 40 percent of the black enlisted men were steward's mates and messmen. By war's end the service also had about sixty black officers, of whom six were women. The Golden Thirteen were the first members of this group. In addition to them and the thirty-six graduates of the V-12 program, a few officers were commissioned as staff specialists: doctors, dentists, chaplains, and civil engineers. With the massive demobilization following the Japanese surrender in 1945, nearly all of the thousands of black personnel who had enlisted for wartime service returned to civilian pursuits. That included twelve of the thirteen men who became officers in March 1944. The surviving members of the Golden Thirteen have indicated in their oral histories that the decisions to leave active service were voluntary. Several have remembered that they were offered promotions if they would remain on active duty.

Dennis Nelson was a "tree-shaker" who did much on behalf of black naval personnel in the years following World War II. He was the only member of the Golden Thirteen to receive a commission as a regular officer and to serve for a full career on active duty. He retired as a lieutenant commander.

Even as they were leaving the service in early 1946, the Bureau of Naval Personnel was removing still further restrictions. One consequence of the segregated concentrations of blacks had been unpleasant racial incidents in several locations. To defuse the potential for further flare-ups and also to alleviate the problems of trying to assign black personnel to only a limited number of billets, the Bureau of Personnel in February 1946 issued a directive that did away with the assignments of black personnel to only certain types of vessels and shore duties. It also did away with segregated housing. A specific part of the directive required reduction of the number of blacks in any ship or station to no more than 10 percent. There were limitations on this integration. With the release of the wartime officers, only three were left on active duty a year after war's end. (John Lee got the first regular commission on March 15, 1947; Dennis Nelson's followed shortly thereafter.) Moreover, the Navy still had the steward branch composed of non-whites. And individual commanding officers, many of whom had grown up in the nearly all-white Navy, still harbored their own particular prejudices.

In 1948 the emergence of a splinter party known as the "Dixiecrats" complicated an already-tough reelection fight for President Harry Truman. He needed the support of black voters to be reelected. He was also concerned about an emerging Cold War in which the U.S. military forces that might be called to combat duty contained large numbers of segregated Army and Air Force personnel. So by Executive Order 9981 of July 26, 1948, he directed the integration of the armed services. In a sense, the Navy was ahead of the trend because it had already moved toward integration at the end of World War II. That movement was evident mostly in the changes implemented after Forrestal became Secretary of the Navy. In 1948, when Truman issued the executive order, Forrestal was Secretary of Defense and in a position to implement it.

Only one member of the Golden Thirteen, Dennis Nelson, stayed in the Navy for a full career. He became a regular officer after the war and served for a time as the Navy's conscience in terms of equal opportunity. He served in the Bureau of Naval Personnel in Washington and made it his business to see that the service moved as quickly as possible to implement official policy. He wasn't senior enough to make such things happen on his own authority, but he was able to function effectively as a thorn in the side of authority.

Nelson was a proud man with an aggressive, sometimes abrasive, personality. He might also be termed a door-kicker. When he saw various doors of opportunity still closed to black naval personnel, he helped kick them open. In doing so, he may have sacrificed his own chances for promotion. He retired from active duty as a lieutenant commander. But the legacy of Dennis Nelson was that the doors were then open for other individuals to walk through as equal opportunity became more and more of a reality.

One specific thing he did was have blacks recalled to active duty in the late 1940s to aid in the effort to recruit new personnel and thus to comply with the integration edict. Among those recalled were John Reagan of the Golden Thirteen and Sam Gravely, one of the V-12 graduates. Coincidentally, the two had been friends while still enlisted men. As mentioned earlier, Reagan served in the fleet during the Korean War, and so also did Gravely. Gravely became a communications specialist and a surface-warfare officer. As the years passed, he moved steadily up the promotion ladder. Gravely was the first black commander, first captain, first rear admiral, and first vice admiral.

In 1949, upon the recommendation of the President's Committee on Equality of Treatment and Opportunity in the Armed Forces (known as the Fahy Committee, after its chairman, Charles Fahy), chief stewards were given the status of chief petty officers. A year later stewards first class, second class, and third class were also given the same status as their general-service counterparts. The fact that the blacks in the Navy were so preponderantly in servant-type jobs was a source of discontent for many years, but this was at least progress. Eventually, the steward rating was done away with, and all food-service personnel were merged in a bureaucratically named rating, mess management specialist, in which race is not an issue.

Still another milestone was the graduation in 1949 of Wesley Brown, the first black officer from the Naval Academy. Like Gravely and the Golden Thirteen, he has done an oral history with the Naval Institute. Although he grew up in Washington, D.C., Brown received his appointment as a midshipman from Adam Clayton Powell, a black congressman from New York. Following his commissioning, Brown pursued postgraduate education and became a member of the Civil Engineer Corps. He made a career of the service, retiring as a lieutenant commander.

During World War II, V-12 had been a supplement to the Naval Academy as a source of new officers. In the postwar years the contract NROTC program was established to provide regular officers in addition to those from Annapolis. And it became yet another source of black officers. For the most part, the units were in large universities, but a few were established in traditionally black schools such as Prairie View A & M in Texas.

Throughout the 1950s and 1960s the Navy was slow to provide opportunities for black personnel. The Navy was legally integrated, so that there were no occupational specialties officially closed off to black members of the service. Even so, the steady promotion of an officer such as Sam Gravely was exceptional. As appendix C demonstrates, the percentage of naval officers who are black is still below the 12 percent of blacks in the nation's overall population, but the underrepresentation was far more pronounced at that time. It wasn't until the late 1960s, particularly when Rear Admiral Draper Kauffman was superintendent, that the Naval Academy really recruited potential black midshipmen actively.

There was also other movement as the seventies approached. President John Kennedy had planted the seed when he made the observation that the military units marching in his inaugural parade in 1961 contained precious few black servicemen. The seed took a while to germinate, however—in part because of Kennedy's death and the war in Vietnam. In the late 1960s, probably at the behest of civilian officials in the Navy Department, a task force was formed to find solutions to the underrepresentation of blacks. The driving force was Lieutenant Commander William Norman, a sort of latter-day Dennis Nelson. Norman and his cohorts established a number of recommendations—some to end negative practices and others to institute positive ones.

One of the individuals called upon to implement the recommendations was another black lieutenant commander, Norm Johnson, who later achieved flag rank. Johnson was appointed in 1968 as a special assistant to Vice Admiral Charles Duncan, then the Chief of Naval Personnel. Johnson was among the first to come up with statistics on the percentages of blacks in various specialties throughout the Navy. He recalls that it was difficult in those days before the widespread use of computers; often it required rounding up data from widely scattered sources. Before that, the detailing of officers seeking to get into special programs such as nuclear power was often done on the basis of looking at the photo in an individual's service record. Given the attitudes of the time, an individual might easily get

Lieutenant Commander William S. Norman, special assistant to the Chief of Naval Operations, briefs Admiral Elmo R. Zumwalt during a meeting in 1971.

shelved even without a fair consideration. Part of Johnson's charter was to see to it that qualified black officers got the opportunities for which their performance qualified them. Another effort was to step up the recruiting of technically capable blacks so that they could get into the hard-skills enlisted ratings; the Navy would thus achieve a much broader distribution of blacks across the spectrum of ratings.

A watershed development in terms of racial awareness was the arrival of Admiral Elmo Zumwalt, Jr., as Chief of Naval Operations in 1970. When he took office, only 5.5 percent of the Navy's enlisted personnel were black, and only 0.7 percent of the officers. Working closely with Lieutenant Commander Norman, the officer involved in the earlier task force, Zumwalt set out to make equal opportunity a reality. He inaugurated racial-sensitivity training and issued a landmark Z-gram titled, "Equal Opportunity in the Navy" on December 17, 1970. It dealt with a variety of topics and is reprinted in Zumwalt's memoir *On Watch*.

In the same book, Zumwalt wrote of a practice that had been in effect on the part of the Bureau of Personnel for years. He told of

Angry sailors display black-power salutes during racial unrest on board the aircraft carrier *Constellation* in the autumn of 1972. Critics contended that Admiral Zumwalt's Z-grams raised expectations and led to several racial flare-ups. His supporters argued that the racial discontent had been simmering for years, that the outbursts would have been much worse if not for Zumwalt's reforms.

taking over a job as officer detailer in 1957: "In the course of briefing me on my new duties, the officer I was relieving told me that the routine for assigning minority officers was to send them to dead-end billets so that their promotion beyond middle rank would be unlikely." They were channeled into the recruiting of minorities and thus often prevented from getting the well-rounded career patterns that would lead to promotion. Zumwalt set about to reverse that way of doing business.

In the course of Zumwalt's four-year "watch" as CNO, the service suffered through a period of racial turbulence, including outbreaks of racial hostility on board ships. Critics charged that Zumwalt's reforms had instigated the unrest by unduly raising expectations for

During World War II, members of the Golden Thirteen were trained as deck officers but not permitted to serve on board combatant ships. This 1974 photo shows Lieutenant (junior grade) Willie Banks of the aircraft carrier *Kitty Hawk*'s deck department.

black personnel. Defenders argued that the Zumwalt changes were long overdue and helped defuse a situation that would have been far worse if not for his policies.

Captain Lee Womack, now the Special Assistant for Minority Affairs at the Navy Recruiting Command, indicates that the problem of proportional representation of black officers has still not been solved. As the tables in appendix C demonstrate, the Navy's officer

Outfitted in his working uniform, Lieutenant (junior grade) Donald Montgomery makes a call from the weapons department office on board the amphibious assault ship *Guadalcanal.*

corps gets whiter and whiter as it moves higher up the rank structure. In part the problem has to do with the mind-set of the officers who write the fitness reports that determine who gets promoted and who doesn't. Statistical analyses of the fitness reports of naval officers show that black officers as a whole receive lower grades than do their white counterparts in such areas as forcefulness, judgment, analytical ability, and command. There is no way the Chief of Naval Personnel can tell individual selection-board members how to vote, but he does issue precepts that tell the board members about these patterns of grading so that they can take this factor into account.

In the late 1970s, when this photo was taken, Commander Mack Gaston was skipper of the guided-missile destroyer *Cochrane*. Since then he has continued to climb the promotion ladder. In 1992, as a rear admiral, Gaston took command of the Great Lakes Naval Training Center, site of the training of the Golden Thirteen in 1944.

Achieving an officer corps that is more nearly representative of the population will be a slow process. As Womack puts it, "It takes twenty years to grow a captain, so we don't expect to see a lot of progress right away." One measure that has been adopted is an affirmative-action program to get more black officers into naval aviation and the submarine service, where they are quite scarce at present. Another inhibiting factor is that blacks represent only about 5.7 percent of each year's crop of college graduates. Those black graduates are the same individuals that the business world is aggressively recruiting in its efforts to comply with civil-rights legislation. The Navy has no quotas per se, but it does have a goal of achieving an officer force that is 6 percent black by the year 2000. To build

Crew members on the deck of the battleship *Missouri* during the course of an open house at Sydney, Australia, during the ship's around-the-world cruise in 1986.

toward that larger number, the service tries to aim for black-officer acquisitions of 7 percent each year.

An organization mentioned in some of the Golden Thirteen's interviews helps the Navy achieve larger numbers of black officers, especially in the higher ranks. The National Naval Officers Association is essentially the professional association for black naval officers. It was established in the early 1970s, during the Zumwalt years. Each year it has a national convention that features workshops to discuss such items as career paths and professional developments. Its collective nature gives it a degree of clout in getting the Navy to pay attention to black points of view and causes. In part the NNOA's expression of concerns led to task-force studies and desired fixes during the 1980s when Vice Admiral Leon Edney and Vice Admiral Jeremy Boorda were serving as Chiefs of Naval Personnel. Another result of the group's cohesion and ability to influence the system is enhanced morale on the part of members of the NNOA.

The organization also has nearly thirty chapters that hold workshops and briefings. The NNOA and its chapters serve as forums for the exchange of information and ideas, and they also foster what has come to be known as "networking" to facilitate the kind of connections that enable individuals to learn about various opportunities. The networking also allows junior officers to get candid advice on how the system works and thus how best to take advantage of it. White officers have had this sort of guidance available for years. Womack refers to it as a network of unofficial mentors or "sea daddies" but is quick to point out that the sea-daddy system does not operate strictly along racial lines. Black officers have white sea daddies and vice versa. The juniors turn for advice to seniors whom they know and trust, often as a result of having served together previously. Even so, there are no guarantees. As Womack explains, "The key to success in this organization is how you perform—period." The advantage of the networking system is to get black officers into the kinds of career-enhancing, high-visibility jobs in which top performance will be rewarded by promotion.

The reunion of the surviving Golden Thirteen members coincides each year with the annual convention of the NNOA. As Womack puts it, they are the role models; they are the pioneers. Because of the success they achieved in 1944 and later in life, they are able to reach out to today's generation of young black officers. As they explain how difficult it was for themselves during World War II, they provide an appreciation of the array of opportunities available to be seized in the Navy of the 1990s. Through the efforts of the Golden Thirteen and their successors, the doors were opened. As they describe that experience, they provide a source of inspiration to those who seek to go through those doors. Nearly fifty years after they were commissioned, the Golden Thirteen still serve the Navy.

Appendix A

Memorandum from Adlai Stevenson to Frank Knox

September 29, 1943

MEMORANDUM TO THE SECRETARY OF THE NAVY

I feel very emphatically that we should commission a few negroes. We now have more than 60,000 already in the Navy and are accepting 12,000 per month. Obviously this cannot go on indefinitely without making some officers or trying to explain why we don't. Moreover, there are 12 negroes in the V-12 program and the first will be eligible for a commission in March, 1944.

Ultimately there will be negro officers in the Navy. It seems to me wise to do something about it now. After all, the training program has been in effect for a year and a half and one reason we have not had the best of the race is the suspicion of discrimination in the Navy. In addition, the pressure will mount both among the negroes and in the Government as well. The Coast Guard has already commissioned two who qualified in all respects for their commissions.

I specifically recommend the following:

(1) Commission 10 or 12 negroes selected from top notch civilians just as we procure white officers, and a few from the ranks. They should probably be assigned to training and administrative duties with the negro program.

(2) Review the rating groups from which negroes are excluded. Perhaps additional classes of service could profitably be made available to them.

I don't believe we can or should postpone commissioning some negroes much longer. If and when it is done it should not be accompanied by any special publicity but rather treated as a matter of course. The news will get out soon enough.

Appendix B

Life Magazine, April 24, 1944

A little more than a month after the commissioning of the Golden Thirteen, a photo of the group appeared in *Life,* which was then probably the most popular magazine in the country. Other than scattered newspaper articles, this was about the only public recognition the new officers got at the time. As Adlai Stevenson had suggested in his memo to Secretary Knox, it was not a development to be accompanied by a lot of fanfare. The photo and brief article about the group are reproduced here.

The same issue of the magazine contained a powerful editorial titled, "Negro Rights." It is reprinted here with the permission of *Life* because it provides an excellent status report on black-white relations in the United States at the time the Golden Thirteen began serving as officers. Notable also were the letters to the editor that were published in subsequent issues as a result of the editorial and the picture of the Golden Thirteen. Some supported the idea of integration and the commissioning of black officers; others were adamantly opposed. The literary rights to the letters still belong either to the letter writers or their descendants, so *Life* is not able to provide permission for their inclusion in this book. Thus, readers interested in pursuing the subject would do well to go to a library and look up the letters sections in the following issues: May 15, 1944 (page 2), and June 5, 1944 (page 2).

NAVY'S FIRST NEGRO ENSIGNS LINE UP ON STEPS AT GREAT LAKES TRAINING STATION FOR FORMAL PORTRAIT. GROUP INCLUDES NEGRO WARRANT OFFICER IN SECOND ROW.

This photograph, taken by Vories Fisher, appeared in the April 24, 1944, issue of *Life* magazine without a listing of the names of the individual officers. The names are as follows: bottom row, left to right, James E. Hair, Samuel E. Barnes, George C. Cooper, William S. White, Dennis D. Nelson II; middle row, Graham E. Martin, Charles B. Lear, Phillip G. Barnes, Reginald E. Goodwin; top row, John W. Reagan, Jesse W. Arbor, Dalton L. Baugh, Frank E. Sublett, Jr.

FIRST NEGRO ENSIGNS

The Navy breaks an old tradition by commissioning 12 enlisted men

The historic picture above shows the first Negroes ever to be commissioned as U.S. Navy officers. A month ago they were all enlisted men. This new Navy policy breaks the tradition that no Negro shall rise above a petty officer rating.

Ten of them have been to college and two have attended specialized schools. Their ages range from 24 to 36. In civilian life they were Pullman porters, bookbinders, mechanics, sheet metal workers, club directors, recorders, guards, instructors, and attorneys.

At present the ensigns are attending indoctrination classes at Great Lakes. Eventually they will command all-Negro crews of patrol boats. Some may even serve aboard the new destroyer escort launched last month which is predominantly manned by Negroes. Soon, 10 more "professionally qualified" Negroes will become staff officers. Then 22 officers will have been created out of 120,000 Negroes serving in the Navy.

NEGRO RIGHTS

THEY WILL COME WHEN THE WHITE SOUTH'S FEAR IS DIVIDED INTO RATIONAL PARTS

The Senate reconvenes, and near the top of its agenda is a problem left over from the Civil War. It is a bill to abolish poll taxes, one of the last remaining legal devices by which most southern states prevent Negroes and poor whites from voting. Even if the Senate passes it, this bill will not give southern Negroes the vote. Neither will the recent Supreme Court decision which declared the Texas anti-Negro primary law unconstitutional. The federal government can chivvy the white South from one extralegal dodge to another, but the southern Negro will never really vote until the southern white man is no longer afraid of him.

The white South neither dissembles nor divides on this point. It is simply aroused to a pitch of frenzied and unanimous resistance to change. In the midst of a war for freedom abroad, we are therefore treated to the threat of a filibuster in the Senate, obscene cries of "nigger-lover!" in the Florida and Alabama primary campaigns, and increasing racial tension throughout the country. In Harlem, which will probably send its first Negro to Congress this year as a result of redistricting, the leading candidate, A. Clayton Powell, is taking a leaf from the southern white's book and is running on a Negro-First platform. ("I will represent the Negro people first; I will represent after that all the other American people.") Never before have Negroes been so outspokenly bitter about America's refusal to give them equal status in the Army, the Navy and industry, and never before have Negro leaders been so active on behalf of Negro rights. America's No. 1 social problem, its great, uncured, self-inflicted wound, is aching violently, perhaps reaching a crisis.

His Vote and Your Daughter

The Negro problem is so complex and so intertwined with all our other national vices and virtues that it is almost incurable in its own terms. It is possible, however, to distinguish between rational and irrational approaches to it, and also to decide what parts of it are primarily of federal concern, and what are primarily a community or personal responsibility.

In this job Americans are lucky to have some very timely expert advice. The Carnegie Corporation seven years ago asked Dr. Gunnar Myrdal, a distinguished Swedish sociologist, to undertake a comprehensive survey of the American Negro, and his study has just been published under the name of *The American Dilemma*. The dilemma, of course, is this: the basic tenets of the American creed make all men free and equal in rights. Yet in fact we deny equal rights to our largest minority, and observe a caste system which we not only criticize in other nations but refuse to defend in ourselves. This makes us living liars—a psychotic case among the nations.

The South has more Negroes and therefore more of the psychosis than the country as a whole. What, exactly, is the South afraid of?

Myrdal finds that the chief white fear is the fear of intermarriage. Other fears he ranks as follows, in the order of their descending importance to the whites: fear of personal and social equality, of joint use of schools and other public places, of equal voting, of equality in law courts, and of equal economic opportunity. In other words, if the South has to change, it will prove least unwilling to give the Negro an equal right to work; next, to give him legal justice; next, the vote, etc.; but it treasures the Jim Crow laws and it will never, never permit intermarriage. However, Myrdal found the Negro ranks his grievances in exactly the reverse order. He wants fair breadwinning opportunities most of all, legal justice and the vote next; but he does not make a major point of segregation, and his ambition to marry whites exists only in the whites' minds.

There would therefore seem to be a basis for progress. But not when all phases of the problem are woven together into a single flag emblazoned "white supremacy." In effect, the North asks the South: "Why won't you let the Negro vote?" The South replies, "How would you like your daughter to marry a Negro?"

Even a moderate, gentlemanly Southerner like Senator Maybank of South Carolina slips this cog of logic. In the Senate last week, he accused "agitators" of trying "to upset our election laws and our customs of segregation." There are agitators who have both these objectives, but the poll tax bill before the Senate does not aim at them. The franchise and segregation are not the same thing. They can be made to seem the same only when the flag of white supremacy wraps them together. That flag conceals the only rational method by which the Negro problem can be ameliorated: the method of dividing it into manageable parts.

The Federal Role

There are only two aspects of the Negro problem which primarily concern the federal government. These are the Negro's political and economic rights. Consider first job and pay discrimination, the thing the Negro hates most and the white treasures least. The federal government's chief way of ameliorating this form of injustice is powerful though negative: refusal to use federal funds, as in war contracts, to perpetuate the caste system. This principle seems rather obvious. But as a practical matter, it is worth remembering that Roosevelt never would have set up the Fair Employment Practice committee if astute Negro politicians had not threatened him with a national Negro march on Washington. And even the FEPC cannot change a nationwide industrial prejudice. It is up to the individuals, corporations and unions who compose our economy, North and South. War industries seem to have a better record on this score in Texas than in Michigan.

The Personal Problem

Political and economic justice for the Negro lie at the end of a long, rough road. And if we get there, the Negro problem will still be with us. The rest of the solution, however, cannot rightly be considered a federal concern.

There are several theoretical solutions to the Negro problem which involve neither intermarriage nor an outrage to the American creed. There is, for example, the theory of "parallel civilizations"—complete equality of opportunity for Negro and white, but complete segregation too. As an overall solution this may or may not work. It is beginning to work in North Carolina, where Negroes vote. It might never work in South Carolina or Mississippi, where the Negro population is much bigger. But nobody knows what will work until they try, and the more experiments, the more discoveries.

Negroes are not uniformly distributed over the U.S. This being so, the problem of their social relations with whites does not call for a federal solution. The problem is both too various and too personal. And anyway, as Lord Bryce said, "good manners cannot be imposed by statute."

If this limitation on federal responsibility were more clearly recognized in the North, the South might be less given to blind fears, and might even start using words like "our institutions" with more precision. The other three-quarters of the country cannot permit the South to disfranchise its Negroes forever. And neither can the South; for all men want to be rational.

Three generations ago the South had a consistent and respectable theory to defend its behavior. The Negro was a lower species of man and his caste was fixed by his Creator. But this theory is no longer respectable; educated Southerners no longer believe it; the white man, says Myrdal, is "losing confidence in the theory which gave reason and meaning to his way of life." That is why Myrdal thinks the southern way of life must and will change. And he adds:

"The Negroes are a minority, and they are poor and suppressed, but they have the advantage that they can fight wholeheartedly. The whites have all the power but they are split in their moral personality. Their better selves are with the insurgents. The Negroes do not need any other allies."

Appendix C

Black Personnel in Today's Navy

Black Senior Officers in the Department of Defense

(All services—numbers and percentages as of June 30, 1992)

Rank	Army	Air Force	Marine Corps	Navy	DoD Overall
Flag/General (O-7 to O-10)	25 6.5%	6 1.9%	1 1.5%	3 1.2%	35 3.4%
Captain/Colonel (O-6)	219 4.6%	98 1.9%	11 1.7%	39 1.1%	367 2.6%
Commander/Lt. Colonel (O-5)	662 6.3%	400 3.3%	46 2.9%	191 2.4%	1,299 4.1%
Lt. Commander/ Major (O-4)	1,935 10.8%	1,199 6.6%	135 4.3%	448 3.3%	3,717 7.1%

Black Officers—U.S. Navy
(As of June 30, 1992)

Rank	Male	Female	Total	Percentage
Flag (O-7 to O-9)	3	0	3	1.2%
Captain (O-6)	39	2	41	1.1%
Commander (O-5)	169	40	209	2.5%
Lt. Commander (O-4)	382	99	481	3.3%
Lieutenant (O-3)	818	291	1,109	4.4%
Lieutenant (j.g.) (O-2)	447	123	570	5.7%
Ensign (O-1)	360	98	458	5.9%
CWO-4 (WO-4)	48	0	48	8.8%
CWO-3 (WO-3)	61	0	61	7.4%
CWO-2 (WO-2)	147	8	155	10.2%

Black Enlisted—U.S. Navy
(As of June 30, 1992)

Rate	Male	Female	Total	Percentage
Master Chief (E-9)	258	6	264	5.3%
Senior Chief (E-8)	672	37	709	6.7%
Chief (E-7)	2,948	229	3,177	8.8%
First Class (E-6)	10,982	1,558	12,540	13.8%
Second Class (E-5)	15,950	3,514	19,464	17.8%
Third Class (E-4)	17,733	3,661	21,394	20.4%
AN/FN/SN (E-3)	14,167	2,897	17,064	23.8%
AA/FA/SA (E-2)	7,159	824	7,983	19.0%
AR/FR/SR (E-1)	3,680	559	4,239	11.2%

Black Totals—U.S. Navy
(As of June 30, 1992)

	Male	Female	Total	Percentage
Officer	2,474	661	3,135	4.3%
Enlisted	73,549	13,285	86,834	17.6%
Total Force	76,023	13,946	89,969	15.9%

The Special Assistant for Minority Affairs, Navy Recruiting Command, provided all of the figures in this appendix.

Index

Photo Credits

Pages 168, 214, 260–61, 262, Great Lakes Naval Training Center
Pages 173, 189, 251, courtesy Jesse W. Arbor
Page 176, National Archives (80-G-300192)
Page 180, National Archives (80-G-300191)
Page 183, National Archives (80-G-240256)
Page 184, National Archives (80-G-240257)
Page 188 left, National Archives (80-G-300195)
Pages 192, 196, 203, 210, 212, courtesy Norman H. Meyer
Pages 204–5, U.S. Naval Institute (James C. Fahey Collection)
Pages 222, 224, 225, 228, 238, courtesy James E. Hair, Jr.
Pages 240, 252, 257, courtesy William S. White
Page 249, National Archives (80-G-300197)
Page 258, National Archives (80-G-412842)
Page 264, Naval Historical Center (NH 95625)
Page 271, U.S. Navy Office of Information,
    courtesy Admiral Elmo R. Zumwalt
Page 272, courtesy San Diego *Union and Evening Tribune*
Page 273, U.S. Navy (Jonathan R. Faser)
Page 274, U.S. Navy (Joe Mancias)
Page 275, U.S. Navy (Kirby Harrison)
Page 276, U.S. Navy (Ron Bayles)
Page 282, Naval Historical Center (NH 95624)

About the Editor

Paul Stillwell joined the staff of the U.S. Naval Institute in 1974 and is now director of the organization's history division. He has a bachelor's degree in history from Drury College, Springfield, Missouri, and a master's degree in journalism from the University of Missouri-Columbia. From 1962 to 1988 he was in the Naval Reserve, including active duty from 1966 to 1969; he served in the tank-landing ship *Washoe County* (LST-1165) and the battleship *New Jersey* (BB-62).

Among his other publications are *USS South Dakota: The Story of Battleship X* (1972), *Air Raid: Pearl Harbor!* (1981), *Battleship New Jersey: An Illustrated History* (1986), the Naval Institute's 1991 engagement calendar *A Century of U.S. Battleships, Battleship Arizona: An Illustrated History* (1991), and *Sharks of Steel* (with Vice Admiral R. Y. Kaufman,1993).

The **Naval Institute Press** is the book-publishing arm of the U.S. Naval Institute, a private, nonprofit society for sea service professionals and others who share an interest in naval and maritime affairs. Established in 1873 at the U.S. Naval Academy in Annapolis, Maryland, where its offices remain, today the Naval Institute has more than 100,000 members worldwide.

Members of the Naval Institute receive the influential monthly magazine *Proceedings* and discounts on fine nautical prints and on ship and aircraft photos. They also have access to the transcripts of the Institute's Oral History Program and get discounted admission to any of the Institute-sponsored seminars offered around the country.

The Naval Institute also publishes *Naval History* magazine. This colorful quarterly is filled with entertaining and thought-provoking articles, first-person reminiscences, and dramatic art and photography. Members receive a discount on *Naval History* subscriptions.

The Naval Institute's book-publishing program, begun in 1898 with basic guides to naval practices, has broadened its scope in recent years to include books of more general interest. Now the Naval Institute Press publishes more than sixty titles each year, ranging from how-to books on boating and navigation to battle histories, biographies, ship and aircraft guides, and novels. Institute members receive discounts on the Press's nearly 400 books in print.

For a free catalog describing Naval Institute Press books currently available, and for further information about subscribing to *Naval History* magazine or about joining the U.S. Naval Institute, please write to:

Membership & Communications Department
U.S. Naval Institute
118 Maryland Avenue
Annapolis, Maryland 21402-5035

Or call, toll-free, (800) 233-USNI.

THE NAVAL INSTITUTE PRESS

THE GOLDEN THIRTEEN
Recollections of the First Black Naval Officers

Designed by Karen L. White

Set in Simoncini Garamond on a Macintosh IIci
Output by BG Composition
Baltimore, Maryland

Display set in Bernhard Tango

Printed on 55-lb. Glatfelter antique cream
and bound in Holliston Kingston Natural
by the Maple-Vail Book Manufacturing Group
York, Pennsylvania